Migration in World History

This fully revised and updated second edition of *Migration in World History* traces the connections among regions brought about by the movement of people, diseases, crops, technology, and ideas.

Drawing on examples from a wide range of geographical regions and thematic areas, noted world historian Patrick Manning guides the reader through:

- the earliest human migrations, including the earliest hominids, their development and spread, and the controversy surrounding the rise of *Homo sapiens*
- the rise and spread of major language groups (illustrated with original maps)
- an examination of civilizations, farmers, and pastoralists from 3000 BCE to 500 CE
- trade patterns including the early Silk Road and maritime trade in the Mediterranean and Indian Ocean
- the effect of migration on empire and industry between 1700 and 1900
- the resurgence of migration in the later twentieth century, including movement to cities, refugees, and diasporas
- the various leading theories and debates surrounding the subject of migration.

Patrick Manning is Andrew W. Mellon Professor of World History at the University of Pittsburgh, where he is Director of the World History Center and Director of the Center for Historical Information and Analysis. He is the author of *The African Diaspora: A History through Culture* (2009) and *Navigating World History: Historians Create a Global Past* (2003). His research includes African population and migration, 1650–1950, and an interdisciplinary history of early humanity.

Themes in World History
Series editor: Peter N. Stearns

The *Themes in World History* series offers focused treatment of a range of human experiences and institutions in the world history context. The purpose is to provide serious, if brief, discussions of important topics as additions to textbook coverage and document collections. The treatments will allow students to probe particular facets of the human story in greater depth than textbook coverage allows, and to gain a fuller sense of historians' analytical methods and debates in the process. Each topic is handled over time – allowing discussions of changes and continuities. Each topic is assessed in terms of a range of different societies and religions – allowing comparisons of relevant similarities and differences. Each book in the series helps readers deal with world history in action, evaluating global contexts as they work through some of the key components of human society and human life.

Agriculture in World History
Mark B. Tauger

Alcohol in World History
Gina Hames

Asian Democracy in World History
Alan T. Wood

Childhood in World History
Peter N. Stearns

Consumerism in World History: The Global Transformation of Desire
Peter N. Stearns

Disease and Medicine in World History
Sheldon Watts

The Environment in World History
Stephen Mosley

Food in World History
Jeffrey M. Pilcher

Gender in World History
Peter N. Stearns

Globalization in World History
Peter N. Stearns

Human Rights in World History
Peter N. Stearns

The Indian Ocean in World History
Milo Kearney

Jews and Judaism in World History
Howard N. Lupovitch

Poverty in World History
Steven M. Beaudoin

Premodern Trade in World History
Richard L. Smith

Premodern Travel in World History
Steven S. Gosch and Peter N. Stearns

Religion in World History
John Super and Briane Turley

Revolutions in World History
Michael D. Richards

Science in World History
James Trefil

Sexuality in World History
Peter N. Stearns

Sports in World History
David G. McComb

The United States in World History
Edward J. Davies, II

Warfare in World History
Michael S. Neiberg

Western Civilization in World History
Peter N. Stearns

Migration in World History

Second edition

Patrick Manning
with Tiffany Trimmer

Routledge
Taylor & Francis Group

LONDON AND NEW YORK

Second edition published 2013
by Routledge
2 Park Square, Milton Park, Abingdon, Oxon OX14 4RN

Simultaneously published in the USA and Canada
by Routledge
711 Third Avenue, New York, NY 10017

Routledge is an imprint of the Taylor & Francis Group, an informa business

© 2005, 2013 Patrick Manning

First edition published 2004

British Library Cataloguing in Publication Data
A catalogue record for this book is available from the British Library

Library of Congress Cataloging in Publication Data
Manning, Patrick, 1941–
  Migration in world history / Patrick Manning. — 2nd ed.
    p. cm. — (Themes in world history)
  "Simultaneously published in the USA and Canada"—T.p. verso.
    Includes bibliographical references and index.
  1. Population geography. 2. Emigration and immigration. 3. Human beings—
Migrations. I. Title.
  HB1951.M28 2012
  304.809—dc23   2012007404

ISBN: 978–0–415–51678–5 (hbk)
ISBN: 978–0–415–51679–2 (pbk)
ISBN: 978–0–203–10070–7 (ebk)

Typeset in Garamond
by Keystroke, Station Road, Codsall, Wolverhampton

Printed and bound in Great Britain by the MPG Books Group

Contents

Illustrations

List of figures

List of tables

Acknowledgments

Chapters 7, 8, and 9 use text from *Migration in Modern World History 1500–2000* CD-ROM with User Guide (Student Version), 1st edition by Manning © 2001. Reprinted with permission of Wadsworth, a division of Thomson Learning: www.thomsonrights.com. Fax: 800 730–2215.

Preface to the first edition

This concise summary of human migration portrays migratory movement as a human habit and as a thread running through the full extent of our history as a species. The book attempts to sustain a single framework, based on migration, for all of human history. The framework I have selected emphasizes identifying human language communities over time, and tracing patterns of cross-community migration linking language groups.

Chapters 1 through 3 present a new framework and a new interpretation of human migration, especially in times before the development of agriculture. These middle three chapters show the significance of cross-community migration during this more recent but rather long time period. Not only river valleys and civilizations but also migrations, portrayed through language communities, characterized this era. Chapters 4 through 6 address the era from the beginnings of agriculture, as much as 15,000 years ago, up to the year 1400 of the Common Era. These middle three chapters show the significance of cross-community migration during this more recent but rather long time period. Not only river valleys and civilizations but also migrations, portrayed through language communities, characterized this era. Chapters 7 through 9 rely significantly on an earlier publication, *Migration in Modern World History, 1500–2000*, a CD-ROM of which I was principal author. These chapters underscore the importance of migration in many aspects of modern world history, and set modern migrations in the context of the full history of human migrations.

The Annenberg/CPB Project provided the support enabling the World History Center at Northeastern University to produce *Migration in Modern World History, 1500–2000* (Wadsworth, 2000), which laid the groundwork for the present volume. I wish to thank Wadsworth Publishing and especially its publisher, Clark Baxter, for permission to present revised versions of the *Migration* CD in these pages. In addition I wish to thank series editor Peter Stearns for suggesting that this volume be written, Lisa Jeanne Graf for her skillful work in creating the maps, Christopher Ehret for his years of counsel on the interpretation of historical linguistics, and the history graduate students at Northeastern University for their commentary on draft versions of the manuscript. The late Joseph H. Greenberg carried on a lifelong campaign of analysis of the classification of languages, and produced an astonishing catalogue of results. The first half of this book presents an introductory explication of some of the historical implications of his linguistic analysis. There is much more to be drawn from his works. I dedicate this work to the memory of Joseph H. Greenberg.

Preface to the second edition

Migration is one of those human patterns that can be seen from the start of the human experience to the present. I have greatly enjoyed learning and writing about this basic human pattern, and I am pleased to see that this little book on a big topic has sustained enough interest to warrant a second edition. I am especially appreciative to Jan Lucassen and Leo Lucassen for their interest in the concept of cross-community migration, as expressed in the first edition, and for their leadership in applying and developing the concept in various historical realms. In addition, I offer thanks to my students at the University of Pittsburgh, who saw that the first edition's narrative of migration as seen through language groups was incomplete, and that more maps were needed to bring the story to the present. Robin Cheung, a fine graphic artist on whom I have relied in other contexts, drew the five new maps, which appear in the final three chapters. Finally, Tiffany Trimmer, a historian with excellent insight into migration theory, kindly agreed to join me in preparing the new appendix on theory and debate. In my opinion, it is an important step to include this theoretical discussion in a history book, even if it arrives only at the end.

Patrick Manning
Pittsburgh, February 2012

A note on the expression of time

This book employs two calendars, one for earliest times and the other for the past five thousand years. For Chapters 2 through 4, the times are expressed in years before the present, or "BP." For Chapters 5 through 9, the times are expressed in years of the Gregorian Christian calendar, as labeled by world historians. From the year 1 of that calendar forward, years are identified as "CE," meaning "in the Common Era." Years before the year 1 are identified as "BCE" or "before the Common Era."

The shift of calendars occurs at the beginning of Chapter 5, at a time five thousand years ago (5000 BP), or three thousand years before the Common Era (3000 BCE).

Chapter 1

Introduction

Modeling patterns of human migration

The history of the world includes remarkable stories of migration in every era. Within the past fifty years, migration from countryside to city in every corner of the world caused the proportion of city-dwellers to expand from one-fifth to over half the human population. Human life, previously rural, has now become dominantly urban. Urban areas of over twenty million inhabitants include Tokyo, Mexico City, New York, Bombay, Istanbul, São Paulo, and Jakarta: of these, only Tokyo and Istanbul had populations of as many as 100,000 inhabitants in 1800.

In the three centuries after the voyage of Columbus – an era often called "early modern" times – some two million settlers crossed the Atlantic from Europe to settle in the Americas. In the same three centuries, nearly eight million Africans were brought to the Americas, most of them in slavery. These populations of immigrants, in complex combination with each other and with the Amerindian populations, created a new social organization on two continents.

In the nineteenth and early twentieth centuries, improved transportation systems and new economic incentives, both positive and negative, enabled some fifty million European migrants to move across their home continent and then to North and South America and beyond. In the same time period, another eighty million migrants moved across East and South Asia, repopulating regions from the Indian Ocean to Manchuria and Central Asia. The continuing long-distance migrations of Africans, including some four million in this period, now appeared minor by comparison.

In times that we call "ancient," more than two thousand years ago, Greek mariners created thriving commercial colonies along the edges of the Mediterranean and Black Seas; in their wake, Rome was able to absorb the surrounding lands into a great empire. In these and earlier centuries, land-based migrations gradually changed the culture of two major subcontinents: people speaking Indo-European languages spread from Central Asia into Iran and northern India, and people speaking Bantu languages moved from what are now Nigeria and Cameroon to many regions of Central, eastern, and southern Africa. In much more distant times the spread of *Homo sapiens* from

Africa throughout the Eastern Hemisphere included – most remarkably and perhaps sixty thousand years ago – voyages across the waters to settle in Australia and New Guinea.

This book provides a concise summary of these and other great migrations. Further, it goes beyond mass migrations, linking large and small migrations to each other and to the broader fabric of human society. It explores the social context from which migrations emerged, showing how migration stems from the very core of human behavior.

Periodic mass migrations provide the tip of the iceberg in migration studies. The large-scale movements – including those we label as migrations of Arabs, Germans, Jews, and Polynesians – consisted in practice of an accumulation of smaller movements that fit into larger patterns with time. The approach in this book is to emphasize the ways in which the individual experience of migrating has been linked to the many other issues and choices in life. Even when the number of migrants has been small, the effects of their movement have been important in technology, social organization, and culture.

This is a study in world history, in several senses. First, it addresses a long time period and explores experiences drawn from many regions of the earth. Second, it emphasizes connections in the human experience. Migration encourages one to think of connections, at least because every migration connects a point of origin and a destination. Third, the book emphasizes migration as an engine for social change, by tracing the dynamics of ideas as well as the movement of bodies. Fourth, it emphasizes at once the continuity and the transformation in migration over time. The book gives a broad interpretation of macro-level change, and shows the connection between global change and local-level histories. Most systematically, I argue that human migration is so fundamental an element of our behavior that it needs to be considered in the study of every aspect of our experience.

The remainder of this chapter introduces a model of human migratory processes. This model – a set of principles and patterns – emphasizes the underlying logic, the recurring choices, and the interacting factors characterizing human migration. As I present it in these pages, the model has five elements that interact with each other: the boundaries of human communities, major categories of migration, the processes of migratory movement, the short-term social development brought about by migration, and the long-term influences of migration. Through the model, I introduce a terminology that will reappear throughout the book, and I identify several patterns of migration that have reappeared throughout human history. In the succeeding chapters, I sketch out the reenactments and the developments in human society associated with migration, for period after period in human history. Although each migratory movement has had its unique conditions and experiences, the underlying habits of human behavior as summarized in the model make it possible to generalize about migrations at the same time as emphasizing their distinctiveness.

Human communities as language groupings

Humans, like most other species, organize their existence into communities. The distinction, however, is that humans have developed language, so that human communities organize themselves around language and not just proximity. Oral communication surely existed among such previous hominids as *Homo erectus*, as it exists among such other species as birds, dolphins, and monkeys. I assume, however, that the development of fully inflected languages, with distinctive grammar and vocabulary, is a development of our own species. According to the recent results of archaeologists and geneticists, modern *Homo sapiens* emerged within the last 150,000 to 200,000 years. In that time, among the members of our species, all those who share a language have been able to communicate in depth with one another. Communication with members of other human communities is possible, but can only reach its potential if one learns the language.

So I am defining a human *community* as the speakers of a given language. The *boundaries* of human communities, over our long history, have been those of language. These boundaries among language communities are not necessarily sharp – closely related dialects and languages may be easily understood. But beyond a certain level of difference, languages become mutually unintelligible, and can only be understood after a period of study and practice. The many different versions of English can be understood with little effort by an English-speaker, but Spanish, in any of its versions, is quite a different language.

Defining a human community as a language community – rather than as an independent family or as an ethnic group – has significant implications for our understanding of history. Most basically, a focus on language shows that early human communities were larger and carried out more communication than is commonly thought. Our usual picture of early human foragers – the "cave man" – assumes that they lived as independent groups of at most a few dozen people. The archaeological record, indeed, shows settlements or camps with groups of this size (often known as "bands") as an important human pattern. But languages, in order to develop and persist, require larger communities. Communities of at least several hundred people, who speak with one another, are necessary to maintain the integrity and continuity of a language. Even for the earliest times of our species, therefore, we must think of human communities not as independent bands, but as collections of families or bands held together through a shared language. Families (and bands), important as they were in the process of migration, were situated within language communities. Home-language community and local genetic community began at much the same magnitude, always bigger than bands. (Migration and intermarriage, of course, enabled some families to stretch across language boundaries.)

What have been the patterns of change in human language communities? We have no direct evidence on the nature of language communities in early times. But the patterns of language change appear to be dependable, and I assume they have existed for all of the history of our species. Changes in vocabulary, pronunciation, and grammar take place according to rules and patterns that cannot have been much different from those we know today. In addition, linguists have made detailed observations on the ways new words and new concepts enter languages according to the experience of each group. Language communities get smaller as groups become relatively isolated, but they must maintain a minimum size of several hundred speakers in order to survive over the long term. At the other extreme, language communities can grow to include millions of speakers if their network of communications is sufficiently intensive. The family trees of language groups reveal the steady divergence of languages from each other, as their speakers become separated in space and time. Yet there are also processes of convergence in language, as with the spread of words for innovations, and when greater communication among people makes one language or one version of a language supreme over others.

The members of each community, bound together by language, also shared a set of *customs*. The very existence of language enabled each community to develop and pass on an extensive set of customs – the many patterns of family, economic, and ceremonial life. Customs too differ from one community to another. Those who move from one community to another must learn not only a new language, but also an accompanying set of customs.

In the world of today we have become accustomed to defining communities as ethnic groups and nations. Yet identification of communities by language, even in today's complex world, is an obvious and useful classification of social difference. The nations in which we claim citizenship are no more than two hundred years old, and the ethnic groups with which we identify, while sometimes older, have been remarkably changeable. Communities of language, in contrast, can be shown to have had long-term stability and steady patterns of transformation. The Germanic languages or the Semitic languages, for instance, can be traced back with some confidence for several thousand years, though the ethnic identities and states of those language communities have changed repeatedly.

For humans today, as for our earliest forbears, migration brings the task of *learning new languages and customs*. This learning is the most specific characteristic of human migration, and it is one of the principal sources of change and development in human ways of life. The knowledge and daily use of multiple languages, far from being a rare exception, is common in the world today and was surely just as common among our ancestors back to the beginning.

Categories of human migration

Following the very brief preceding definition of human language communities, I now move to define migration within and among these communities. I identify four categories of human migration. Three of these are quite similar to patterns of migration for other animals, especially mammals. The fourth category is rather unique, and accounts for a substantial amount of human history.

Home-community migration involves movement of individuals from one place to another within the home community. That is, the offspring of one family move to another family to find mates. Home-community migration is necessary for reproduction of the species, in order to maintain a sufficiently wide genetic pool. For humans, these movements consist most basically of young men and women moving from one family to another in marriage. Thus, many and perhaps most humans experience home-community migration, as they start new families of their own. But the circumstances can vary widely. In patrilineal, agricultural systems, it may be the case that young men grow up on the farms of their fathers, inherit a portion of the land, and never move from it. Such an arrangement requires, therefore, that women move from one family to another and from one farm to another, to marry the men and produce the next generation. In matrilineal agricultural systems, in contrast, the tendency is for the women to stay with the family into which they were born, and for men to move from one family to another. Both systems work.

Colonization is the departure of individuals from one community to establish a new community that replicates the home community. This type of migration is the primary means by which an animal species extends its geographic range: it involves moving into unoccupied territory or expelling previous occupants. Usually, the colonists settle in an environment very similar to that of their home community, and thereby maintain the same style of life. The expansion and contraction of the range of North American wolves provides an example of the positive and negative sides of colonization. Among humans, colonization takes place occasionally, especially for communities that are thriving. The colonists settle and begin new communities without having to learn new languages or customs. The initial movements of humans into Australasia and the Americas are important examples of colonization. (Of course, the variety of environments in Australasia and the Americas suggests that simple colonization does not tell the whole story of the spread of humans to those vast regions.)

Whole-community migration is the displacement of all the members of a community. Some species migrate habitually, usually in an annual cycle – whales, elk, and certain birds – and all but a few laggards in those communities participate in each movement. These migrations move communities among alternating ecologies, enabling them to complete their life cycle. Humans do not have an inherent or universal pattern of community migration – they do not generally migrate as whole communities. However, some communities – nomadic communities, as we call them – do migrate habitually, often adopting the habits of the grazing animals they have come to dominate or the fish they pursue. They often take their homes with them – their animals, their tents, and their other belongings. This pattern, known as transhumance, may have been fairly common for early human communities in the days before settled life began. Another pattern is that whole communities may migrate in order to flee a natural disaster such as famine or a human disaster such as expulsion from their homeland.

Cross-community migration consists of selected individuals and groups leaving one community and moving to join another community. This pattern is followed universally by humans, and rarely by other species: language communication among humans provides the basic reason for this distinct pattern of migration. All human communities experience out-migration by members of their population who go to other communities. The migrants leave their home communities for various reasons – to benefit the home community, to benefit themselves, to escape the home community, or because they have been forcibly removed. At the same time, the home community accepts in-migrants from other communities who find a local role to play for either a short or long time. The rates and directions of migration may vary significantly, but the practice in general is universal among humans.

The existence of language and the distinctions in language among human communities give a particular character to the cross-community migration of humans. For wolves, antelope, and whales, the various communities lack distinct languages, so that movement of an individual from one community to another would appear to be easy. But since these mammals encounter almost exactly the same society when they migrate from one community to another, their migrations bring few benefits and, indeed, few results at all. Humans who migrate to new communities, in contrast, must learn new languages and customs. At the same time, these migrating humans can introduce new language and customs to their host communities. This is distinctively human behavior, and it is the reason migration in human history is not only a story of the spread of humankind, but also a story of the transformation of human life again and again.

Table 1.1 summarizes the four main categories of migration and their usual characteristics among humans. Cross-community migration, though it is only one of four types of migration, influences every aspect of human migration because it creates and spreads changes. For instance, cross-community migration changes home-community migration so that the latter serves not only for biological reproduction but also enables a division of labor. Further, cross-community migration spreads new technology, so that colonization can include settling in new environments. And cross-community migration may encourage whole-community migration, for instance by building connections between nomadic and settled populations.

Migrations, whether of long or short distance or duration, are central to the human experience. Most humans think of themselves as staying put, within their home community. In fact most people take part in home-community migration, even if they tend not to think of their localized movements among families as "migration." In contrast, only a minority leave their home community, and their migrations may occupy only a brief portion of their lives.

Table 1.1 Categories of human migration

Home-community migration
    Function: broaden gene pool by moving within community
    Species following this pattern: all species
    Human pattern: mostly female migrants

Colonization
    Function: extend range of species
    Species following this pattern: all species
    Human pattern: mostly male migrants

Whole-community migration
    Function: alternate among ecological settings
    Species following this pattern: some species
    Human pattern: annual or occasional displacement of community

Cross-community migration
    Function: share community experience
    Species following this pattern: *Homo sapiens* only
    Human pattern: mostly male migrants

Nonetheless, the categories of colonization, whole-community migration, and cross-community migration combine to provide one of the major forces for historical change.

Because the categories of migration are quite distinctive for the individuals who make those various types of move, this book will present individual stories of migration to illustrate the experience of each type of migration as it was repeated or transformed over time. This is in fact one of the lessons of world history: even when exploring such broad processes as the earliest or most recent settlements of the Americas, it is important to keep an eye on the individual experience as well as the overall pattern.

Cross-community migration: processes and institutions

Why do individual humans migrate? What results does migration bring? The basic answers to these questions must be sought through investigation of the migrants, their families, their communities, and the other communities of humans who might be seen as potential sources of benefits or dangers.

The first reason for individuals to migrate is the hope that their personal situation will improve. This may mean escaping an unhappy situation brought by social oppression or economic deprivation, or it may mean the possibility of achieving a higher status after completing a voyage, either at home or abroad. A second reason for migrating is that individuals can hope to bring benefit to their family: the migrants may be going to retrieve needed resources, learn new skills, or bring back help. In recent times this means sending cash home; in earlier times it meant going to hunt or to retrieve needed minerals. A third reason for migration is Samaritan – the migrant may hope to contribute additional resources or benefits to the receiving community. This motivation is perhaps most easily seen for religious missionaries, who move to new communities with the desire of spreading their faith, but can also be seen for people who move to spread new technologies. A fourth reason for migrating, for some people at least, is the pleasure of voyaging and the pleasure of learning new places, new people, and new ideas.

The decision to migrate, however, may not be in the hands of the individual migrant. Sometimes it is made by leaders of the family or the wider community: many were the children forced to accept decisions by their parents to migrate. Other migrants were impressed into military forces, expelled from their homeland, or taken into captivity by raiding parties.

Migration, if it often generates hope, always brings its cost and dangers. The most obvious cost of migration is the mortality brought by displacement. Whatever the normal rate of death in a community, it is likely to be higher if members of that community become migrants. Hunger, thirst, disease, storms, injuries brought by accidents, disputes in the course of travel, and encounters with warfare and piracy all raise the risk of dying once one begins to travel away from home.

For those who survive, migrants must go through the effort of learning a new language and new customs, on the road and especially in a new community. Even after mastering the basics of communication, the migrant must go through the effort of social initiation, joining and finding an adequate place in a new community or household. This process, known variously as "seasoning," "socialization," and "acculturation," is an essential step in the successful completion of any act of migration.

Each category of migrants has a predominant demographic profile. Home-community migrants are mostly female, as males are more likely to stay attached to the households of their parents. Colonists are more often male than female, and are dominantly young adults. Whole-community migrants, also known as nomads or transhumants, reflect the overall demographic profile of the home community.

Cross-community migrants are generally rather small in number, as a proportion of their home community. Most of the migrants are young adults, and most of them are male. While the reality of cross-community migration is often complex, I offer this simple typology of four commonly used terms to summarize most such migration: settlers, sojourners, itinerants, and invaders. *Settlers* are those who move to join an existing community that is different from their own, with the intention of remaining at their destination. (Note the distinction I am making between *settlers*, who move to a different community as an act of cross-community migration, and *colonists*, who are settling in an act of colonization of new territory by their home community.) *Sojourners* are those moving to a new community, usually for a specific purpose, with the intention of returning to their home community. Somewhat different from sojourners are *itinerants*, who move from community to community, but who have no single home to which they expect to return. A further category is *invaders*, who arrive as a group in a community with the objective of seizing control rather than joining. These four basic categories of cross-community migration can contribute, depending on the individual experience of migrants, to a much more complex pattern of migration in practice.

Migrants may journey on their own, making their own way through the stages of migration. More often than not, however, the movement of cross-community migrants is facilitated by *networks*: chains of people who facilitate their movement and their settlement at the end of the journey. Migratory networks, as we will see, are important to the success of cross-community migration.

Networks of people have been developed for many purposes. Here my interest is to describe the general characteristics of a certain category of networks: *cross-community networks*. Such networks, involving cooperation across distance and across boundaries of language and culture, facilitate the movement of migrants from one place to another. The migrants themselves, willingly or not, are a part of the network, but the network depends primarily on others who encourage the movement of migrants.

Migratory networks rise and decline according to need, and they may be rather less permanent than the communities they link. But successful networks, able to move significant numbers of migrants among communities, take on a life of their own. The functions to be performed within a migratory network begin with recruiters, who seek people in one community to go to another. If they seek voluntary migrants, their job is to persuade potential migrants of the benefits of moving; if they seek involuntary migrants, their job is to locate and perhaps to seize candidates. A second function is that of dispatchers, those who make arrangements for sending migrants on their way. As before, this task is performed differently if the migrants are involuntary rather than voluntary. A third element of the network consists of facilitators for travel. These include guides, guards to protect against piracy, ships' crews for migrants going by sea, teamsters for migrants going by caravan, and people to provide food and shelter along the way. Of the hostels along the way, perhaps the most important is the hostel at the destination of the migrant. There one locates those who will assist in seasoning, the process of learning the language and customs of the destination, and also the biological seasoning brought by the differences in disease environment and cuisine. In the course of this seasoning, the migrant establishes an identity – a name and a description – in the community of destination. A final element in the network provides the connections to work, enabling the migrant to gain acceptance as a person who can enter the community and take up a role within it.

While individual migrants may move without networks, any movements of large numbers of migrants soon create networks to organize the process of movement. Since these networks stretch across space and across community boundaries, they are not easily named or incorporated. And since patterns of migration are more variable than communities, it is more difficult to define and theorize networks than communities. Yet these networks have been central to maintaining links among communities, and links among communities provide a key aspect of human history. So this book will include a substantial emphasis on networks facilitating migration as well as on the migrants that have passed through them. For the early twentieth-century migrants from South China and Italy, chains of migrants and facilitators eased the passage of new migrants in their journey. A less benign network of warriors, merchants, and sailors facilitated the migration of African slaves in early modern times; Turkish migrants relied on military and familial networks as they worked their way from Central Asia to Anatolia starting in the eighth century CE.

Habits of migration and short-term social development

In addition to stories of migration itself, in its multiple categories, the book offers stories of human *development* through migration. By development, I mean the complex process of transformation in human society. The concept of "development," like that of "progress," is problematic. The danger in using these terms lies in the common practice of using them to propose a smooth picture of human advance, ignoring or underplaying the crisis, chaos, disaster, destruction, hatred, and occasional evil that have accompanied every stage in human history. Even accounting for all of these negative turns in life, however, some version of the notion of "development" is necessary for any long-term account of human history. The very notion of "history" would make very little sense if it failed to account for some sort of "development."

Here, for instance, is a simplified set of imagined circumstances to display the impact of migration in world history. An existing social system might thrive and expand, perhaps through colonization of new areas. Ultimately the community might encounter limits on its resources, either as its population expands or as its resources shrink (through natural changes or depletion by humans). This challenge might lead to out-migration of some of the deprived, taking their knowledge, skills, and anxieties with them to other communities. Or it might provoke remaining members of the community to create innovations in technology and social organization. The innovations, if they are successful in meeting the challenge, can be implemented at home, or they can be carried into colonies or passed on to people in other communities. The results of these succeeding processes are such that life in an affected community, while not necessarily better, almost surely becomes different. By this definition, migration is associated with development in human society. These varying circumstances, taken together, provide a pattern (and perhaps a cycle) of social changes.

Language, distinguishing humans so sharply from other species, is important in spreading innovations within human communities, and thereby in causing communities to differentiate and become more distinct. Cross-community migration, by linking these diverging communities, performs two functions. First, cross-community migration spreads innovations from community to community in much the same way as language spreads innovations within communities. Second, as cross-community migration brings new resources and new ideas into a receiving community it stimulates further innovation. This contribution of migration to the creation of new ideas (not just their spread) has perhaps been underemphasized in previous analysis. The new ideas, once created, are spread within communities by language and among communities by migration.

In sum, while migration often brings benefits to individual migrants and their families, the benefits of migration at the aggregate level are equally important. The exchange of language, customs, and technology leads to innovations, as different ideas are brought into contact with each other. Then the innovations themselves are spread through the process of migration. Known goods and services are spread among communities by migration. In addition, the movement of people speeds the movement of plants, animals, and minerals in the wake of humans, and some of these have beneficial effects for the receiving society.

At the same time, however, there are also costs of migration at the aggregate level. Migration always spreads disease, and sometimes it spreads massive contagion, bringing waves of death to all connected communities. Migration also spreads other contagions – plants and animals that change the ecology of the receiving region, making them less habitable. And while migration leads to the development of new innovations, it also spreads past innovations, and the result of this is sometimes to cause the disappearance of human communities and ways of life. In language, for instance, migration both creates new languages and causes the disappearance of existing languages as communities come into contact.

This pattern of development, stimulated especially by language and cross-community migration, helps explain how it is that *Homo sapiens* has spread into an incredible range of different ecologies without undergoing any but the tiniest steps in biological evolution. Language, migration, and the resulting evolution of human society and technology have given us the patterns of human history, with endless change and transformation. Yet all those changes remain based on certain fundamental habits, common for all human history. That is, the dynamic of families sending, splitting, and moving – and learning – remains similar. At the same time, the character of human history in every era differs from that in the era before, because the learning and the expansion keep changing human society in all but its most basic character.

Long-term consequences of migration

The elements of human migratory behavior, as described in the first four elements of this model – human language communities, their principal categories of migration, the processes facilitating migration, and their social development – will appear repeatedly in the chapters below. In addition, the long-term results of migration that are the fifth element of the model will also emerge from the unfolding story.

Cross-community migration is valuable mainly because of the differences among human communities. Cross-community migration, in turn, generates changes that lead to further differences among communities. Paradoxically, however, at other times cross-community migration leads to greater similarity among communities. Cross-community migration is a favored behavior, at the species level, because it creates and spreads changes in human society.

Let us begin at a very wide level, and consider the broadest historical patterns associated with migration. The populations that we know as modern *Homo sapiens* emerged in eastern and southern Africa some 200,000 years ago. Our ancestors dispersed progressively as they colonized the African continent, then all of Eurasia, Australasia, the Americas, and ultimately every piece of land on earth. The resulting pattern, associated intimately with this dispersion, is *differentiation*. For many millennia those differences grew steadily, as humans developed new languages, new technologies, new philosophies, and entered an ever-wider range of ecologies. Human communities, in occupying new territories with distinctive ecologies and resources, changed their technology, their social organization, and their beliefs. Languages diverged because of separation in time and space. Even human physical attributes differentiated, partly in response to "genetic drift" resulting from separation, and partly through genetic adaptations to different environments. Cross-community migration performed the functions of creating new ideas through making new connections, and carrying new ideas and new technologies from one place to another.

On the other hand, processes of interaction have tended consistently to counteract the patterns of dispersion and differentiation. Human communities, though separated and distinguished from each other, have nonetheless remained in contact and in mutual dependence. For instance, the interactions of farmers, herders, and fishers have caused sharing of resources among communities, while the interactions of conquerors and their subjects have strengthened some communities at the expense of others.

The pattern of development and transformation in the lifestyle of a single species is peculiar to humans. The dispersion, differentiation, and interaction of human populations combined to create innovations that generated a remarkable social evolution, which has proceeded much more rapidly than biological evolution. The continuing development of human society brings about *convergence*. Throughout human history, the movement of people has brought tendencies toward convergence that run counter to the processes of differentiation. Especially in recent centuries, migratory movements have led to increased sharing of new technology. Common languages and calendars, similarly, have spread widely in recent times.

The big transformations in human society are seen most obviously through technology: fishing, boating, hunting, agriculture, metal-working, commerce, and writing are just a few. But the developments in human ideas, artistic expression, and social organization are just as important to human existence as these technological advances. And the changes in human society are measured not simply in events that can be traced to a crucial moment, but often in the complex interplay of forces over time. Thus, the long-term patterns of migration become not just a historical result but an influential factor in themselves, affecting the details of individual and group decisions in later times. This is the lesson, for instance, of Jared Diamond's investigation of the long-term consequences of the domestication of plants and animals. Similarly, the types of long-term changes to be explored in this study of migration include social differentiation, convergence, cumulation of developments, and long-term influence of early changes, as well as periodic major changes in society. Historians have many types of change to analyze.

The long-term inheritance of earlier migrations provides the base from which any new set of movements arises. For instance, the smallest human communities may not have changed much in size, but the largest communities have grown greatly in scale. The elements of the migration model persist across the whole 200,000 years of the existence of modern *Homo sapiens*, but they have influenced each other differently at every turn.

Conclusion

This world-historical analysis of migration identifies a common set of migratory processes and patterns of behavior for all of human history. To keep track of the various elements of migration, I have organized them into a model with five elements of analysis. These elements address the boundaries of human communities, four basic categories of migration, the processes of cross-community migration, the role of migration in social development in the short term, and the long-term impact of migration.

How do the elements of migration interact, according to the interpretation emerging from this model? I begin by defining human communities in terms of language, which draws attention to the distinction of cross-community migration from other categories of migration. Then I trace all four types of migration within and across community boundaries – home-community migration, colonization, whole-community migration, and cross-community migration. I classify the migrants as colonists, settlers, sojourners, itinerants, invaders, and as whole communities. In this exploration, I focus especially on the interplay of institutions of migration: families within and across communities, migratory networks, and the migrants themselves. The analysis of cross-community migration (more complex than other sorts of migration because it depends on human social institutions) shows how it interacts with colonization, whole-community migration and home-community migration. The innovations brought by cross-community migration generate social development, and these in turn lead to new processes of migration. In turn, the long-term results of migratory processes create the conditions in any community that set the opportunities for migration.

The objective of this book is to illustrate the recurring patterns of human migration and social reproduction, and to show how they underlie the pattern of endless reformulation, innovation, and exploration that characterizes our species. The book is an attempt to explain the transformations of human society through a focus on the tried-and-true habits – the instincts – that have so dependably brought transformation in human life. Based on this framework and these objectives, let us now explore migration in world history, at global and local levels, as presented in eight consecutive time periods.

Further reading

This book focuses on a long-term analysis of a single theme in history, and thus is concerned as much with continuity and reproduction of human situations as with change and transformation. James Burke (a biologist) and Robert Ornstein (a psychologist) trace a major theme in culture through a similarly long time in *The Axemaker's Gift: A Double-edged History of Human Culture* (New York, 1995). For a presentation on the theme of migration over a shorter time but with a wider range of resources in CD-ROM format, see Patrick Manning, *Migration in Modern World History, 1500–2000* (Belmont, Calif., 2000). The theme of urbanization over time is addressed in Tertius Chandler, *Four Thousand Years of Urban Growth* (Lewiston, New York, 1987). For an introduction to the investigation of migration through multiple disciplines, see Jan Lucassen, Leo Lucassen, and Patrick Manning, eds., *Migration History in World History: Multidisciplinary Approaches* (Leiden, 2010); the introductory chapter is a helpful overview. Another introduction to migration studies over the long term is Christiane Harzig and Dirk Hoerder with Donna Gabbaccia, *What is Migration History?* (Cambridge, 2009).

Language communities have provided essential frameworks throughout the existence of modern humans. Merritt Ruhlen has provided an accessible overview of languages and language communities in *The Origin of Language: Tracing the Evolution of the Mother Tongue* (New York, 1994).

Migration of communities and migration across community boundaries are general characteristics of animal species, but they take specific forms for humans. An excellent introduction to human migration in the past three thousand years is Robin Cohen, *Global Diasporas: An Introduction* (Seattle, Wash., 1997). For a good analysis of the social functions of cross-community migration in recent times, see Fredrik Barth, *Ethnic Groups and Boundaries: The Social Organization of Culture Difference* (Oslo, Norway, 1969).

On the association of migration with social development in the short term (that is, within a few human lifespans), the work of the Danish anthropologist Ester Boserup has been influential. In *The Conditions of Agricultural Growth* (Chicago, Ill., 1965), Boserup analyzed processes of agricultural change in East Africa, and drew out lessons that have been applied widely.

Migration in one time period can also bring consequences that are influential in much later times. The most influential recent analysis of long-term effects of early migration is Jared Diamond, *Guns, Germs, and Steel: The Fates of Human Societies* (New York, 1997). For another thoughtful interpretation of long-term processes of change, including the consequences of migration, see Graeme Snooks, *The Dynamic Society: Exploring the Sources of Global Change* (London, 1996).

Chapter 2

Earliest human migrations, to 40,000 BP

Archaeologists (including paleontologists studying human skeletal remains), human biologists, ecologists, and geneticists have developed a relatively detailed and coherent narrative of human evolution. It begins, about seven million years ago, with the origin of the first hominids in eastern and southern Africa, and the biological separation of these species from the other great apes. Then it traces the gradual succession of new hominid species and their slowly changing lifestyles. This story results from combined and interdisciplinary work of a wide range of scholars, and it has been clarified by considerable debate. Studies of skeletal structure, technology, living patterns, and genetic composition have been crucial in explaining the development of hominid populations.

The latest stage in human biological evolution has been identified brilliantly by the recent work of geneticists: the change was the emergence of our own species of *Homo sapiens* some 200,000 years ago, in the same African regions where the first hominids appeared. Geneticists, in addition to showing that modern *Homo sapiens* developed in Africa, argue that our species then spread to occupy all the world, displacing all other hominids in the course of their great migration. The debates over the verification and the implications of this interpretation continue, mostly between geneticists and archaeologists. (Some archaeologists have responded with skepticism, emphasizing the possibilities that modern humans emerged in several regions, or that *Homo sapiens* intermarried significantly with other populations, such as Neanderthals in Europe.)

New sources of evidence and new lines of argument are sure to add to the discussion of the emergence and spread of modern *Homo sapiens*. In particular, as I argue here, the factors of language and migration have been under-emphasized in interpreting this last stage of human evolution. The analyses of linguistic and migratory patterns combine to provide insights that both geneticists and archaeologists must take very seriously in evaluating their understanding of the origin and spread of *Homo sapiens*. Adding and linking the factors of language and migration can clarify the points of origin and directions of travel for large-scale migrations.

This chapter traces hominid evolution from the time of *Australopithecine* divergence from great apes to the occupation of the Old World tropics by *Homo sapiens*. It summarizes the current understanding of archaeological and genetic findings throughout the period up to 40,000 years ago. In addition, I give particular emphasis to an interpretation of the migration of *Homo sapiens* based on linguistic information and on the characteristic human patterns of migration described in the previous chapter. Two sections in the middle of the chapter address the questions of how we know about earliest human history and where scholars disagree. I describe the methods and debates in archaeology and genetics, and give particular attention to the methods of linguistic analysis, especially the implications of present language distributions for past migrations.

Our species of *Homo sapiens*, for most of the time it has existed, has been a tropical species. Warm climates and warm waters are our homeland. The initial stages in human colonization of new territories consisted, therefore, of expansion from the East African homeland to accessible tropical areas in Africa, Asia, and Oceania. These migrations are the topic of the concluding sections of this chapter.

Early hominids: eastern Africa and the Old World

The hominid story begins with geological changes about seven million years ago. Prior to that time, great apes had developed in forested areas of Africa, South and Southeast Asia. But with a major geologic upheaval along eastern Africa from the Red Sea to South Africa, the chain of mountains punctuated by the Rift Valley appeared, and the region to the east of the Rift became dry savanna rather than forest. The winds carrying moisture eastward from the Atlantic Ocean lost most of that moisture as they reached the new range of mountains, so that eastern Africa, along with the Arabian Peninsula, became much drier than before.

In the million or so years after this ecological change, new species diverged from the great apes of Central Africa and developed in the drier regions of the east. These species lived primarily on the ground rather than in trees, and developed an upright stance and bipedal movement. (Walking on two feet is not unusual for animals in general – if one considers birds, kangaroos, and dinosaurs – but it is quite rare among mammals.) Thus developed the order of hominids.

The earliest hominids have been labeled as belonging to the genus *Australopithecus*, and they included *A. afarensis* and *A. rhodesiensis*. These early hominids ranged from what is now Ethiopia to South Africa, but also as far west as Chad, and they appear to have survived primarily by foraging vegetable matter. They had brains of some 500 cubic centimeters in volume. Included among them is the specimen known as Lucy, found at Hadar in Ethiopia and dated between three and four million years ago, who is shown to have walked firmly upright.

Hominids lived for several million years before developing stone tools. The earliest known tool assemblages date as far back as roughly 2.6 million years ago. These Oldowan tools (from Olduvai Gorge in Kenya, where they were first documented), also known as "pebble tools" or "core-choppers," include small tools that have been lightly worked, usually to create a sharp edge on one side, so that they could be used as scrapers. The physical characteristics of the toolmakers had changed sufficiently for archaeologists to label these beings as a separate genus, so the genus *Homo* was confirmed, and among its early species was identified *Homo habilis*, "able man" or "man the toolmaker." *Homo habilis* had a brain of 800 cubic centimeters in volume, and remains of this species have been found especially at lakesides, in contrast to the earlier *Australopithecus* remains, which were found especially along rivers. The geographical range of *Homo habilis* remained much the same as before – the grasslands of eastern and southern Africa – though climate and micro-ecology continued to change and exert their influence on the lives of hominids.

A new species, *Homo erectus*, emerged in East Africa nearly two million years ago. With brains that began at 800 cubic centimeters in volume, these hominids coexisted for a time with *Australopithecenes* and with *Homo habilis*, and by one million years ago had become the only surviving hominid species, with brains that expanded to a volume of 1,200 cubic centimeters. *Homo erectus* was able to spread into new areas. The process of these migrations, in the terms I have proposed in the previous chapter, was that of colonization. That is, small groups left the home society to form equivalent communities in ecologically similar territories. Eventually, communities of *Homo erectus* were able to live in areas that did not have the same ecology as the East African homeland. They were able to occupy West Africa and North Africa, and they were the first hominids to move beyond the African continent. Remains of *Homo erectus*, dated to more than 1.5 million years ago, have been verified for Jordan, the Caucasus, Java, and South China.

A new technology substantially strengthened the adaptability of *Homo erectus*. Roughly one and a half million years ago, the Acheulian or "hand axe" technology emerged in East Africa, and it seems to have been associated especially with *Homo erectus*. These hand axes or biface tools were chipped elegantly on all sides, creating an effective scraping tool that fit easily into the hand. The Acheulian hand axes remained the tool of choice for over a million years, until just over 100,000 years ago. (Hand axes did not spread east of India, however: the communities of *Homo erectus* in Southeast Asia continued to use Oldowan or core-chopper tools, perhaps in association with tools of bamboo.) Only about 500,000 years ago did *Homo erectus* manage to occupy the cooler, forested lands and the more difficult terrain of Europe.

Homo erectus gradually experimented with a second major new technology, the control of fire. The difficulty of distinguishing natural from controlled fire in the archaeological record is considerable, but by 200,000 years ago some sites in Europe and in Africa give a fairly clear indication that they were hearths, where controlled burning took place, presumably for heating and cooking.

With the passage of time, ecological fluctuations brought more or less rain and ice to various regions of the Eastern Hemisphere: glaciers expanded and melted about every two hundred thousand years. Meanwhile, the development of new hominid species continued both inside and outside of Africa. From western Europe to the region surrounding the Caspian Sea, communities of *Homo neanderthalensis* (Neanderthal Man) emerged some 200,000 years ago, and left a remarkable record of their activities in caves, showing that they had well-designed hearths and that they buried their dead.

Though hominids had spread to many areas in the Eastern Hemisphere, the African continent remained their most propitious environment, and the populations in Africa were surely larger than elsewhere. It was there, as before, that the major new development took place.

Homo sapiens: from biological to social evolution in Africa

Beginning perhaps 200,000 years ago, the story of hominid evolution took a crucial turn. One of the new species, *Homo sapiens*, proved to have particularly adaptive characteristics, and was able to expand at the expense of all competitors. The bodies of the new species were quite similar to *Homo erectus*, the brain was only a little bit larger, and the shape of the skull changed modestly. Perhaps the larynx had become significantly more flexible. The most remarkable aspect of the new species was that its modest biological changes were sufficient to set in motion a whole new dynamic. That is, within the past 200,000 years, the principal changes have been not biological evolution but the social evolution of humanity, accompanied by the expansion of the population size and the geographical range of *Homo sapiens*.

A group of geneticists and molecular biologists at the University of California, Berkeley, conducted sampling and examination of human DNA from groups all over the world, focusing on mitochondrial DNA, a component of human cells passed only through the female line, from each mother to all her children. By comparing the relative differences in composition of mitochondrial DNA, they found that the differences were greatest within Africa and thus concluded that the ancestors of human populations were in Africa. By estimating the rate of change in genetic composition, they projected that communities of *Homo sapiens* could be traced back 200,000 years; journalists rhetorically labeled an "African Eve" as the mother of all humanity. The inevitable debates revealed the need for modification in the initial analysis, but in general the results have remained stable, and are now confirmed by other studies. Genetic analysis of certain cellular components governed only by the Y (or male) chromosome confirms both the time and the region of human origins. Recent archaeological finds show remains physically indistinguishable from modern humans to have existed in Ethiopia as long ago as 160,000 years.

The geneticists have gained their two main points: *Homo sapiens* emerged in Africa, and *Homo sapiens* displaced all other hominids – in Africa and then throughout Eurasia. But the centrality of genetics in determining the African origins of *Homo sapiens* does not mean that genetic studies are sufficient to determine the patterns of human migration and development from that time forward. The story of human expansion from eastern Africa to the world, while confirmed in its outline, needs to be filled in with detail. As I will argue, understanding social processes and not just the biological residue of our history is necessary to reconstruct the major steps in human expansion.

The principal advantages of this new hominid species over its competitors, I believe, were that *Homo sapiens* had fully articulated language and a pattern of cross-community migration. These two new strengths provoked a steady stream of social changes by creating communities in which learning and social transformation could be cumulative. The emergence of *Homo sapiens* did not bring biological evolution to an end, for the same processes that have slowly brought about changes in species continue to work their mysterious effects. But among *Homo sapiens* new processes of social evolution emerged, propagated, and transformed themselves with lightning speed.

The lifestyle of the first communities of *Homo sapiens* must have been very like that of neighboring communities of *Homo erectus*: life particularly along waterways, production and use of stone tools with Acheulian technology, gathering vegetable and animal matter from land and water, and gaining meat primarily by scavenging. This new human population, in order to develop and maintain itself, required at least several thousand individuals, in the view of population geneticists. (Thus the "first humans" would have been part of an evolving community, rather than isolated individuals.) The social communities of humans were far smaller than this biological total, but to sustain their emerging languages they must have had at least several hundred members.

The initial differences among human communities in languages and customs may have been small by present-day standards. Yet the early communities of *Homo sapiens* developed a basis for moving into new regions by putting their discoveries into words, communicating with other communities, and combining old and new ideas. Once in new regions, groups of humans could become even more different from other communities yet retain some contact with the activities and developments of the parent communities.

As human communities grew and spread, they were confronted repeatedly by a choice: between concentrating at water's edge and ranging across open grassland. Earlier hominids had faced this choice, and tended to stay close to waterways. Humans, as they developed new technologies and explored new ecologies, found new ways to benefit from life in the grasslands and from life at water's edge. Studies of human evolution have long tended to emphasize hunting and the grasslands; to achieve some balance, I want to emphasize the continuing importance of rivers, lakes, and the ocean in early human society. Gatherers found a rich variety of plant and animal life along the seashore, along rivers, and at lakeside. Humans are likely to have been swimmers from the first, and to have developed rafts and boats. Though the evidence is indirect, maritime archaeologists have shown the logic of the construction of the first watercraft: logs might serve as rafts, but more practically the gathering and bundling of reeds – available at water's edge throughout the tropics – provided materials for lightweight and maneuverable craft.

In their choice of ecological specialization, human communities could choose to concentrate on life along the waters, or to move out of the valleys and into surrounding higher lands, or to sustain communities with a division of labor between members exploiting each of these environments. The balance of human reliance on the produce of the soil and the produce of the waters has been adjusted in each new region and with each new technology.

Improvements in stone technology began to accumulate, in association with improved practices in hunting and fishing. The practice of decoration began, as has been shown with ostrich eggshells etched with wavy lines or punctured with holes for stringing, as revealed in early South African sites.

All of these patterns of change are consistent with – and can only be explained by – the practice of cross-community migration. Migration was no longer limited to the exchange of persons within a community, the episodes of colonization by small family groups, or the occasional flight of a whole community from disaster. In addition, young people (and probably mostly males from the start) now left their home community to visit or join other communities, learning the language and culture of those with whom they settled, and learning as well as introducing ideas about technology, culture, and social relations. The question of who stayed at home and who left to voyage was posed for every generation. The flow of cross-community migrants served to keep different communities, even distant ones, in contact with one another. At the same time, the connections among distant communities, if they ceased to be reaffirmed through migration, might lapse entirely. At a larger scale and in a later time, similarly, the connections between Asia and North America were to lapse and be forgotten to most.

The first hundred thousand years of human existence brought a substantial change in population distribution. In the period up to 60,000 BP ("before the present," or 60,000 years ago), African populations moved from being centered in the savannas of eastern and southern Africa, where their hominid ancestors had always been most numerous, to being centered in the east–west belt of the northern savanna between modern Sudan in the east and Senegal in the west. Four great language groups are based in the African continent, and reflect the placement and movement of people for tens of thousands of years. I believe that recent language distributions can be projected back with sufficient confidence to say that as of about 60,000 BP, the Khoisan languages were based in the savanna areas of eastern and southern Africa, where humans had first evolved. The Nilo-Saharan languages were based in the middle Nile Valley, and the Afroasiatic languages were based in a nearby region of the middle Nile Valley. The Niger-Congo languages were centered to the west of the last two, and included groupings both east and west of Lake Chad. All of these were areas where hominids had lived before, but the regional emphasis had now moved from eastern and southern Africa to the grasslands and waterways of the northern savanna. In addition, and in continuity with earlier hominid patterns, we must assume that humans populated the shores of the Indian Ocean and the Red Sea.

How do we know? Methods for analysis

All of the assertions above draw on research and analysis in several disciplines. It is time to address the terrains and the methods of these disciplines. Evidence on early human communities and their movements comes principally from four great areas of study: archaeology, genetics, historical linguistics, and anthropology. (Many other fields – such as plant biology, geology, and ecology – play supporting roles.) Archaeology, itself a multidisciplinary field of study, has long maintained pride of place in analysis of early human development, because of its excavation and direct analysis of human relics. Genetics (in association with molecular biology) is only one of several fields in biology that has proved relevant to the study of human evolution, but it has become particularly powerful, and is likely to have even greater impact as the additional results of the Human Genome Project become apparent. Yet genetics, while a powerful tool, is still a crude one. The results of genetic study of mitochondrial DNA and Y-chromosome analysis, the two strongest sets of evidence for the emergence of *Homo sapiens* in Africa, have not yet been linked in detail to analyses in other disciplines. Historical linguistics, in contrast, has undergone nearly two centuries of analysis, often in combination with archaeology. Still, the historical analysis of language and language communities continues to develop through new research and theory.

In a very real sense, none of our evidence on the distant past comes from a direct experience with the past. All of the evidence is available in the present. For language and genetics, we sample evidence on language and DNA from living people, and project these results into the past. Sometimes we can investigate earlier evidence – as when remnants of written texts and bodily remains from early times become available for analysis. In archaeology, too, the materials that we investigate have survived into the present – but archaeological analysis is restricted to the tiny portion of surviving past materials that we have unearthed.

Archaeologists locate the surviving physical remains of earlier times, and estimate the dates of their creation. Archaeology gives us, for early *Homo sapiens*, information on human physical conditions, ecological conditions, technology, living patterns, and connections to other communities. For archaeology, evidence is unearthed from past human communities rather than collected from present communities. Archaeology provides eclectic information on many topics, though the information is limited by the small size of the digs. The evidence includes human remains, ecological conditions, and material culture. These sometimes produce indirect but rarely direct information on language and genetic composition.

Genetics provides information on the genetic composition of present and past communities. For historical or evolutionary studies, the information is collected in the present (from today's cells) and projected into the past. The logic or model of projecting current evidence into the past is thus crucial in the completion of a genetic-historical analysis: I will emphasize two issues in modeling. First, given that each individual has two parents, one's ancestry goes back along many paths. That is, the "tree model" in genetics goes in two directions: from one ancestor to many descendants, and from one descendant to many ancestors. (Actually the reality of genetic ancestry does not spread as widely as the model, because individuals play multiple roles in the family tree.) Nevertheless, two types of recent genetic evaluation have sought to simplify the analysis, and make it more parallel to linguistics, by focusing on sex-linked characteristics of mitochondrial DNA and Y chromosomes. But despite this simplified modeling for certain analytical purposes, the fact is that human reproduction is sexual. As a result humans, in contrast to languages, must have ancestors on many branches of the family tree. A second issue in genetic modeling is that the geneticist, in collecting samples from people today, makes assumptions about what past populations they are descended from. For example, geneticists may assume that people living today in isolated areas of Southeast Asia are direct descendants of the earliest populations in that area. Such assumed relationships come from evidence other than genetic data, and if the assumptions are imprecise or incorrect, the analysis and conclusions will be deficient.

Historical linguists study the languages spoken today, and from them make estimates about the ancestral languages from which they descended. Where possible, linguists also work from written records on languages in earlier times. For linguistics (as for genetics), we assume that present data give us the remnants of earlier communities. But the definition of "earlier community" is different in each case. For language, it is assumed that each language has one parent. As noted above, in genetics a person has more and more ancestors as one goes to earlier generations, while a language has a single ancestor at each stage. The "tree model" of languages presents the range of languages descended from an ancestor, and indicates relationships with other languages descended from the same ancestor. Because of the single-ancestor characteristics of the linguistic "tree model," language gives more evidence on path of migration than does genetics, because it allows for less possibilities. Some further principles and techniques in language analysis are described further in the next section, because they are applied widely in this book.

Anthropology is the study of human communities, especially their social and cultural practices, and especially for small communities. The anthropological subfield of ethnology (also known as ethnography) focuses on analysis of communities through direct observations. Ethnography includes the description of cultural practices in communities. To the extent that one can think of these cultural practices as being inherited, ethnologists have commonly proposed the equivalent of "tree models" for cultural practices, and have hypothesized the cultural practices of ancestral populations based on observations of recent populations. For migration, in contrast, major ethnological studies are rare, because the tendency in anthropology has been to study groups in isolation from each other. The work of Danish ethnographer Frederik Barth on West African populations in the 1960s, however, gained wide attention for his emphasis on the shifting identities of people as they crossed ethnic boundaries in the course of their life.

One hopes that these four types of analysis will each contribute to a consistent overall picture of human history. But the various disciplines need not provide identical results to be useful and accurate records of the past. For instance, genetic change and linguistic change in a population need not go together. It is common to find cases where there has been major language change and small genetic change in a community. As an example, the Celtic-speaking Gauls of France adopted Latin under Roman rule (a scant two thousand years ago), with little genetic change. The opposite pattern of major genetic change and small language change, though less common, can also be found: once English, Spanish, and Portuguese were established as the main languages of the Americas, immigrants from all parts of Africa and Europe adopted those languages as they settled in the Americas.

In three of the four fields – archaeology, genetics, and linguistics – much effort has gone into dating the past. Researchers have attempted to establish the dates for their observations on natural phenomena, human remains, language, and technology. Dating is both relative and absolute. All three fields are relatively strong in their ability to identify relative chronology, but there remain substantial doubts on absolute chronology. Far more effort has gone into dating archaeological findings than into dating the changes in language and genetic composition. Much archaeological dating relies on elaborate comparisons of various sorts of data. The most basic archaeological technique for dating is stratigraphy: that is, the depth and order of the strata or layers of earth and other remains under which a given artifact or set of human remains is buried in an excavation. Dating is also conducted by comparison to the surrounding plants and animals, features of the earth, and indications of climate. To these processes of relative dating, archaeologists have added techniques for absolute dating. Radiocarbon dating, based on analysis of carbon associated with artifacts, provides evidence of absolute dates of the artifacts up to 50,000 years ago. A similar process, potassium-argon dating, can give evidence of absolute dates for remains of 500,000 years ago or more. The newer technique of thermoluminescence addresses part of the gap between these two main procedures, and other techniques are under development. Overall, archaeologists and their colleagues have addressed the dating of the human past with great seriousness. Their work, however, proceeds slowly and with an inevitable bias: most analyses underestimate the actual age of the changes they seek to identify.

Dating in genetics and linguistics focuses not on the dating of specific humain remains, as in archaeology, but on estimating the time of separation of groups into subgroups – gene pools or language groups. Relative dating is straightforward in genetics: once the immense task of establishing the sequence of elements in the proteins and DNA under study is completed, it is not difficult to state the degree of difference between individual samples. As noted above, these differences can be projected from today's individuals to past populations if the succession of populations is modeled appropriately. Then, to the degree that one can assume a steady rate of genetic change creating separations among populations, one can turn this relative dating into absolute dating. Such estimation is the basis for the geneticists' assertion that *Homo sapiens* emerged some 200,000 years ago.

In linguistics, the relative difference among languages is somewhat more difficult to determine than is the case in genetics, because of the complexity and variability of language. Short lists of common words (for numbers, body parts, and social roles) have been remarkably successful as sources of information on the relative difference among languages. But in addition, languages have grammatical structures that vary greatly, and they also include words borrowed from other languages – each of these factors may reveal information relevant to the relative difference among languages. While work is sometimes slow, the application of these principles is promising. Linguists working on certain major language families – Indo-European and Nilo-Saharan, in particular – have been able to show that the several subgroups of these families separated not all at once in a single dispersion, but one by one over a long period of time.

For languages, there has been little progress in estimating the absolute dates of major changes. One procedure to estimate the absolute dates for separation of languages, known as "glottochronology," compared languages on a standard list of some 200 words, and projected the date of separation of the languages based on the proportion of similar words. This procedure, which in any case was considered to be applicable to changes within five thousand years, rapidly became controversial and its use declined. More recently, linguists have sought to identify absolute dates in using techniques inspired by archaeology: using a wide range of associated data to estimate the dates of diverging language communities. These include using the words for techniques, plants, animals, and social organization (including borrowed words) and correlating these with archaeological data.

Archaeologists are often conservative in estimating the age of their finds and the age of the larger processes they document. For their specific finds archaeologists combine several dating techniques, and do not rush to adopt the oldest date. For the larger processes, archaeologists commonly date the beginning of a phenomenon with the oldest known discovery. But since archaeological work is necessarily incomplete, the earliest record may not have been discovered. Linguists are conservative in their own way: they are willing to offer dates for divergence of language communities for the last several thousand years, but are reluctant to do so for earlier times. Geneticists are the least conservative, and have been willing to project relatively early dates for the phenomena they study.

Using language to analyze migration

The work of assembling the broadest overview of human languages has only recently come to be undertaken seriously, and completing the task will require detailed work by hundreds of linguists. The task of determining the chronological depth of the various language phyla or groupings will be difficult, and our methods are very crude so far. Thousands of individual languages have been lost in recent times, and more were lost in earlier times. Sometimes the disappearance of a language resulted from the populations dying out, but more commonly it resulted from the populations adopting other languages. By a similar logic, one can imagine that not only individual languages but whole groupings or phyla of languages have ceased to exist, as their populations became absorbed into others in which the populations managed to reproduce themselves more successfully.

Joseph Greenberg has done more than anyone else to assemble a picture of the main groupings of human languages. Over a long career, he classified the languages of Africa, the Americas, much of Eurasia, and parts of the Pacific. Greenberg wrote extensively on the methodology of language classification. Such classification began with the work of Sir William Jones, who in 1786 published a description of what became known as the Indo-European family of languages, distinguishing this family from other languages of the Old World. Historical linguists from Jones to Greenberg have learned to interpret language change through three broad types of processes: the "genetic" origin and change of languages, the "borrowing" of words, and the mutual influence of languages. For all the complexity of underlying detail in the world's thousands of languages, these three principles are very instructive in understanding language change.

First, the "genetic" origin and change of languages. Languages change over time at a relatively constant rate – both in their vocabulary and in their grammar. Languages are related to one another "genetically," in that one ancestral language can give birth, over time, to daughter languages, which in turn give birth to other languages with time. (For instance, one can predict the grammar and vocabulary of ancient Latin by working back from patterns in the languages known to have descended from Latin.) Classifying languages consists of comparing words and structures of languages to each other, to develop an interpretation of language "families." For any two languages, one seeks to answer two sorts of question: whether the two can be seen to have a common ancestor and, if so, how closely they are related to each other and to the common ancestor. (In making these comparisons, it is usually best to compare numerous words and structures in the analysis of any two languages, and numerous languages in the analysis of their grouping.)

Second, the "borrowing" of words. While most words in a language are inherited from the ancestral language, some words are borrowed from other languages or even from other families. In English, while our basic words for numbers and body parts are inherited from Old English and earlier languages, our word for "minister" comes from French, our word for "algebra" comes ultimately from Arabic, and our word for "tea" comes ultimately from Chinese. In the twentieth century, the term "OK" came to be spoken in many different languages. Each of these word borrowings thus reflects a movement of ideas, of artifacts, and of people. In general, the borrowing of words is parallel to and reflective of the borrowing of technology and ideas. Borrowing and loaning of words are thus linked to cross-community migration.

Third, the mutual influence of languages. Languages spoken in the immediate proximity of one another, even when they are of quite different families, often adopt some of the same characteristics in the grammar and modes of expression. This can be seen as the logical result of having numerous multilingual individuals, who move from one language to another commonly, and who develop patterns of expressing themselves similarly even though the vocabulary and grammar of their various languages differ fundamentally. One example from southern Africa stands out: the Khoisan languages are almost unique in containing several implosive sounds. For instance the !Kung people of Namibia pronounce their name with an implosive click (!) from the roof of the mouth. Several nearby Bantu languages, while greatly different in grammar and vocabulary, have adopted the click sounds. For instance, the Xhosa people of South Africa pronounce their name with a click (x) from the side of their mouth. In contrast to the borrowing of individual words, these are examples of languages exchanging types of sounds or organizations of expression.

These three basic principles of linguistics show the range and flexibility of linguistic analysis. The principle of genetic origin emphasizes the uniqueness of each community of speech. But the principles of borrowing and of mutual influence of languages assume that people will be crossing the boundaries of these communities all the time. The study of linguistics, therefore, takes into account the human patterns of migration and interconnection in its most basic principles.

Despite the disappearance of many individual languages and probably of some major language phyla, the surviving evidence of language is of great help in determining the paths of early human migration. It is clear that all the major language groupings go back further than the development of agriculture. (The language groups of Australia and New Guinea, which evidently stem from the initial settlement of those regions as much as 60,000 years ago, provide the best example of the longevity of some language families.) In this chapter, therefore, I will rely especially on linguistic evidence to suggest the patterns of migration for the period from perhaps 100,000 years ago to about 40,000 years ago. In the next two chapters, I will return to language evidence to trace the migrations of humans in the time from 40,000 years ago to 15,000 years ago, and then in the early agricultural era, from 15,000 to 5,000 years ago.

Figure 2.1 shows the approximate geographic distribution, in about the year 1500, of twelve language groups, into which all of the world's many thousands of languages surviving at that time can be classified. The Dene-Caucasian (including Sino-Tibetan) and Eurasiatic language groups had the largest number of speakers; the Niger-Congo and Austric groups had the largest number of languages. As will be shown below, this distribution of the world's languages contains a great deal of valuable information about human populations and migrations in much earlier times. (The map has been drawn based on language distribution in 1500, because migration since then has changed the pattern of language distribution greatly.)

In a technique commonly used by historical linguists, I will now demonstrate how the distribution of languages can provide information on the geographic points of origin and the path of migration of populations and their languages. The full determination and verification of the points of origin and the paths of movement of populations and their languages are complex and require the assembly of expertise drawn from many fields. But through a simple technique, the *principle of least moves*, a lay person can make quick and remarkably valuable estimates of the points of origin and direction of migration of past populations. Only two sorts of information are required, and both of these are provided by linguists in many cases: (1) a genetic classification of related languages, distinguishing the broader groupings of languages for earlier times from the narrower groupings of more closely related languages for more recent times; and (2) a map showing the locations of populations speaking these same languages and groups of languages.

Let us take the example of speakers of the Portuguese language. Where was the homeland from which their ancestors came? Linguists have classified Portuguese as a Romance language, and have identified the major other Romance languages as Spanish, French, Italian, and Romanian. The idea of using the principle of least moves to locate the homeland of a group of languages is as follows: (1) on the map in Figure 2.2, locate and mark the point that is the geographical center for each language; (2) locate the point that minimizes the distance moved to each of these points. Thus, if we placed points at the geographic center of Portugal, Spain, France, Italy, and Romania, then our estimate of the point of origin for the whole language group would be somewhere in northwestern Italy. This is the point from which the total length of the lines drawn to each of the language centers would be minimized. In fact,

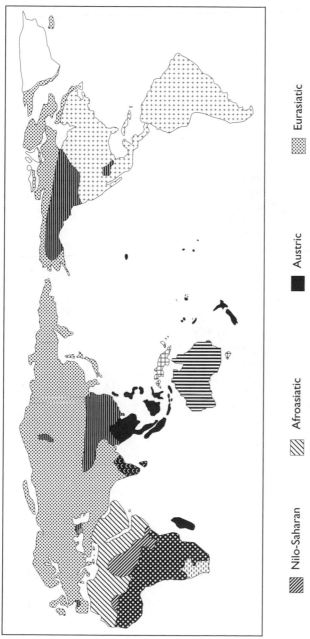

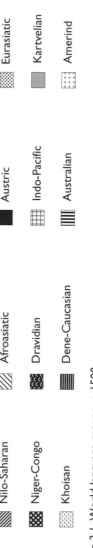

▨	Nilo-Saharan	▨	Afroasiatic	■	Austric
▨	Niger-Congo	▨	Dravidian	▦	Indo-Pacific
▨	Khoisan	▥	Dene-Caucasian	▤	Australian

▨	Eurasiatic		
▨	Kartvelian		
▨	Amerind		

Figure 2.1 World language groups, c. 1500

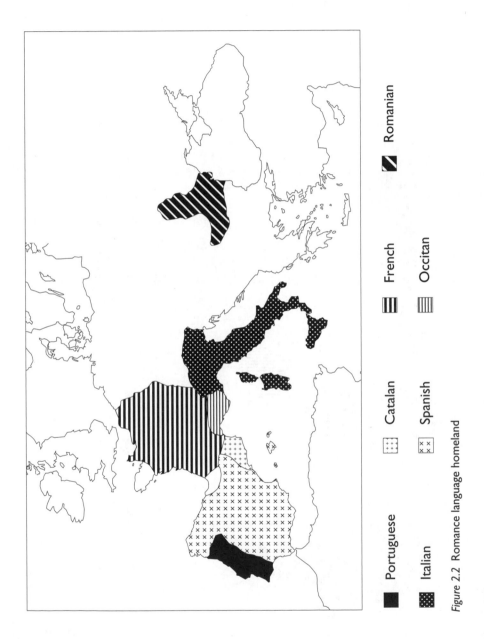

Portuguese

Italian

Catalan

Spanish

French

Occitan

Romanian

Figure 2.2 Romance language homeland

it gives a pretty good representation of the fact that Latin-speaking Romans, especially from the northern half of Italy, colonized all of these areas over two thousand years ago, and launched the process leading to the languages of today. (Perhaps the most significant demonstration of this principle was Joseph Greenberg's use of it in the 1960s to show that the Bantu-speaking populations, covering almost the entire southern third of the African continent, had first emerged in southeast Nigeria, where their nearest linguistic neighbors were also located.)

This statement of the principle of least moves is highly simplified, and in this presentation has left out a great deal of available information. For instance, there were many more Romance languages than the five I listed; the center of origin for Portuguese or any of the other languages can be located more precisely by accounting for the various dialects within the language; there are huge populations speaking Portuguese, Spanish, and French outside of Europe (though these are known to have grown up in recent centuries), and so forth. Nonetheless, this simple least-moves approach enables the lay reader to participate actively in the interpretation of past human migrations through study of evidence on language classification.

If we can trace the ancestry of Portuguese-speakers back more than 2,000 years through analysis of Romance languages, can we trace it further? Romance languages are one of the categories in the Indo-European language family. The other main categories are Germanic, Celtic, Greek, Albanian, Slavic, Baltic, Anatolian, Indo-Iranian, and Tocharian. As shown in Figure 2.3, the least-moves estimate for the Indo-European homeland is near the shores of the Black Sea. One must guess at the time frame, but I will affirm that the origin of this group must go back before the development of agriculture, to at least 15,000 years ago. In fact, linguists and archaeologists have debated fiercely the question of the location of the Indo-European homeland, and also the timing of Indo-European origins. But our simple least-moves estimate is sufficient to get us into the thick of the argument – it is precisely one of the main areas proposed by scholars as the Indo-European homeland, and is definitely within a thousand kilometers of any of the candidates for the homeland.

Continuing back into the deeper past, we may ask whether Indo-European was part of a broader and earlier grouping of languages. Indeed, the answer is yes, and the most authoritative summary is that of Greenberg, who identified the super-family of languages he has labeled Eurasiatic. The Eurasiatic super-family comprises seven major families of languages of Eurasia and the Arctic, of which the Indo-European languages are but one. As I will show in Chapter 3, the least-moves estimate of the Eurasiatic homeland is near the Pacific coast of north Asia.

This completes my compressed methodological summary on the use of linguistics in interpreting migration history. It is now time to apply it.

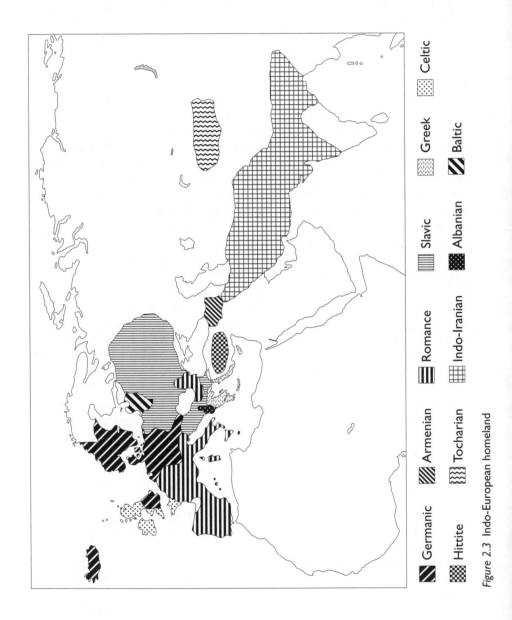

Germanic · Armenian · Romance · Slavic · Greek · Celtic

Hittite · Tocharian · Indo-Iranian · Albanian · Baltic

Figure 2.3 Indo-European homeland

Peopling the Old World tropics, 100,000 to 40,000 BP

Homo sapiens migrated into region after region of the world, concluding with the occupation of the Americas. As noted in earlier sections of this chapter, this migration began with the differentiation of *Homo sapiens* populations within Africa (the emergence of four major language groups being a major indication of their divisions), and the development of new technologies and social systems allowing humans to occupy a steadily wider range of ecologies. Then one stream of migrants, relying on water's-edge technology including the use of boats, crossed the narrow waterway between Ethiopia and Yemen (less than 20 kilometers at the time) and expanded eastward: these migrants colonized the Indian Ocean coast with relative ease, and from that vantage point gradually spread to the interior of islands and mainland areas. Earlier populations of *Homo erectus* provided little resistance to the migrants, and may not have been numerous in the coastal zones along which the settlers moved.

Perhaps the most remarkable step of this migration was the movement across what is now the Indonesian archipelago to the lands that are now New Guinea and Australia. The only way to get to New Guinea and Australia was to cross stretches of open ocean of at least 100 kilometers, yet archaeologists have shown that humans had achieved that task up to 60,000 years ago through dating of human remains and artifacts in Australia.

An essential part of the information for creating this interpretation comes from the work of geologists. Their work has demonstrated that the earth went through a long cooling phase between about 130,000 and 20,000 years ago, after which it warmed rapidly. During this long era of cooling the polar ice pack grew, ocean levels declined, and the climate became steadily drier because so much water was in frozen form. Figure 2.4 shows the summary results of recent research, using measurements from the island of Barbados to estimate the rise and fall in sea level over that time. It suggests that in the time from 80,000 to 60,000 years ago, sea level was from 60 to 80 meters lower than it is today. Thus the migrants who first worked their way eastward along the tropical coast were on a coastline that has since been inundated by the rise in waters at the end of the Ice Age. Those lower sea levels revealed an expanded Southeast Asian subcontinent which the geologists have called Sunda. The lower waters also linked Australia and New Guinea into a continent that geologists call Sahul.

Even with the maximal amount of land revealed by low levels of the ocean, there still remained a task of island-hopping that required distances of perhaps 100 kilometers by boat. The boats may have been reed craft or bamboo rafts. The crossing was made not once but several times, according to genetic evidence showing differences within the populations of Australia and New Guinea. After making this crossing, the settlers were able to spread throughout Sahul.

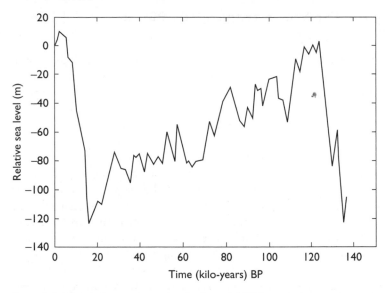

Figure 2.4 Global changes in sea levels, from 140,000 BP to the present

Source: Edouard Bard, Bruno Hamelin, and Richard G. Fairbanks, "U-Th ages obtained by mass spectrometry on corals from Barbados: sea level during the past 130,000 years," *Nature* 346 (6283): 456–458, August 1990.

I think that this idea of a water's-edge migration from Africa to Australia, from perhaps 80,000 to 60,000 years ago, is more than plausible. If a technology were developed that enabled humans to prosper at the boundary of tropical ocean and land of somewhat varying rainfall, there were thousands of kilometers of coastline of similar ecology from the Horn of Africa to Sahul. Gathering vegetable and crustacean nourishment, and perhaps fish, would have been the basis of subsistence. Boats would have been a necessary part of life. The result was that Indo-Pacific and Australian language groups, and probably the ancestors of Sino-Tibetan, Austric, and Dravidian groups, were set in place by 60,000 BP. Figure 2.5 summarizes the evidence on distribution of tropical language groups, with a dot placed at the homeland (the least-moves center) for each major language group.

What were the languages of those who left Africa and headed east along the coast? They could have been in any of the four language groups of Africa today, or of yet another language group that has since disappeared. Of the current African language groups, I would argue that the Nilo-Saharan languages were the most likely source of the eastward migrants. I base this estimate on the geographical distribution of Nilo-Saharan languages, for which the homeland would appear to have been within reach of the Red Sea coast; and on the significant emphasis of Nilo-Saharan speakers in more recent times on what Christopher Ehret has called an "aquatic culture." As a second candidate for

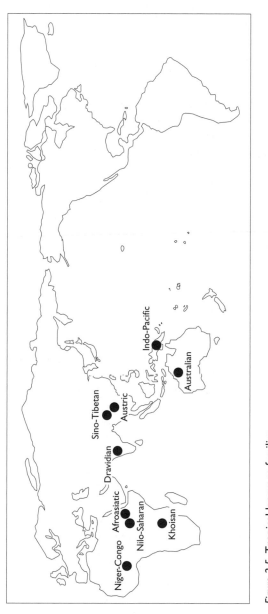

Figure 2.5 Tropical language families

the origin of the eastward migrants, I would suggest the Afroasiatic languages: these too appear to have a homeland along the frontier of modern Ethiopia and Sudan, and were geographically well placed to send migrants eastward.

Two other groups are less likely candidates as the source of colonists in Asia, but cannot be excluded. For the Niger-Congo languages, their homeland appears to be rather far to the west (at least as far as Kordofan in western Sudan), but many of the Niger-Congo-speakers in recent times have emphasized life at water's edge. For the Khoisan languages, the Khoisan-speakers of today live rather far from the East African coast, and have very little involvement in boating. (On the other hand, genetic comparisons suggest Khoisan-speakers are closer to Asians than other African groups, though this might reflect recent rather than early connections.)

If the Nilo-Saharan languages were the source of the eastward migrants, then one would expect ultimately to find all the tropical Asian and Oceanic language groups to be related to Nilo-Saharan, presumably as daughter language groups. These would include Dravidian, Sino-Tibetan (or Dene-Caucasian), Austric, Indo-Pacific, and Australian. The continuing work of language classification is almost sure to clarify these linkages.

(As a skeptical note on this vision of human occupation of the tropics, I should note that the islands of Madagascar and the Comoros, off the southeast coast of Africa, were not occupied by humans as part of the initial human expansion, and may not have been settled by humans until some three thousand years ago. Madagascar and the Comoros, however, each lie some 400 kilometers from the African coast, a far greater distance than those crossed by mariners crossing from Africa to Arabia or from Sunda to Sahul.)

Were the migrants motivated by a pioneering spirit as they moved eastward along the tropical coastline? Was their pattern of migration mainly a colonization of empty territory rather than an overlapping set of cross-community migrations? Certainly the evidence remaining in New Guinea and Australia of the multiple migrations across the open ocean conveys the image of an aggressive campaign to expand. Yet I do not think that humans can carry out relentless campaigns of expansion for thousands of years. If we turn to more recent examples of groups with great activity in migration – the Polynesians, the Vikings, the Phoenicians, and, more recently, the Scots and the Lebanese – we see that their campaigns of migration could last as much as several hundred years, and then gave way to patterns involving far less long-distance migration. On the other hand, if we think of the Phoenicians and the Lebanese as related, we might argue that certain populations alternate between periods of active colonization and periods of less aggressive cross-community migration.

I propose to resist the temptation of picturing the peopling of the earth as a series of campaigns of colonization, in which bands of settlers focused deliberately on conquering new lands until the frontier was closed. Such campaigns of colonization surely took place, but they are not the whole story: they were part of a wider and more complex pattern of human movement and interaction. Any "pioneering spirit" that seized hold of a population for a time was associated with a technology, a way of life, and a specific adaptation to the environment. It would have developed out of cross-community migration that combined ideas to bring the pioneering social order into existence.

Conclusion

The confirmation of the African origins of *Homo sapiens* has stimulated a rethinking of the relationships among world regions. It has generated a multidisciplinary effort to clarify and unify our understanding of the processes by which humans spread throughout the world. This discovery affirms unmistakably the unity of human populations, yet draws attention to human differentiation into communities that came to vary greatly in language, in culture, and in aspects of their physical appearance. In my analysis of these issues, I emphasize the clarification of the human past that can be brought by fuller attention to the history of language groups and to the detailed patterns of human migration.

So I want to return to the types of migrant I have identified, to consider how these types of individual migration might have facilitated the overall process of human occupation of the earth's surface. Migration of whole communities was usually a migration of desperation rather than of hope: most often, it consisted of refugees driven out by drought or by conquest. Colonization was perhaps the most optimistic mode of migration. Human patterns of migration from one language community to another differed from the migration of all other species, and enabled a rapid occupation of the world. Immigration reflected and brought the strengthening of existing communities more than the creation of new ones. Conquest reflected the attractiveness of existing communities, if not their strength. Sojourning might have been to areas of concentrated population, or to distant sources of desirable resources. Itinerants, always small in number, may nonetheless have brought key services or information. These four patterns of cross-community migration sustained the larger pattern of human colonization. They facilitated the succession of human technologies and social organizations, such as littoral gathering, boating, hunting, and building, that permitted colonization of new lands.

In analyzing the patterns of human migration, it is important to maintain attention to a basic issue of lifestyle: the balance of human dependence on the soil and on the waters. Too often it has been assumed unthinkingly that man is a terrestrial species, when the connections to rivers, lakes, and oceans may have been central. In this book I will attempt to keep track, at each stage of the argument and the story, of the proportion of population in terrestrial and watery lifestyles, and keep track of which has the newest technological advances.

One further point is to draw attention to the controversy, still unresolved, about the pace of change in human evolution. Scientists, in debating the evolution of humans and that of other animals, are divided into two main camps. One side argues that evolution has mainly been a slow and steady process of change; the other argues that periods of rapid change, occurring from time to time, account for a large portion of total genetic change. So I must articulate my stand on the balance of evolution and revolution in human genetic and social change.

In my interpretation, assuming that we of *Homo sapiens* differ from all our predecessors in having a fully articulated language and a pattern of inter-community migration, I have treated these developments as a revolutionary rather than evolutionary change. Whether these patterns developed in a rapid burst of change or slowly over many thousands of years is still impossible to say. But once these new characteristics were firmly in place for *Homo sapiens*, no further great changes in human nature were necessary to explain the outlines of historical change from that time to our own. The patterns of migration across communities and the translation of ideas were sufficient to bring an accelerating stream of innovations, so that humans developed layer upon layer of technology, art, and social structure. This pattern of accelerating innovation through discussion and migration began, I argue, not with industrialization and the rise of science two hundred years ago, not with the beginnings of agriculture some 10,000 years ago, but more than ten times longer ago than that.

Further reading

The evolution of early hominids provides background to the evolution and migration of modern *Homo sapiens*. For this background, a concise summary is presented in the early chapters of Peter Bogucki, *The Origins of Human Society* (Oxford, 1999), and a more detailed review is available in D. W. Phillipson, *Archaeology of Africa*, second edition (Cambridge, 1993).

For archaeological studies of the evolution and spread of *Homo sapiens*, the above studies are also useful. For a good general review of the emergence and spread of *Homo sapiens*, see Steve Olson, *Mapping Human History: Genes, Race, and Our Common Origins* (Boston, Mass., 2002). In addition, paleontologist Chris Stringer is joined by Robin McKie to present a lively and controversial analysis, *African Exodus: The Origins of Modern Humanity* (New York, 1998). A detailed and important review of the archaeology of modern *Homo sapiens* is Sally McBrearty and Alison S. Brooks, "The Revolution that Wasn't: A New Interpretation of the Origin of Modern Human Behavior," *Journal of Human Evolution* 39 (2000), 453–563.

Other methods of analysis for study of early human migration include genetics, linguistics, and anthropology. For a detailed but accessible review of the genetics of *Homo sapiens* that includes some linkage to language, language development, and problems of dating, see Luigi Luca Cavalli-Sforza (trans. Mark Seielstad), *Genes, Peoples, and Languages* (Berkeley, Calif., 2001); a more thorough presentation of the genetic analysis of human populations is to be found in L. Luca Cavalli-Sforza, Paolo Menozzi, and Alberto Piazza, *The History and Geography of Human Genes* (Princeton, N.J., 1994).

On archaeological methods of dating, Bogucki, *Origins of Human Society*, includes a good discussion of methods of dating with regard to the earliest human remains in Australia.

For an overview of language in history, see Merritt Ruhlen, *The Origin of Language: Tracing the Evolution of the Mother Tongue* (New York, 1994). I follow Ruhlen in many parts of his argument, but not on his close association of Afroasiatic with Eurasiatic languages. The most authoritative work on the historical study of language, with particular attention to African examples, is Christopher Ehret, *History and the Testimony of Language* (Berkeley, Calif., 2011). Also on the languages of Africa, see Bernd Heine and Derek Nurse, eds., *African Languages: An Introduction* (Cambridge, 2000). Joseph Greenberg's pioneering classifications of major language groups of the Old World tropics are summarized in *The Languages of Africa* (Bloomington, Ind., 1963); and "The Indo-Pacific Hypothesis," in Thomas A. Sebeok, ed., *Current Trends in Linguistics*, vol. 8 (The Hague, 1971), 807–871.

The idea that early humans migrated especially by water has been emphasized by those who have studied Australia and New Guinea. For studies of later times that give insights into the likely practices of early maritime life, see Paul Johnstone, *The Sea-Craft of Prehistory* (Cambridge, Mass., 1980); Jon M. Erlandson, "Ancient Immigrants: Archaeology and Maritime Migrations," in Jan Lucassen, Leo Lucassen, and Patrick Manning, eds., *Migration History in World History: Multidisciplinary Approaches* (Leiden, 2010), 191–214; and Christopher Ehret, *The Civilizations of Africa: A History to 1800* (Charlottesville, Va., 2002).

Chapter 3

Peopling northern and American regions, 40,000 to 15,000 BP

By 60,000 BP humans had become a set of communities expanding their activities along coastal and inland areas of the tropics from West Africa to the South Pacific. The lifestyle of these humans likely depended on the gathering of animal and vegetable materials from water's edge – oceans, rivers, and lakes. It appears, however, that this technology was not adequate for life in the cooler or drier climates of regions north of the tropics. Humans remained restricted to the tropics until they developed techniques for living under different ecological conditions.

Occupation of temperate regions required development of a technology based on gathering of different sorts of vegetable materials and associated with hunting of large animals. The new technology included better spears and (later) throwing sticks, techniques for isolating large animals, and sewing to make clothing for cold weather as well as to sew hides around wooden frameworks for boats. These techniques, once developed, allowed for rapid occupation of the northern two-thirds of Eurasia. Once gaining the ability to live comfortably in temperate zones, whatever their point of entry from the tropics, humans spread easily to occupy the lands and water's edge from the Atlantic to the Pacific.

The ability to occupy northern Eurasia prepared humans for entry to North America, either on foot or by boat. As they entered the Americas, humans found no hominid competitors. But as had been the case in Australia and northern Eurasia, they did encounter megafauna – in this case large mammalian species – and the expansion of humans correlated neatly with the disappearance of the megafauna. The archaeological remains of early humans in the Americas have been sparse so far, indicating that populations were either late to arrive or slow to grow. I believe that the linguistic evidence argues for an early occupation of the Americas – before the last great Ice Age.

Between 30,000 and 15,000 BP, the earth experienced one more wave of cooling: massive sheets of ice formed at both poles and extended to cover most of Europe and North America. Sea level fell by 40 meters (see Figure 2.4). The small human population in northern Eurasia and the smaller population in the Americas had to withdraw to more southerly regions, and every human population had to adjust to a climate that was cooler and also drier (since so much water was frozen).

The outlines of the human movement north of the tropics and into the Americas are the subject of this chapter. Among the key issues are the routes, the timing, and the technology of the human movements north. As in the previous chapter, I will argue that linguistic evidence, in combination with evidence from archaeology and other disciplines, gives us important clues on these movements.

Peopling northern regions, 40,000 to 30,000 BP

The explanation of the human movement eastward from Africa along the fringe of the Indian Ocean to the Sahul continent, as presented in Chapter 2, is a rather straightforward analysis, once its basic presumptions are accepted. The evidence of archaeology and genetics, confirmed by that of language, gives a consistent picture of the tropical expansion of *Homo sapiens*.

Reconstructing the human occupation of northern Eurasia and the Americas, in contrast, is a complex problem. It involves the sorting out of several possible routes of migration, and requires resolving conflicting evidence on genetics, archaeology, and language. The overall scenario I propose is as follows. As late as 40,000 BP, *Homo sapiens* remained restricted to the tropical areas of Africa, Asia, and Oceania. By 30,000 BP, *Homo sapiens* had expanded to occupy all of Eurasia, displacing previous hominids (*Homo erectus* in the eastern half of the hemisphere and Neanderthals in the western half of the hemisphere), and had established communities in North America though probably not yet in South America.

Much of the basic information about this northern stage of human expansion remains to be established; for instance, there are many who argue that the Americas were not occupied by humans until perhaps 15,000 years ago. And while the Alaskan region of entry into North America seems inescapable, the possible routes for the occupation of northern Eurasia from the tropics would seem to be numerous. As I will argue, the evidence on language does much to clarify these and other issues.

In the analysis to come, I contrast regions of linguistic commonality with regions of linguistic diversity. The main regions of linguistic unity, as shown in Figure 3.1, are in northern Eurasia and the Americas. The most impressive region of linguistic unity is Eurasia, where the single large language family of Eurasiatic is spoken today from the Atlantic to the Pacific and even to the Indian Ocean. A close second in linguistic unity is the Amerind languages, which expanded without interruption to occupy all of South America and most of North America (though they have since lost out significantly to Indo-European languages). A third pattern of linguistic unity, characterized by a wide scattering of related groups, is the Dene-Caucasian languages.

In contrast, I want to point out four major centers of linguistic diversity: regions where the existence of distinct but related languages in a small area

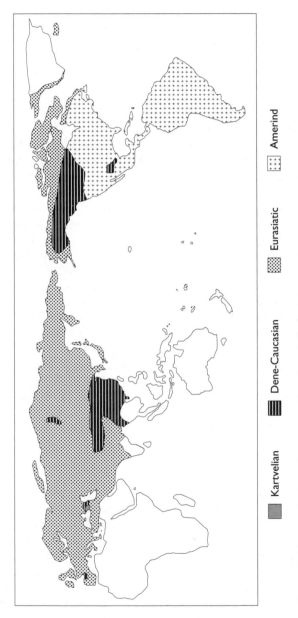

Figure 3.1 Language families of temperate Eurasia and the Americas

Kartvelian ▦ Dene-Caucasian ▓ Eurasiatic ▨ Amerind ⠿

gives the impression that these were regions from which migrants left. (The reader may consult Figure 2.1 in the previous chapter to locate these regions.) One such region of diversity is the Caucasus. There in the low mountains between the Black and Caspian Seas, we find the North Caucasian languages (including modern Chechen) and Kartvelian languages (including modern Georgian) – each related only distantly to other languages – and representatives of the Indo-European and Altaic families of Eurasiatic languages. The Caucasus has received wide attention as a possible center of human dispersion. For instance, the use of "Caucasian" as a racial term stems from an eighteenth-century argument that the Caucasus was the home of a pure, "Caucasian" race, and from nineteenth-century assertions that the same region was the homeland for the Indo-European languages. Since geneticists now argue that the characteristics of "race" are genetically superficial rather than of any depth, the relevance of the Caucasus for racial analysis has become dubious; however, the relevance of the Caucasus for its linguistic diversity remains significant.

A second region of linguistic diversity has received far less attention. Within the great linguistic commonality of the Eurasiatic languages, the greatest diversity of languages is to be found on the northeast Asian coast, where four of the seven subgroups of Eurasiatic appear to have their homelands. (See Figure 3.2.) Joseph Greenberg's recent work emphasizes the significance of this region: I accept his analysis, but acknowledge that more study is needed to confirm it. The Gilyak and Chukotian language groups have not been studied in great detail, and recognition of Korean, Japanese, and Ainu as a single group is recent. The Altaic languages exhibit the greatest diversity in the eastern part of their range, suggesting that the group emerged in the east. A least-moves estimate of the homeland for Eurasiatic as a whole places it near the Pacific coast, and suggests that the Eurasian steppes may have been settled from the east rather than from the west. The Indo-European languages, while now the largest and most populous group within the Eurasiatic family, are also the most far-flung from the apparent homeland. They may have begun, therefore, as western outliers among the Eurasiatic-speakers.

A third region of linguistic diversity goes further back in time: the homeland of Sino-Tibetan and Austric languages in southwest China. All four of the major subgroups of the Sino-Tibetan languages are represented in today's southwest China, along the major rivers of Southeast Asia. In much the same areas, and only slightly downriver, are the homelands of the Austric languages (more commonly discussed in their four constituent subgroups, Austroasiatic, Miao-Yao, Dai, and Austronesian). This center of linguistic diversity appears to be a region from which early migrants spread in all directions, since languages stemming from this homeland are now spoken in all areas of Asia and beyond.

The fourth region of linguistic diversity goes even further back in time: it is the middle Nile Valley, where Afroasiatic and Nilo-Saharan language groups

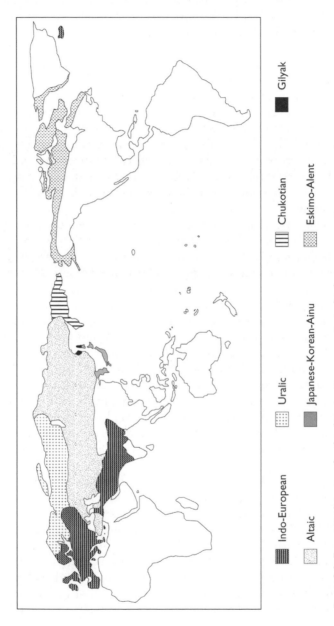

Figure 3.2 Eurasiatic language family, showing its seven principal subgroups

Indo-European   Uralic   Chukotian   Gilyak

Altaic   Japanese-Korean-Ainu   Eskimo-Aleut

have their homeland, and where a small but important group of Niger-Congo languages is located just to the west. The middle Nile was arguably the region that started the whole process of expansion to the east 80,000 years ago; in addition, it may also have been a source of expansion to the north in later times.

The archaeological record shows *Homo sapiens* as inhabitants of temperate Eurasian regions from the Atlantic to the Pacific beginning about 40,000 BP – somewhat later for the arctic fringe of Eurasia. There had been a pause, it appears, between the occupation of the tropics by 60,000 BP and the movement into temperate Eurasia. Some sort of breakthrough in technology and perhaps social organization was needed to enable significant numbers of humans to move north.

With this introduction, let us turn to an investigation of the Eurasiatic languages, the family of languages now occupying the great majority of the territory of Eurasia. The map of Eurasiatic languages, as proposed by Greenberg, covers such an immense area that one is readily tempted to view it as reflecting a rapid move to occupy all of northern Eurasia, stemming from a single region in the tropics. This is a first approximation to the argument that I will make, though I will also add a number of complications to the story. The identification of this large family (sometimes called a super-family) of languages is a substantial accomplishment: it is a major advance over the previous century's emphasis on Indo-European languages, now shown to be one of seven constituent groups of Eurasiatic language. The history of the Eurasiatic language group goes back much further and includes a far wider range of populations than does its Indo-European subgroup. Linguists have suspected this possibility for some time: Greenberg's analysis of Eurasiatic paralleled the work of a series of European-based scholars (working particularly in Russia) who developed the term "Nostratic" to refer to the combination of Indo-European, Altaic, Uralic, and other language groups. A great recent accomplishment lies in the developing consensus between the school of Greenberg and the school of linguists working with the term "Nostratic." In practice, all are now in agreement that the Nostratic or Eurasiatic family does not include the Afroasiatic, Dravidian, or Kartvelian families. (There does remain the difference that Greenberg has given more emphasis to the languages of the Pacific coast than have the Nostratic scholars.) Thus we have a widely accepted consensus on the composition of a language family covering most of Eurasia.

The next stage in unraveling the puzzle of occupying the temperate regions is analyzing the languages of the Americas: Greenberg's results are summarized in Figure 3.3. Prior to his classification of Eurasiatic, he published in 1987 a classification of the languages of the Americas. His identification of Amerind as a single family encompassing the great majority of American languages brought a stormy response from Americanist linguists who declined to accept the existence of this larger grouping of languages. Important

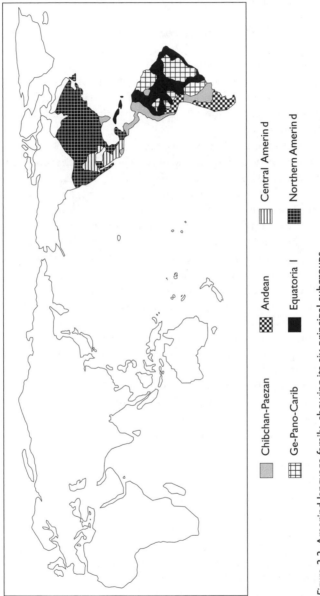

Chibchan-Paezan   Andean   Central Amerind

Ge-Pano-Carib   Equatorial   Northern Amerind

Figure 3.3 Amerind language family, showing its six principal subgroups

statements from each camp appeared as a result, and one must wait for the debate to run its course; but for this book I have unhesitatingly accepted Greenberg's classification because its patterns fit so well with those accepted for languages elsewhere in the world.

Greenberg argued that Amerind is a sister group to Eurasiatic. (If he had seen Amerind as a daughter group, he would have classified it along with Eskimo-Aleut as a subgroup of Eurasiatic.) This classification implies that Eurasiatic and Amerind are both descendants of some ancestral stock, one that linguists can presumably seek out. Thus, if Eurasiatic came into existence in about 40,000 BP, perhaps among fishers and hunters of the northeast coast of Asia, then one is prompted to argue that Amerind arose at much the same time, among hunters and fishers of the same region who continued to move north and east. Amerind-speakers moved across the Bering straits to the Americas, either on a land-bridge during the Ice Age, or by sea before it. Greenberg's own clear opinion was that Eurasiatic and Amerind both emerged about 15,000 BP among populations that occupied lands given up by receding glaciers. On the other hand, genetic evidence, as summarized by Cavalli-Sforza, tends to support the earlier date of about 35,000 BP for the settlement of the Americas and also for the occupation of temperate Eurasia. I too accept the earlier period as the time for expansion of these languages. Figure 3.1 shows Eurasiatic and Amerind, along with the other language groups of the temperate and American zones.

To these two large groupings of languages beyond the tropics we may now add a third. Linguists John Bengtson and Merritt Ruhlen have made the case for a grouping that they call Dene-Caucasian. They find a family relationship among five sets of languages that are widely separated geographically: Sino-Tibetan, North Caucasian, Basque (in the Pyrenees of Spain and France), Yeniseian (isolated languages in northeast Siberia), and the Na-Dene languages of North America. Three of these groups – Basque, North Caucasian, and Yeniseian – can easily be seen as remnants of earlier populations that lost ground to expanding Eurasiatic-speaking groups. The Na-Dene group of North America, in contrast, clearly arrived in North America after the Amerind-speakers, and found its advance into the continent limited by the previously established populations. Sino-Tibetan, meanwhile, is much more a tropical than a temperate language group, in that most of its subgroups are located in the subtropical highlands of the Southeast Asian river valleys.

The evidence for the Dene-Caucasian language family suggests that there have been at least two waves of advance by humans into the Eurasian temperate zone: first by Dene-Caucasian-speakers, and then by Eurasiatic-speakers. To clarify this possibility, it is important to establish the place of the Sino-Tibetan languages in the larger Dene-Caucasian family. In Chapter 2, I argued that Sino-Tibetan was one of the founding families left by the eastward-moving colonization of the tropics. Under this assumption, the other groups listed in Dene-Caucasian are in practice part of Sino-Tibetan. But if Sino-Tibetan is only part of a larger family, one may have to look beyond Southeast Asia for the location of its homeland. A different homeland would lead to a different interpretation of paths of migration.

Let us turn explicitly to exploring the four main possible routes for the occupation of temperate Eurasia. First, as implied above, there is the argument for migration up the Pacific coast. Maritime peoples of the Southeast Asian tropics, in advancing northward, could have gradually accommodated themselves to the changing seaside species. (The importance of seafood in the cuisine of Korea and Japan today may thus be the reflection of an ancient tradition.) At a region of the coast opposite Hokkaido and Sakhalin, these coastal populations may have developed the techniques of hunting, boating, and gathering that made possible life on the steppe. They could then have moved west, spreading out and diverging to become the various Eurasiatic-speaking populations. The Amur River Valley presents the interesting possibility of a waterway by which coastal peoples could gain acquaintance with the steppes. This approach focuses on the concentration of Eurasiatic subgroups on the northwest Pacific shore: Korean-Japanese-Ainu, Gilyak, Chukotian, and, nearby, Altaic. In this case, Eurasiatic would most likely have descended from Austric. Other possible linguistic ancestors include Sino-Tibetan and Indo-Pacific.

I believe that a new type of boat – skin boats – assisted the migrants who moved from the tropics into northern Eurasia. To make such boats, animal skins are sewn and stretched over a wooden framework: the modern Inuit kayak is a fine example. Skin boats have the advantage of being light and portable; they ride high in the water and keep their passengers dry. Maritime archaeologist Paul Johnstone has noted the distribution of such boats all over northern Eurasia and into arctic North America: it is rather precisely the distribution of the Eurasiatic languages.

I suggest that skin-boat technology was invented along the northeast Asian coast some 40,000 years ago, perhaps in the Amur River Valley. Reed boats, probably the main watercraft of populations moving north along the Pacific coast, had the disadvantage of exposing mariners to the cold waters of the north. The invention of skin boats required the ability to hunt large animals effectively, and also required awls to puncture the skins and sew them together with either animal or vegetable ties, plus the ability to construct a sturdy wooden framework. The new boats could have been tried out in rivers, and then extended to use in the seas. With portage from river system to system, migrants combining hunting and fishing were able to use skin boats to occupy region after region of temperate and arctic Eurasia.

A second path to the north was from the Sino-Tibetan homeland to the Eurasian steppes. This trail would have led from what is now South China, with the migrants moving up and down various river valleys and learning how to live in progressively drier zones that brought changing systems of rains. Movement eastward toward the Pacific should have been easy at any point, but movement westward was easy only north of the Himalayas, from the latitude of the Huang He River. In effect, then, these migrants may have followed what later became the Silk Road to reach and settle in Central Asia, the Caucasus, and Europe. This might have been the path of Dene-Caucasian speakers as they moved north from a tropical homeland, then branched out east and west as they reached the grasslands. But the present wide dispersion of the communities speaking Dene-Caucasian languages leaves it difficult to reconstruct the timing and the steps of their migration.

A third path to the temperate zone might be labeled the Nile–Fertile Crescent–Caucasus path. This path, centering on the "Fertile Crescent" of present-day Israel, Syria, and Iraq, is often assumed to be the path by which humans left Africa and settled the Eurasian heartland: for instance, geneticist L. L. Cavalli-Sforza, in his authoritative survey of the genetics of human migration, has assumed that this was the path for the human migration out of Africa. It is a plausible route, but when examined in detail it reveals three types of difficulty in the linguistic, ecological, and genetic arguments in favor of such a route. I can state the ecological point concisely, while the other two points must be explained at greater length. The ecological differences between the middle Nile and the Fertile Crescent or Caucasia – the differing vegetation, temperatures, and patterns of rains – while easily surmounted by human technology in more recent times, were not necessarily easy for humans to overcome 60,000 years ago. We need clearer archaeological documentation of *Homo sapiens* in the Fertile Crescent before 40,000 BP than is now available to be confident that this was the main route out of Africa.

The linguistic difficulties are mainly that the most recent linguistic analyses give no clear support to the Nile–Fertile Crescent–Caucasus route, in contrast to the linguistic logic behind the first two routes. This point is worthy of some comment because it contradicts earlier linguistic analysis claiming that such links could be shown. The Semitic languages are spoken in southwest Asia and northeast Africa. Because the Semitic languages were so influential in the development of writing and such important texts as Hammurabi's legal code and the Hebrew Bible, scholars of the nineteenth century sought to link Indo-European languages to Semitic. And since social-scientific analysis in the nineteenth century focused especially on racial identity, there was reason to try to link Semitic-speakers to Indo-European-speakers on the grounds that both were part of a Caucasian race, based especially on assessment of skin color. Scholars seeking to identify a "Nostratic" group of languages related to Indo-European, in their early work, revealed a continuation of this thinking. They correctly included Altaic, Uralic, Korean, and Japanese in this larger grouping, but also sought to include Semitic and Dravidian in what have been shown to be incorrect classification within Nostratic. (The relationship of Kartvelian to Eurasiatic or to Afroasiatic languages remains unresolved.)

The most recent analysis shows that Semitic, ancient Egyptian, and Berber language groups reflect three relatively recent separations from languages centered in the middle Nile Valley. Their movement north might have been about 15,000 years ago, at the end of the Ice Age, rather than earlier. The other groups of Afroasiatic languages – all centered south of the Sahara and all spoken by dark-skinned peoples – are closer to the Nile Valley homeland. A movement 40,000 years ago from the Afroasiatic homeland to create a Eurasiatic homeland would have been a long journey indeed – especially if we accept, as I have argued, that the Eurasiatic homeland was in the east of Asia rather than the west. Further, while Greenberg asserted that Eurasiatic and Amerind were sister stocks, descended from a common ancestor, few linguists have argued that Amerind is closely linked to Afroasiatic. In consequence, Eurasiatic and Amerind are most likely descended from the languages of Southeast Asia. Thus Afroasiatic (including Semitic) has no close linguistic relatives in Europe, West or Central Asia.

A further difficulty with the Nile–Fertile Crescent–Caucasus route is in the genetic evidence. Although genetic evidence is commonly argued to support the case for a path of migrants from the Nile Valley through the Fertile Crescent and to Eurasia generally, I think the historical projections of genetic evidence need to be recalculated. In particular, the current projections contain a consistent bias that underestimates the genetic distance among populations geographically close to each other and exaggerates the genetic distance among geographically distant populations. Cavalli-Sforza's extensive research and careful summaries show a serious attempt to correlate work from all fields of study contributing to the study of early humanity. Yet there remain curious results that do not fit in. Systematically, the most isolated populations are those calculated as having the greatest genetic distance from others, and hence as being the oldest. As a result, he estimates the divisions among populations in the central parts of Eurasia as being relatively recent. In another curious decision, Cavalli-Sforza uses inherited racial terms to classify phenotypes, though genetic work has made clear that physical appearances represent a small part of genetic difference: a look at his map of the Americas, showing the differences of skin color with region, suggests strongly that environment and not just heredity affects human phenotype.

There is, finally, a fourth path from tropical to temperate Eurasia that can be advanced on linguistic grounds: the path leading from the Dravidian-speaking zone of the Indian Ocean littoral across the mountains and northward. In more recent times other populations have migrated in the opposite direction, from Central Asia into India, so it is possible that a previous migration might have gone northward. I know of no serious attempts to make this case in either archaeological or linguistic terms, though one could imagine the possibility that Eurasiatic languages are descended from Dravidian. The route from tropical waters to temperate grasslands, however, was rather short in this case.

Here is my assembly and summary of the complex possibilities out of which we must reconstruct the human occupation of temperate Eurasia. Overall, I would argue that there were three substantial migrations from the tropics to temperate Eurasia, and one cannot yet be certain about their relative timing. A movement overland or in part along rivers in the valleys east of the Himalayas from South China to the eastern Eurasian steppes may have given birth to a temperate population. This group, speaking Dene-Caucasian languages, made initial adjustments to life in temperate zones. The second substantial migration moved north along the western Pacific shore. This movement led to formation of the Eurasiatic language group, which then spread to displace or assimilate earlier groups except for some Dene-Caucasian remnants. At the very least, the linguistic diversity of the north Pacific coast suggests that it was a place of early settlement and a homeland for groups of migrants. Third, a northward movement of African-based Afroasiatic-speakers may have contributed to settlement of temperate Eurasia. If such a move took place in relatively early times, the migrants might have moved along the Mediterranean and Black Sea coasts, though the linguistic evidence suggests that Afroasiatic migration beyond Africa was relatively late.

I think that Eurasiatic and Amerind both had their origins on the western shores of the north Pacific. Amerind then spread into the Americas, before the last Ice Age took hold in 35,000 BP, while Eurasiatic spread westward across the Eurasian steppes. I think that both groups relied on boats as well as on the soil; they stayed close to rivers as they moved inland, and they hunted large animals as well as small on land and at water's edge.

Regardless of the outcome of my hypothesis, it is clear that Eurasiatic and Amerind must be compared with other major language groups, to see if an affiliation can be identified. The full list of candidate groups from which Eurasiatic and Amerind might have sprung includes: Nilo-Saharan, Afroasiatic, Dravidian, Sino-Tibetan (or Dene-Caucasian), Austric, Indo-Pacific, and Australian. Of these I think Austric is the most likely parent or affiliate of Eurasiatic, but that assertion is based so far on geographic proximity rather than on any detailed linguistic comparison.

One important issue that I have skimmed over is the interaction of *Homo sapiens* and other hominids. The linguistic evidence discussed above, while it does not give a definitive answer to how temperate Eurasia was occupied, provides important background for understanding the ways in which *Homo sapiens* encountered and displaced previous hominids. Especially for Europe, we have evidence to help clarify the story of the competition of *Homo sapiens* for space with hominid predecessors, especially with *Homo neanderthalensis* in Europe. The genetic evidence, so far, indicates little interbreeding of the two closely related hominid populations. A likely scenario is that the incoming *Homo sapiens* occupied the best lands, grew in population, and reduced the preceding populations to marginal life and then to disappearance. Some intermixture could have occurred within this scenario.

Old World movements during the last Ice Age, 30,000 to 15,000 BP

Up to this point, I have argued that all the major language groups had come into existence by 30,000 years ago. By this logic, the era during and since the last Ice Age has been a time of adjustments in regional populations rather than a period of filling empty lands. Here is a review of the eleven major Old World language groups that exist today, giving my estimates of the placement, division, and movement of subgroups of each, as they emerged from 30,000 to 15,000 years ago. I will begin with the nine groups of the Old World tropics, and then turn to the groups of temperate Eurasia. In a subsequent section I discuss migration in the Americas.

The Khoisan languages remained centered in East Africa, though groups in southern and southwestern Africa formed, apparently in association with expansion into those areas. In the savanna and also in the forests of West Africa, there developed seven major subgroups in Niger-Congo languages, as people became specialized in life in different ecologies. The Nilo-Saharan languages, located in the eastern two-thirds of the Sahara and lands south of the Sahara, diverged into three large groups – one along the middle Niger River, one in the Sahara, and one in the grasslands west of the Nile. In addition, Nilo-Saharan languages included sister groupings in grasslands east of the Nile, and languages of the Nile Valley itself. In this period, as perhaps before, the speakers of Nilo-Saharan languages gave particular emphasis to an aquatic culture, living from the proceeds of rivers and lakes.

Afroasiatic languages, also with a homeland in Africa's eastern savanna lands, broke into several major groups in this time. The groups included Omotic (in western Ethiopia), Cushitic (in Ethiopia and Somalia), Chadic (in Nigeria and Chad), and a northern group including subgroups of Berber (in northwest Africa), Egyptian (in the lower Nile), and Semitic (in the Fertile Crescent). The importance of listing all four of these groups is to confirm that the parent group of Afroasiatic languages had its origin in the middle Nile Valley of Africa, and not in Asia.

For the tropics outside Africa, the language groups broke similarly into subgroups and spread to adjoining areas. The Dravidian languages diverged into northern and southern groups living on the Indian subcontinent. The Austric languages, with a homeland in the river valleys of what is now southwestern China, diverged into four major subgroups: the Austroasiatic, Miao-Yao, and Dai language groups, remaining in the middle valleys of the great rivers of southeast Asia, and Austronesian languages, which developed among populations that had moved downriver and expanded from the lower Yangzi Valley. The Sino-Tibetan languages are the largest constituent of the far-flung Dene-Caucasian family. Sino-Tibetan, with a homeland directly adjoining that of the Austric languages in the middle valleys of the great rivers, divided into several groups that remained in the same region or went further west and upriver, and the Chinese, a language community that moved down-river to the lower Yangzi Valley.

The Indo-Pacific languages were spoken by people who may have occupied most of the mainland of Sunda (in the times before rising waters submerged much of that subcontinent), and who populated the great island of New Guinea and the surrounding archipelago. Indo-Pacific-speakers were notably strong as mariners, as they lived on islands throughout the Indonesian archipelago. The Australian languages show greatest diversity in the tropical areas of northern Australia, but the pattern of language subgroups also reveals the eventual migration into the desert regions and the temperate areas of southern and eastern Australia.

In the northern zone of Eurasia, the Eurasiatic languages diverged into their constituent groups. Chukotian, Gilyak, and Korean-Japanese-Ainu in the east; Altaic in the east and center, Uralic in the north; and Indo-European in the far west. Most recently, Eskimo-Aleut spread to the extreme northeast.

Migrations in the Americas to 15,000 BP and after

The story of migrations in the Americas has quite naturally tended to be told separately from the occupation of the Old World. Evidence of linguistic classification provides a way to minimize this separation, and to emphasize the parallels and the direct connections of American migrations with those of the Old World. As I have suggested above, the arrival of humans in the Americas was tied to the occupation of northern Eurasia. The obstacle to entering the Americas was not the short oceanic space that sometimes separated Siberia and Alaska, but the difficulty of living that far north. The solution to the riddle of living in the Arctic surely involved the construction of boats able to cross the frigid waters of the region. More fundamentally, the ability to move into the Americas, either on foot or by boat, depended on the broader ability to find food and shelter at this latitude. For this reason, it is most logical to hypothesize that humans occupied arctic North America at much the same time as they occupied arctic Eurasia.

Once in North America, the exploring and expanding human populations faced a different problem from any of their ancestors. Heretofore, the direction of migration had been from the tropics to new tropics, and then to temperate zones and ultimately to arctic regions. The first discoverers of America, in contrast, were born and bred in cold regions. They and their migrant offspring had gradually to learn the techniques of life in warmer regions. They faced the task of learning new ecology after new ecology as they moved south and east, until they reached at last the limits of South America. One may ask rhetorically whether the American settlers carried some sort of deep social memory that enabled them to retrieve the experience of tropically based ancestors many generations earlier, and to solve the problems of life in the tropics. Even without such a mysterious social memory, humans after 30,000 BP had a generally higher level of experience and technology with which to face their problems than their distant ancestors.

At the beginning, migrants in the Americas benefited from a windfall. As earlier in Australia and surely in other areas, the newly arriving humans faced not only the difficulty of learning a new environment, but also the windfall of discovering large animals unprepared for human skills in hunting. The disappearance of megafauna in Australia, northern Eurasia, and in North America, in times coinciding with their occupation by humans, may be more complex than a simple hunting-to-extinction of these great animals by recently arrived humans, but they surely reflect the reorganization of the ecology to adjust to the impact of humans.

The distribution of subgroups within the Amerind languages provides a clear and logical picture of the advance of human settlement into the Western Hemisphere. Distribution of the language groups shows that they were established well before the development of agriculture, and that numerous migrations occurred both before and after the rise of agriculture.

Speakers of the Northern Amerind languages spread to occupy the great majority of what is now the United States, plus large areas to the north and south. The homeland for this grouping, based on the distribution of its subgroups, was in what is now the Pacific northwest of the US – perhaps in the valleys of the Columbia and Snake Rivers. A second family is Central Amerind, a grouping of peoples of the highlands that ultimately expanded to encompass the Rocky Mountains from Utah through the Sierra Madre in central Mexico. The homeland from which the Central Amerind languages expanded appears to be in the Sierra Madre in Mexico.

The Chibchan-Paezan languages are now spoken in Central America and northwestern South America. The distribution of these languages suggests a homeland in the lowlands of northern Colombia. To the south is the Andean language group, with a homeland in the central Andes (perhaps in modern Peru), and speakers of Andean languages extending all the way to the tip of South America. In a remarkable parallel to the language groups of North America, there is first a group of languages centered in lowland river valleys near the Pacific (the Northern Amerind group in North America, and the Chibchan-Paezan group in South America), and an adjoining (and presumably subsequent) group of languages centered in highlands (Central Amerind in North America and Andean in South America).

The remaining families of Amerind are east of the mountainous chain of the Andes. In the great valleys of the Amazon and the Orinoco, the grasslands and forests through which these rivers flow, and the grasslands south of the Amazon Valley, the Equatorial-Tucanoan and Ge-Pano-Carib language families have spread out from homelands in the lower Orinoco and Amazon valleys, respectively, to cover almost the entirety of the land space east of the Andes.

Two further language groups round out the basic categories of migrants to the Americas. The Na-Dene languages emerged in North America, in a migration of people speaking languages related to Sino-Tibetan. Cavalli-Sforza has estimated on genetic evidence that these groups settled in this region in about 15,000 BP. The Na-Dene languages, with a homeland in what is now the Alaska panhandle, include two main subgroups: those of the Pacific coast (notably Haida) and those of the Athabascan grasslands south of the Canadian permafrost. The latter group dispatched to the south migrants whose descendants spoke Apache and Navajo languages. Then, following the settlement of Na-Dene-speakers, Eskimo-Aleut-speakers colonized the arctic fringe of North America. This most recently developed subgroup of Eurasiatic arrived with their specialization in boating, hunting, and fishing – in open waters of the Pacific for the Aleut-speakers and along ice-bound coasts for Eskimo-speakers.

While the homelands of the six major subgroups of Amerind can be identified from the evidence of language classification, as indicated above, there remains much work to be done in postulating the succeeding migrations from those centers to other regions of the Americas. The following rapid summary suggests some of the stories that remain to be told about migrations in the Americas from 15,000 BP to 5000 BP.

The Northern Amerind language family eventually expanded to include almost all of North America outside the highest elevations. From the homeland in or near the Columbia Valley, one group moved eastward, splitting into those who emphasized the forests (later including the Algonquians), and those who emphasized the plains (later including the Sioux, the Iroquois, and the Cherokee). Two other groups established communities in California. Of these, the group now known as Penutian sent out migrants that became the Maya in Yucatan and the Choctaw and others of the northern Gulf of Mexico. Second, the group known as Hokan sent out groups that settled both the Pacific and Atlantic coasts of Mexico.

The Central Amerind languages, which took form in the highlands of northern Mexico, extended their influence as far north as Utah, as far east as Oklahoma, and as far south as Oaxaca. It is notable, however, that the gap between the Rockies and the Sierra Madre, in what is now Arizona and New Mexico, is a region where several linguistic groups have left their traces: several subgroups of Northern Amerind, populations speaking Na-Dene languages, and speakers of Central Amerind languages. This arid but accessible region became a remarkable zone of confluence and mixture.

The Chibchan-Paezan languages, with their homeland in northern Colombia, eventually sent migrants great distances in all directions. They became the dominant languages of Central America south of the Maya and of the Pacific coast well into Peru. At greater distance, members of this family include Timucua (formerly spoken in north Florida), the Yanomani language of the Amazon basin, and some languages of the southern Andes. The Chibchan-Paezan core area was certainly at the heart of the domestication of food crops in South America.

The Andean languages appear to have formed in the mountains of Peru. Later speakers of the languages moved to the northern Andes and, perhaps still later, others moved all the way to the southern tip of South America, and also to colonize the prairies of Patagonia. The Inca Empire, when it formed many centuries later, united many Andean-speaking peoples, but it also governed peoples speaking languages of the Chibchan-Paezan and Equatorial-Tucanoan groups.

The two language groups that dominate eastern South America, between the Andes and the Atlantic, reveal a complex history of repeated migration, with modern patterns that make it difficult to identify their homelands. The Equatorial-Tucanoan languages, including such languages as Arawak of northeastern Brazil and Tupi of the central Brazilian coast, may have taken form in the middle or upper Amazon Valley. The Ge-Pano-Carib languages may have taken form in the lower Orinoco Valley or the Guianas. Each of these groups, however, has sent settlers all over the forests and grasslands of eastern South America.

This rapid exploration of the early history of Amerindian populations through study of linguistic history shows that there is a fascinating history that can be retrieved through this approach. Linguistic information provides the outlines of a history of migration and social change greatly different from previous histories. It includes some surprises and some major changes, and it provides an interpretation far more complex, yet far more comprehensive, than the previous picture. The languages of the Americas, previously studied mostly by scholars who analyze two or three languages at a time, need also to be compared in large groups, at the level of large language families. Such work will probably result in revisions of Greenberg's proposed membership in the categories, but not major changes in the categories themselves. Determination of the relative age of the linguistic groupings is a complex task, but one of particular importance.

Further, this summary of migration and differentiation of Amerind language stocks needs to be compared with that for the parallel group of Eurasiatic languages. The six subgroups of Amerind have had somewhat different experiences than the seven groups of Eurasiatic, but one can hope to gain much by tracing the parallels and the distinctions in the histories of these two sister families.

I will return to the various groups of Amerind-speakers in the next chapter, to discuss the development and spread of agriculture through their populations. Here I want to emphasize that most of the American migrations described in this chapter took place before the development of agriculture. For instance, while Penutian-speaking people of southern Mexico were important in the domestication of maize, the ancestors to their languages were first spoken in Northern California. Similarly, the languages of the islands and coasts of the Caribbean Sea include four of the six Amerind groups, suggesting repeated migrations into the Caribbean region. Similarly, the complexity of the language groupings along the Pacific coast of North and South America suggests that groups sailed in both directions along this coast.

Conclusion

This chapter has reviewed what I like to call the third and fourth stages in human migration. While the first two stages of human migration populated the African continent and populated the Old World tropics, the next two stages filled the temperate areas of Eurasia and filled the Americas. The humans occupying the Americas encountered widely different ecologies: from the arctic zone through temperate North America to the tropical regions of North and South America and the Caribbean, and finally to the temperate regions of South America and its highlands. The evidence of language has provided essential clues on the timing and direction of these migrations.

Because humans now lived in such a remarkable range of places and environments, it is relevant to ask what effect these varying environments may have had on human individuals and human societies. On the latter point, anthropologists have given considerable study to the variations in human social organization with ecological setting. The interpretive difficulty is that they must use observations on societies in the recent past to make judgments on the organization of societies thousands of years ago.

For the effect of environment on individuals, we are dealing with the question of "race" in human history. The movement of humans around the planet brought some minor evolutionary differences in such features as size, shape, skin color, hair, and facial features. These features may have been adaptive in times when populations were mostly restricted to single regions, but are less significant today.

Can the history of migration provide us with information about the nature of race among humans? Yes, it can. In today's parlance, Africans often get lumped together as a single "Negro race," yet the work of human biologists has shown that there are more genetic variations among Africans than there are among all persons born outside of Africa. That is, the distinctions we have called "race" are matters of *phenotype* (outward appearance) rather than *genotype* (genetic composition). So the distinctions of "race," while surely genetic in that they are reproduced over the generations, reflect only a modest portion of human genetic composition.

Of course, after the last few centuries of racial strife and categorization, humans are not likely simply to drop the topic of race from discussion just because scientists have verified that racial differences are superficial. Indeed, we can hope that the discussion will continue productively, through historical and biological study of the emergence and significance of phenotypical differences among human populations. If, as most everyone assumes, phenotypical differences among humans result from their having lived in different environments – the most obvious case is skin color and the degree of exposure to the sun – most of these differences go back no further than about 40,000 years. Knowing more about the path and the timing of human migrations around the world will help us collect new 'information on the development of varying human phenotypes. On questions about the ideology of race and racial discrimination, however, we can go back no further than our own modern times in which these ideas were developed and implemented.

Further reading

The basic analyses of linguistic classification for northern Eurasia and the Americas are Joseph Greenberg, *Languages of the Americas* (Stanford, Calif., 1987), and Greenberg, *Indo-European and its Closest Relatives*, 2 volumes (Stanford, Calif., 2000–2002). A recent statement on methods is Christopher Ehret, *History and the Testimony of Language* (Berkeley, Calif., 2011). A more accessible summary, including the argument for an early migration associated with Dene-Caucasian languages, may be found in Merritt Ruhlen, *The Origin of Language: Tracing the Evolution of the Mother Tongue* (New York, 1994); see also Patrick Manning, "*Homo sapiens* Populated the Earth: A Provisional Synthesis, Privileging Linguistic Evidence," *Journal of World History* 17 (2006), 115–158.

A great deal of the genetic evidence on the human occupation of temperate Eurasia and the Americas is summarized in L. Luca Cavalli-Sforza, Paolo Menozzi, and Alberto Piazza, *The History and Geography of Human Genes* (Princeton, N.J., 1994). The importance of boats in northern Eurasia and the Americas is set forth in Paul Johnstone, *The Sea-craft of Prehistory* (Cambridge, Mass., 1980); I have projected some of his arguments into times earlier than he proposed. For genetic and other techniques in study of very early migrations, see Jan Lucassen, Leo Lucassen, and Patrick Manning, eds., *Migration History in World History: Multidisciplinary Approaches* (Leiden 2010).

Determining the paths of migration from tropical to temperate zones of the Old World relies significantly on zones of linguistic diversity. Broad analyses of zones of linguistic diversity include, for what is now south China, Paul K. Benedict, *Sino-Tibetan, a Conspectus* (Cambridge, Mass., 1972) and Peter Bellwood, *Prehistory of the Indo-Malaysian Archipelago*, rev. edition (Honolulu, Hawaii, 1997); and for the Nile Valley, Christopher Ehret, *A Historical-comparative Reconstruction of Nilo-Saharan* (Cologne, Germany, 2001), and Ehret, *Reconstructing Proto-Afroasiatic* (Berkeley, Calif., 1995).

For the Americas to 5000 BP, the works of Greenberg, Ruhlen, and Cavalli-Sforza (et al.) noted above are the principal sources of my analysis. The archaeological evidence for the Americas, meanwhile, is faint for early times, and does not yet support the early dates for human occupation proposed by genetic or linguistic analysis. See, for instance, Gary Haynes, *The Early Settlement of North America* (Cambridge, Mass., 2002).

Chapter 4

Agriculture, 15,000 to 5000 BP

In the period from 15,000 BP to 5000 BP, agriculture developed in several regions of the world. Agricultural development was mainly a long process of experimentation and discussion that led eventually to a new organization of work, though it was punctuated by at least one era of rapid change. Over the long term the result was an impressive advance in technology, an expansion and redistribution of human population, and new patterns of migration. This chapter reviews the rise of agriculture by exploring three related issues: Where and when did agriculture develop? How did agriculture develop? How did agriculture spread from one place to another?

The last of these three questions, in turn, poses a major issue in migration: what patterns in migration did agriculture stimulate? Did the early farming peoples expand at the expense of other populations, colonizing great new territories? (This is the "human-colonization model" for the spread of agriculture.) Or did the practice of farming spread from population to population, so that pre-existing groups continued to exist? (This is the "crop-migration model" for the spread of agriculture.) We may seek genetic, linguistic, archaeological, and anthropological evidence to develop a response to the question. I argue that the evidence of language, in particular, suggests that neither pattern dominated. The human-colonization model (also known as "demic" migration) predominated in the cases of rice production in Southeast Asia and yam production in Central Africa. But crop migration predominated in other cases, such as the expansion of wheat production in the Middle East and Europe and the spread of maize through the Americas.

This chapter traces what I am calling the preconditions for agriculture and the first two waves in the domestication of plants and animals. First, I discuss early experiments with plants and animals, focusing on five world regions where significant early experimentation with intensive food gathering laid the groundwork for agriculture and actual food production. Second, I argue that crucial stages in the domestication of plants were synchronized in at least six regions of the earth because of rapid climatic changes at the end of the Ice Age. In this first wave of agricultural domestication, at least ten major crops developed in those regions. In the same era as the domestication of plants, though not always in the same order, came domestication of animals, development of new techniques in fishing, and new handicrafts, most notably the development of pottery. The result came to be a substantial increase in productivity, so that the populations living from agriculture, herding, and fishing grew in comparison to other populations, and a whole new set of social dynamics came into being. After thus tracing the development of agriculture, I then trace the migration of farmers and of agricultural practices in several areas of the world.

Third, and after these food-production breakthroughs in a few regions, the new ideas were tried out in increasingly comprehensive fashion, with innovations in every environment. In this second wave of agricultural development – over the next five millennia, from 10,000 BP to 5000 BP – agriculture spread to many and perhaps most areas of the world, along with herding and new techniques in fishing. For this period, I discuss the expansion of the earlier agricultural centers and then trace the rise of four new hearths of agricultural development. As in the previous section, I then analyze the spread of agriculture from these hearths to other regions, relying especially on linguistic evidence. In the fourth section of the chapter, as a reminder that life at water's edge was central to human existence even in this era of agricultural innovation, I discuss the interplay among agricultural, pastoral, and aquatic life that emerged in this time period.

The archaeologist V. Gordon Childe, writing in the 1920s, coined the terms "Agricultural Revolution" and "Urban Revolution" to summarize the transformations of this era. In developing those terms, he wrote especially about the eastern Mediterranean and the influence of that region on Europe; his terms continue to serve well in drawing attention to the importance of agriculture and cities in changing the basis of human societies. Nevertheless, recent research has tended to contradict two of the impressions Childe created: that the eastern Mediterranean was the unique site of the invention of agriculture, and that the rise of agriculture and cities was rather sudden. Scholars are now showing, instead, that there were long preludes to the development of agriculture and that and similar developments took place in several areas of the world.

Jared Diamond, in his recent review of the rise of agriculture, has argued that long-term advantages accrued to those language communities which were first to develop each set of crops. In effect, he has presented agricultural development as a principal cause of substantial population growth and migration. I offer here a contrasting interpretation in which I argue that, although the spread of agriculture was central to human development, cross-community migration spread agriculture too rapidly for the founding agricultural communities to achieve the dominance that Diamond suggests they have had throughout history. Diamond, a physiologist, has joined with archaeologist Peter Bellwood to argue that the pattern of human colonization was the main migratory response to agricultural domestication; the geneticist Luigi Luca

Cavalli-Sforza has made similar arguments for "demic migration" as the process for the population of Europe. As I will argue below, crop migration was roughly as common as human colonization in spreading agriculture, and the basic practice of cross-community migration underlay all of these broader patterns for the expansion of agriculture.

Preconditions: experiments with plants and animals

There is evidence of intensified practices of food gathering as early as 15,000 years ago. The regions that are candidates for this sort of activity include northeast Africa and adjoining western Asia, Southeast Asia (including South China), West Africa, Mesoamerica, New Guinea, and perhaps other regions. For these regions it seems possible that the inhabitants supplemented their gathering of food with relatively intensive harvesting of certain plants.

The best-developed of these interpretations is for northeast Africa, where linguistic evidence shows that Nilo-Saharan-speakers and Afroasiatic-speakers expanded their gathering of grasses. In the same region, Nilo-Saharan-speakers developed an association with cattle, while the Afroasiatic-speakers (who lived in Asian as well as African portions of this region) developed an association with sheep and goats.

In four well-watered tropical regions, well-established populations were positioned to experiment with intensive food-gathering. In West Africa, populated by speakers of Niger-Congo languages, there developed a practice of intensive harvesting of tubers. This practice, now known as "vegeculture" or "planting agriculture," involved placing a portion of a harvested tuber back in the ground so that it would sprout again. New Guinea was a second area where people may have experimented with tuberous vegeculture. For Southeast Asia, among speakers of Austric and Sino-Tibetan languages, it seems likely that both these types of experiment were tried from early days. The grasses that are wild relatives of rice were available in much of South and Southeast Asia. Harvesting of the wild grasses of the region would lead eventually to domestication of rice, and harvesting of the wild tubers would lead eventually to development of several types of yam.

The area from southern Mexico to northern South America is the other main region in which such early experiments of intensive gathering may have taken place, focusing on various types of squash. The dates for such experiments may have been as early as 15,000 BP, and arguably centered among peoples speaking Chibchan-Paezan languages. This Mesoamerican and South American region ultimately developed a rich agricultural tradition with numerous major cultigens.

How do we know about these early developments? First, we naturally hypothesize that there must have been some antecedents to the development of full-scale cultivation of crops, including a long if only partly conscious process of breeding and selection of the best varieties. Second, we rely on evidence in language, which gives clear hints of early experiments and borrowing of domestic animals among the Nilo-Saharan- and Afroasiatic-speakers. Third, the results of archaeological digs, botany, and genetics have helped in locating the origins of cultigens.

Nevertheless, the evidence is thin and inconclusive. It is difficult enough to verify the existence of full-scale agriculture from the archaeological record ten thousand years ago. The archaeologists, by their discipline and temperament the most cautious about speculation, are generally the last to agree that the remains of burials or trash heaps show the use of grasses or yams in a first step toward agriculture. One problem for all of these cases is that the exact foyers for development of new crops have not been verified by archaeological findings. We know from paleobotanical and genetic studies the wild ancestors of the domestic crops, and can therefore limit the region from which domesticates came. But we cannot yet pinpoint any points of development. It is therefore very important for the understanding of early human history to organize more study of domestication of tropical cultigens. For reasons both environmental and political, archaeological investigation is better funded and more productive of results in temperate zones.

Nevertheless, archaeological work, though slow and expensive, may be expected to provide a continuing flow of information on early agriculture. An example of the benefit of continuing investment in archaeological research is the case of Papua New Guinea, where teams of archaeologists (based principally in Australia) have recently confirmed the cultivation of taro and bananas in highland valleys as long ago as 10,000 BP. This new work now confirms Papua New Guinea as one of the original sites of the invention of agriculture. In general, understanding of the early chapters of human history requires much more archaeological study of tropical regions.

Agriculture and pastoralism: the first wave

The domestication of plants and animals – the development of agriculture – has fascinated analysts for centuries. Only in the twentieth century did dependable evidence begin to accumulate, as botanists searched for the nearest wild relatives of domestic cultigens, and as archaeologists searched for remnants of early cultivation. The Russian botanist N. I. Vavilov heroically scoured the continents in the 1920s and 1930s for evidence on early agriculture. The debates ranged widely, and the evidence has continued to be uneven. With time, better dating techniques and new types of evidence (including linguistics) became available. There is not yet a consensus. The picture that I present in these pages is not accepted by all. But it presents my expectation of what will be borne out by studies in time.

In the relatively short time between about 13,000 and 10,000 years ago, agriculture sprung up in six regions of the world. Collectors became farmers in each of these areas, systematically planting as well as harvesting their crops. Among the main crops developed in this period were wheat in the Fertile Crescent, sorghum in the middle Nile, rice and yams in Southeast Asia, yams in West Africa, taro and bananas in New Guinea, and squashes in northern South America.

What set the timing for this series of developments? It was a sharp set of climatic changes, in the best estimate of recent analysts. The rapid end of an Ice Age that had lasted twenty thousand years interacted with the slow developments in human experiments with plants and animals. From about 15,000 BP, temperatures rose in many parts of the world. (See Figure 2.4 for the reflection of these temperature changes in changing sea levels.) Polar ice caps melted, the levels of the oceans rose by hundreds of feet, and rainfall rose, leading to new vegetation everywhere. As food supplies expanded, so did populations of humans (and other animal species too, no doubt).

Then in another sharp change known as the Younger Dryas, temperatures declined in a period that has been dated as from 12,900 BP to 11,600 BP. The temperature declines are revealed in ice cores, tree rings, and other records. One explanation for this decline is that the melting of North American glaciers in the previous era of warming brought a flood of cold waters to the North Atlantic, and interrupted the northward flow of the warm Sargasso Sea, thus bringing cooler temperatures to all the oceans and to landmasses as well. The results of temperature decline brought declining rainfall and sudden shortage of food supplies. In places where humans had no extra resources or insufficient originality, the results were a decline in population, falling back to earlier levels. But in some places, humans were able to respond to the crisis by intensifying their collecting activities and turning them into the innovation of planting as well as harvesting. This new approach was far more laborious, but when the results were successful, they permitted the population to sustain itself and grow.

An additional factor facilitated the development of agricultural techniques in several regions: mountainous regions – or, more specifically, regions with sharp variations in altitude within a small region – brought a significant advantage. The range of altitudes meant a range of climates, so that neighboring groups could develop a range of different and complementary crops. Further, if the climate became suddenly warmer or colder, farmers could adjust by ascending or descending the mountains and continue to grow the crops they knew well. The combination of these phenomena explains why agriculture developed at virtually the same time in several areas of the world.

Figure 4.1 indicates the early agricultural complexes discussed for six world regions, and also indicates the language groups of the peoples who led in these agricultural innovations. The language groups correspond not to the fourteen major groups of world languages, but to certain subgroups of these languages that are thought to have been spoken by the groups leading in agricultural innovation.

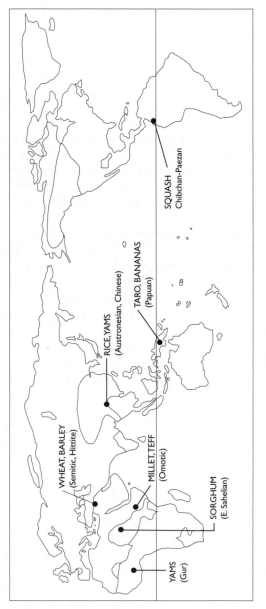

Figure 4.1 Agriculture and language, 15,000–10,000 BP

The best-documented case of the breakthrough from initial experimentation to full scale agriculture and food production is that of wheat, developed on the highlands of the Anatolian Peninsula and the adjoining lowlands of the Fertile Crescent. Archaeological results have confirmed the overlapping species of wheat that were domesticated. Many of these lands were inhabited by speakers of the Semitic group of Afroasiatic languages; some may have been inhabited by speakers of the Hittite group of Indo-European languages. Another grain, barley, developed in virtually the same region under similar conditions.

At the southern end of the Mediterranean region in which grasses had earlier been gathered, people of the Eastern Sahelian group of Nilo-Saharan languages, living in the area west of the middle Nile, used similar experience to develop the cultivation of sorghum. The area in which these farmers developed their crop, now part of the Sahara Desert, is also a somewhat mountainous area. The evidence of archaeology and linguistics also indicates that these people were early producers of pottery and early herders of cattle, which were native to the region. Further up the Nile Valley (to the south), another group of Afroasiatic-speakers, those speaking Omotic languages, developed different crops in the area at the edge of the Ethiopian highlands: millet (a grain crop domesticated from widely available wild species), teff (a local grain), and enset (a plant related to the banana of which the stalks are edible).

Christopher Ehret has shown the interactions among these groups to have been surprisingly complex. Cattle were domesticated by the Nilo-Saharan-speakers who became farmers of sorghum; with time they came also to herd goats and sheep, with techniques they learned from nearby Afroasiatic-speakers. Still later, donkeys were domesticated in the Red Sea Hills, and became the first pack animals. In sum, food development by different groups of Afroasiatic-speakers shows that the Afroasiatic language group as a whole had already expanded for other reasons.

Quite a different story of experimentation and later domestication of grasses took place in Southeast Asia. It is widely agreed that rice, yams, and bananas were all domesticated in Southeast Asia, but insufficient botanical and archaeological research has been completed to give us precise locations for the first farming of any of these crops. The wild grasses from which domestic rice was developed grow throughout the region from north India to south China; the research has not yet been sufficient to pinpoint the main centers of its initial development. Similarly, the various wild yams closely related to *Dioscorea alata*, the principal yam cultivated in Southeast Asia, flourish throughout Southeast Asia.

The distribution of languages in two groups gives us a hint as to where archaeologists and botanists should search. For both the Sino-Tibetan and Austric language groups, the distribution of language subgroups is clustered tightly around a single area: the highlands of Yunnan. Through this remarkable region of deep gorges pass rivers that lead to every area of Southeast Asia. The Yangzi River and the Salween River flow parallel within 200 aerial kilometers of each other in Yunnan, yet the Salween flows into the Indian Ocean in Burma while the Yangzi discharges into the East China Sea over 3,000 kilometers to the northeast. Between these rivers flow such other major rivers as the Mekong and the Red. Most of the subgroups within Sino-Tibetan and Austric languages are represented by populations living (or documented as having lived) within this region. It is thus a major center of population dispersal, and as such a prime candidate for a region of agricultural innovation, from which populations may have spread because of their new technology. It may be that experiments with rice (at higher elevations) and with yams (at lower elevations) permitted the launching of agriculture, and that rice, yams, and the Southeast Asian species of bananas were originally closely associated. (On the other hand, it is also possible that these crops also developed in a pattern more like that of the Eastern Mediterranean, where crops such as wheat and sorghum developed in distinct regions that were nonetheless in contact with each other.)

Recent studies of the Indo-Pacific-speaking region of Papua New Guinea confirm its importance as a center for the domestication of taro and bananas. The bananas domesticated in New Guinea are of a different variety of bananas than that of Austric-speaking Southeast Asia; and taro, a root crop that later became important throughout the Pacific, was domesticated from local wild ancestors. In addition, sugar cane appears also to have been domesticated by the Indo-Pacific-speaking people of the island. As in other cases, the highland areas and the variation in altitude may well have contributed to the development of agriculture. For New Guinea, given its distance from other regions, the development of agriculture was virtually unquestionably a local innovation rather than a borrowing from other areas.

The development of West African yams, especially *Dioscorea rotundata*, led at a certain point to systematic planting and cultivation of these yams instead of the simpler process of replacing in the ground segments of yams earlier harvested. Perhaps, as is often assumed, the full development of agriculture in this region took place rather late in the game. On the other hand, it is equally possible that the absence of sufficient archaeological investigation in West Africa combines with the subtle nature of the transition from vegeculture to agriculture to deprive us of clear confirmation. Among the reasons I make the prediction of an early West African transition to agriculture are that the same region eventually brought domestication of oil palm, guinea hen, various species of millet, rice, earth peas, gourds, and other cultigens. The Gur-speaking, Mande-speaking, and Kwa-speaking groups of Niger-Congo may have been especially important in these agricultural developments.

As a sixth early center of agricultural domestication, I propose the northwest coast of South America, among the Chibchan-Paezan-speaking peoples. Of the four early New World hearths of agriculture, this is the one most centrally placed, most ecologically varied, and most likely to have been able to spread agricultural practices to neighboring areas. Far more archaeological analysis has gone into study of the origin of maize in Mexico, but dates on these studies do not go back beyond 10,000 BP. I propose, therefore, that systematic farming of squashes and perhaps other crops began in the coastal valleys that now make up part of Colombia, during the Younger Dryas cooling episode. According to this view, we may summarize by saying that each of the regions sustaining substantial human populations, in Old and New Worlds, experienced the beginnings of agriculture in the aftermath of the last Ice Age.

This is an appropriate point at which to review the assertions of Jared Diamond that this early agricultural development, some ten to thirteen thousand years ago, has done much to set the direction of human population and power ever since. Diamond has emphasized two points on which I wish to concentrate: one about cause and one about effect. As for cause, he has emphasized the importance of great east–west stretches of land as the source of a helpful variety in ecologically similar crops, so that the strongest of them can develop in disease resistance and productivity. In his view, the great stretch of temperate lands of Eurasia was privileged above all others as the source of crops and of human cultivators. As for effect, Diamond has argued that the language groups of the populations that first domesticated plants and animals have been privileged, and have grown at the expense of all others. As he argues it, the initially larger populations that resulted from agriculture then both elicited and survived diseases preying on their dense populations, so that immunities among these populations (especially Europeans) were much higher than those of other populations. The rest of history, as Diamond tells it, has been structured by the biological and demographic dominance of Eurasian populations over all others, as a result of neither their intelligence nor their culture, but from their biological inheritance. In short, Diamond highlights a human-colonization thesis for the spread of agriculture.

While Diamond's analysis is a bold and intriguing assertion of the long-term influence of the developments at a crucial turning-point, the evidence summarized above suggests some nuances that should be applied to it. First, the changes brought by agriculture, no matter how fundamental, were not sufficient to override the results of all previous human migrations. The basic placement of major language groups in most of Africa, Asia, the Americas, and probably Europe was set in the era before agriculture: as I will argue, agriculture affected the distribution of subgroups of the great linguistic families rather than the placement of the families as a whole. Second, if the east–west expanse of wheat-growing lands became populous, so also did the east–west expanses of rice-growing lands in Asia and the east–west expanses of sorghum- and millet-growing lands in Africa, each of which developed populations carrying both diseases and immunities to them. The American lands too became densely populated, and maize had come to be produced over much of the hemisphere by the time of Columbus. (Diseases and immunities, however, did not develop as fully in the Americas.) Third, as I will argue in the next section, the patterns of migration among farming and non-farming peoples offer reasons why the inventors of agriculture did not gain the historical dominance that Diamond suggests they ought to have achieved. An adequate explanation of agricultural dispersal needs to be somewhat more complex. In short, to Diamond's statement of cause (availability of east–west ecological regions) and effect (colonization by the founding agricultural populations), one must add three further statements: a statement of preconditions (the preexisting location of populations and language groups), an additional effect ("crop migration" in which agriculture moves from community to community), and an underlying mechanism motivating both patterns of agricultural dispersal.

The last point is particularly important. The social mechanism underlying agricultural dispersal is the human behavior of cross-community migration, which led at once to broad patterns of colonization and crop migration. Agricultural communities, as they developed, sent migrants into adjoining language communities, and of course received migrants from other communities. Migrants from agricultural communities brought agricultural practices with them as they settled in different language communities, learning from their hosts the ecological details that enabled them to adjust their farming to local conditions. Such community mixes could lead in two directions. If the immigrants were numerous or prestigious enough, the local community adopted the language and culture of the immigrants, and the change would later appear to have been colonization from the agricultural homeland. On the other hand, if the immigrants spread the new techniques effectively enough, the local community adopted agricultural practices and absorbed the immigrants, and the change would later appear to have been crop migration without migration of people. In both cases, an underlying pattern of cross-community migration led in some cases to the appearance of colonization and in other cases to the appearance of crop migration.

This debate over the demographic implications of agriculture is significant for our understanding of human population. The contrasts in the implications of the two main patterns of agricultural dispersal – human colonization and crop migration – lie in the resulting degree of human diversity. Advocates of the human-colonization thesis presume that much human biological and cultural diversity was lost as farmers marginalized and absorbed non-agricultural peoples. They also presume that diseases and immunities to disease were concentrated in the expanding agricultural peoples. Advocates of the crop-migration thesis presume that the diversity in human populations tended to be retained even with the spread of agriculture. The crop-migration thesis presumes that diseases and immunities were distributed somewhat more equitably among human populations. In either case, cross-community migration (and not simply colonization) was central to the spread of agriculture.

While I argue for a lesser degree of replacement of early populations by migrant farmers than Diamond, I do not wish thereby to contradict his argument about disease communities. Microbes attack humans of any language group, so that populations living near to each other and communicating with each other, whether their language and ancestry are the same or different, become a single disease community. The most remarkable case, therefore, is the middle zones of the Americas, where a long-established, dense, agricultural population developed, but where human diseases developed to a far lesser degree than in Eurasia and Africa. Had other such American diseases developed in addition to syphilis, the Columbian exchange might have led to equivalently disastrous epidemics in the Old World as well as the New. Diamond's emphasis on the ecological variety of the densely populated parts of the Americas (and not just the isolation of the Americas) seems important in explaining why Americans had such a fragmented disease community.

Agriculture and pastoralism: the second wave

Once agriculture was first developed as a response to crises, subsequent agricultural changes were mainly through innovation and emulation, rather than responses to crisis. What I am calling the second stage of agricultural innovation includes two main types of activity: the continued elaboration of crops and techniques in the initial agricultural centers (as with improvements in wheat and rice production) and the later establishment of new centers of agricultural innovation (in the Americas and North China).

For the elaboration of existing centers of agricultural development, as indicated in Figure 4.2, let us begin with the further innovations in Southeast Asia. The initial development of rice cultivation, which I have assumed took place in the inland areas of Southeast Asia, relied principally on cultivation under rainfall. Another innovation of this region was the stilt house, a light but sturdy dwelling suitable at once for life on hillsides and in wet areas, which later spread throughout mainland and island Southeast Asia. But further developments emerged: I believe that the development of paddy cultivation, in which rice was grown under water, took place in areas now known as South China, and in the hands of people speaking both Chinese and proto-Austronesian languages. The domestication of the water buffalo and the harnessing of water buffalo to the construction and care of paddies for rice brought a great expansion in the productivity of rice cultivation, and led to the expansion of the two populations concerned.

The Chinese-speaking populations remained in South China, and gradually spread north to occupy what is now North China. The Austronesian-speaking populations, while many remained in what is now South China, also carried their new technology across the waters. Linguists have shown that Austronesian-speaking populations moved first to Taiwan, then to the Philippines, then south into the Indonesian archipelago, and both east and west from there. These Austronesian-speakers were rice-planters, but they were also mariners, having developed outrigger canoes. In addition to rice, they planted yams and bananas; they lived in stilt houses. As Austronesian-speaking agriculturists spread into the Indonesian archipelago, they displaced and

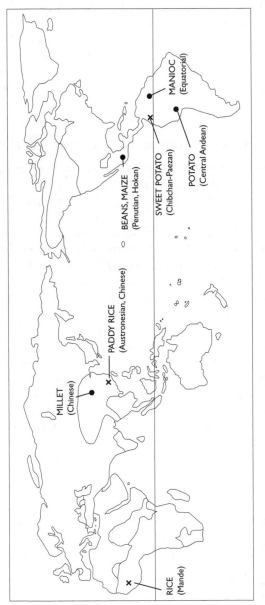

Figure 4.2 Agriculture and language, 10,000–5000 BP

absorbed previous inhabitants, who presumably spoke Indo-Pacific languages. To the east, as the migrants reached New Guinea and the adjoining Bismarck Islands, however, they encountered more Indo-Pacific-speakers, only now as a dense population of farmers. The interchange of the two groups led ultimately to a new cultural synthesis and to the settlement of the Pacific, as will be described later. To the west, the Austronesians who moved through the Indonesian archipelago eventually returned to the mainland, occupying the Malayan Peninsula. Meanwhile, the populations speaking the other branches of Austric languages, having shared in a similar agricultural complex, spread rice-growing throughout mainland Southeast Asia.

In fact, the expansions of Chinese-speakers and Austronesian-speakers provide the best cases to support the argument of Diamond that the inventors of agriculture colonized new territories and prospered at the expense of other groups. The Chinese and Austronesians were improvers rather than inventors of agriculture, but they spread rice cultivation and themselves far and wide. Nonetheless, several other groups speaking Sino-Tibetan and Austric languages also occupied large areas of Southeast Asia using rice agriculture. Meanwhile, Dravidian-speakers in India also took up rice cultivation, perhaps at this time and perhaps earlier.

The wheat- and barley-growing system of Southwest Asia experienced a second-stage expansion at least as successful as that of the rice-and-yam system of Southeast Asia. The development of plows, pulled by oxen, rendered the cultivation of wheat more efficient, and wheat cultivation came to be adopted by more Indo-European speakers and by Dravidian-speakers in addition to Semitic-speakers. Additional crops based on grasses developed, as oats were developed by Indo-European speakers. Grapes were domesticated near the shores of the Black Sea, and production of wine gradually worked its way west.

Yet the expansion of wheat production does not fit Diamond's model as neatly as does that of rice. If the initial leaders in wheat cultivation spoke Semitic languages, one might expect to find Semitic-speaking peoples expanding to all the lands in which wheat grows well. Or if an ancestral Indo-European population had spread outward from the Fertile Crescent through wheat cultivation, we would see its reflection today in one large group of Indo-European speakers, or else in a series of subgroups that migrated outward as spokes from their initial center. Instead, the distribution of Indo-European subgroups is associated more clearly with different ecological regions, from Germanic and Baltic in the north to Armenian and Indo-Iranian in the southeast. This distribution suggests that Indo-European-speakers were in place before the development of agriculture, and that agricultural practice spread from group to group.

In the Saharan and Sahelian regions of Africa, the expansion of agricultural practice led to domestication of several new crops: pearl millet, watermelon, calabash, and especially cotton were to assume substantial importance in the times to come. In woodland West Africa, yam cultivation expanded and provided the base for further innovation – developing domestication of guinea fowl, oil palm, raffia palm, voandzeia (an earth pea), blackeyed peas, and rice. In the Indus Valley, adoption of wheat cultivation was soon accompanied by development of sesame, eggplant, and domestication of the humped Zebu cattle. Later in the process of domestication, horses were domesticated in Central Asia, and two varieties of camel were domesticated.

The squash-based agricultural hearth of the northwestern coast of South America diversified with time. New crops domesticated by Chibchan-Paezan-speakers out of local varieties included sweet potato, tomato, beans, peanuts, and a variety of cotton. In developments complementary to this diversification, the second wave of agricultural development brought the rise of three distinctive agricultural systems among other New World language groups, living in the Caribbean coast of Mexico, the Caribbean lowlands of Venezuela, and the highlands of South America. The farmers in three new agricultural hearths were close enough to the tropical Pacific coast to have been aware of the practice of agriculture there, but the new hearths relied on quite different cultigens and practices of cultivation.

The second-wave development of maize in southeastern Mexico, among populations of subgroups of Northern Amerind-speakers (the Hokan and Penutian groups), brought into existence one of the most productive of all food crops. Detailed archaeological work shows the stages of development of maize from tiny kernels to substantial cobs. Along with maize were domesticated varieties of beans which provided a fortuitous nutritional complement to maize, enabling the populations to grow significantly in numbers. Maize subsequently spread into many regions in North and South America. The overall pattern for the spread of maize is clearly dominated by crop migration rather than colonization.

In the lowlands of northern South America, along the Caribbean coast of Venezuela, manioc, a root crop, developed as the primary source of calories. Domestication of this crop required development of techniques for removal of prussic acid, a poisonous component of the tuber. (Expression of liquids from the tuber did the trick.) Manioc spread throughout eastern South America in a mix of colonization by Equatorial-speakers and crop migration. Other crops domesticated in this region included arrowroot, cacao, and pineapple. As with other tropical areas, the archaeological work conducted has not yet been sufficient to determine the precise times and places of domestication of these crops. But the sheer number of the crops and their importance in human nutrition in subsequent times should be sufficient to draw our attention to the early achievements of the Equatorial-speaking peoples of northern South America, even if they seem to have created no great or lasting empires.

Further south, at Andean altitudes thousands of meters above sea level, a second-wave creation of a new agricultural center brought development of potatoes (tubers) and quinoa (a grain). Also in the highlands the llama was domesticated as a pack animal and a source of fiber for weaving, and guinea pigs were domesticated for food. The development of these crops permitted the rise of a remarkably dense population for such a high altitude, a population perhaps denser than that of the Himalayas. Potatoes did not spread far until, in the age of maritime contact, they could be planted in temperate areas at higher latitudes.

A final major center of second-wave agricultural innovation is that of North China. This center of temperate climate is best labeled as the Huang He (Yellow River) Valley, but often it is simply listed as "China" and thus conflated with the tropical agricultural development of South China. North China's early agriculture, based on domestication of local millet, is relatively well known because of intensive archaeological study in that region. I believe, however, that the agriculture of North China will ultimately be shown to be quite separate from and later in origin than that of South China. Sorghum also came to be grown in North China, though it may be that the ultimate origin of the sorghum was northeast Africa. With the passage of time, techniques for growing rice were developed for this region, and the full range of crops enabled the region's population to grow. Thus it was that the people of North China, long in an outlying corner of the Chinese-speaking region, were able to grow in population and establish a set of states that would later expand and dominate the southern regions from which their ancestors had come.

Life at water's edge

After all this concentration on the rise of agriculture and the accompanying domestication of animals, it will not do to neglect the importance of life at water's edge in the history of human food production and the history of migration. It may be that, in this era, man's mastery over the soil grew more rapidly than his mastery over the waters. But the importance of life at water's edge continued, as did the interaction of tillers of the soil and harvesters of the waters. There were fishers on all the waterways, and human populations remained concentrated in proximity to rivers, lakes, and seas. The quality of watercraft inched ahead. The skin boats of Eurasiatic-speakers are attested in rock sculptures in Norwegian fjords, and in drawings of craft navigating Central Asian rivers. The Austronesian-speaking migration to island Southeast Asia was accomplished with the outrigger canoe, powered by sails as well as oars. The peoples of woodland North America developed bark canoes, sturdy and almost as light as skin canoes, with which they navigated the great inland waterways of their homeland. On the tropical Pacific coast (and also in highland lakes of South America), reed boats carried substantial loads, sometimes through difficult surf. Dugout canoes developed for the Amazon Valley also carried people among the Caribbean islands. And in the normally calm waters of the Mediterranean and the western Indian Ocean, plank boats supplemented and replaced dugouts and laid the groundwork for larger-scale shipping.

Despite all these changes in fishing and boat handling, there may not have been advances in fishing or gathering from rivers, lakes, or oceans to match the advances in agriculture and pastoralism of the era addressed in this chapter. As a result, the proportion of the human population living away from the waters grew. Farmers and herders relied on access to water, though in different ways. Their houses, too, tended to face the waters when possible. The days of mankind's principal reliance on the waters were now passing, but the importance of life at water's edge continued, as did the interaction of tillers of the soil and harvesters of the waters.

Conclusion

Agricultural change, launched over ten thousand years ago in several regions of the world, has continued ever since. Some of the early crops have maintained and expanded their initial importance: wheat, rice, maize, millet, manioc, yams, and bananas. But new crops have developed with every age, and new varieties of the old crops continue to appear.

The spread of agriculture to every area of the world was partly through colonization by the original developers of agriculture, but it was equally the result of crop migration. Both these processes of agricultural dispersal depended on a long-term pattern of cross-community migration. Not uncommonly, the ideas of agriculture spread more rapidly and more thoroughly than farming communities could move. Small numbers of migrants, in discussion with those experienced in the lands where they settled, could learn together how to implement agricultural practices in each new area.

Agriculture surely brought a substantial growth in human population. How rapidly did human population grow? When did Africa cease to hold the majority of human population? Perhaps at some time in this period, as populations in Asia, Europe, and the Americas expanded in their areas of settlement. African populations were growing as a result of innovations in agriculture, animal husbandry, and fishing, but populations in other regions were also able to grow. While humans of this era were certainly more numerous within the tropics than in temperate areas, the gathering mastery of temperate zones expanded populations in northern Eurasia, and American populations grew in both temperate and tropical regions. The expanding size and concentration of human populations enabled the development of new diseases that would limit the growth of human populations. Meanwhile, despite the growth and shifts of population as a result of agriculture, the pre-agricultural distribution of population, as reflected in language groups, remained significant.

As the technology of agriculture and variety of crops advanced over several thousand years, concentrations of population grew and fostered a division of labor and often a social hierarchy. Regions of early concentrations of population included Mesopotamia, Nubia, Egypt, the Mediterranean, highland Mexico, Peru, Ethiopia, the lands of the Maya, and the valleys of the Indus, Yangzi,

Huang He, and Niger. These are the places archaeologists have thrived on, because of the richness of their remains. Yet in the chapters to come, I will seek to set these centers in the context of the rural areas between them, and often give primacy to the rural areas. Even in our own twenty-first century, when urban areas have at last come to sustain the majority of the human population, we still rely fundamentally on those in the rural areas, and we escape to commune with the rural areas (especially watery terrains) whenever we get the chance. We have five thousand years more of history to work through in this little book, and most of it will deal with the majority of humans who lived outside of cities.

Further reading

The pathbreaking summaries of archaeological knowledge by V. Gordon Childe still retain their importance as overviews of early agriculture and urbanization. See V. Gordon Childe, *New Light on the Most Ancient East: The Oriental Prelude to European Prehistory* (London, 1934). The earliest major study of plant domestication was N. I. Vavilov (trans. Doris Love), *Origin and Geography of Cultivated Plants* (Cambridge, 1992), first published in 1926.

On the experiments with plants that preceded their actual domestication, see Carl Sauer, *Seeds, Spades, Hearths, and Herds: The Domestication of Animals and Foodstuffs*, second edition (Cambridge, Mass., 1972); and Christopher Ehret, *The Civilizations of Africa: A History to 1800* (Charlottesville, Va., 2002).

On domestication of wheat, see Daniel Zohary and Maria Hopf, *Domestication of Plants in the Old World: The Origin and Spread of Cultivated Plants in West Asia, Europe, and the Nile Valley*, third edition (New York, 2000). On sorghum in northeast Africa, see Ehret, *Civilizations of Africa*. On yams in West Africa, see D. G. Coursey, *The Yam* (London, 1967). On domestic animals, see Roger A. Caras, *A Perfect Harmony: The Intertwining Lives of Animals and Humans throughout History* (New York, 1996). For an authoritative overall view of agricultural domestication which is nevertheless cautious about assigning early dates to domestication in tropical areas, see Jack Harlan, *The Living Fields: Our Agricultural Heritage* (Cambridge, 1995).

On the first wave of agricultural development, Jared Diamond, *Guns, Germs, and Steel: The Fate of Human Societies* (New York, 1997), provides an interpretation of agricultural domestication and its consequences. For an extension of this approach, see Jared Diamond and Peter Bellwood, "Farmers and Their Languages: The First Expansions," *Science* 300 (2003), 597–603. See also Lynda Shaffer, "Southernization," *Journal of World History* 5 (1995), 175–191. Others have offered comments in subsequent issues of *Science*.

The second wave of agricultural development, since 10,000 BP, started with extension of existing agricultural centers. Colin Renfrew, J. P. Mallory, and L. L. Cavalli-Sforza have debated the patterns of expansion of wheat and barley farmers among Indo-European-speakers: Colin Renfrew, *Archaeology and Language: The Puzzle of Indo-European Origins* (London, 1987); J. P. Mallory, *In Search of the Indo-Europeans: Language, Archaeology, and Myth* (London, 1989); and L. L. Cavalli-Sforza, *Genes, People, and Languages* (Berkeley, Calif., 2001). Peter Bellwood has analyzed the expansion of rice cultivation among Austronesian-speakers in *The Prehistory of the Indo-Malaysian Archipelago*, rev. edition (Honolulu, Hawaii, 1997). The second wave of agricultural development also included new agricultural centers; these are discussed in the proceedings of a Smithsonian Institution conference: C. Wesley Cowan and Patty Jo Watson with the assistance of Nancy L. Benco, *The Origins of Agriculture: An International Perspective* (Washington, 1992).

Chapter 5

Commerce, 3000 BCE to 500 CE

The period from 3000 BCE to 500 CE was at once a formative period for today's societies and a time of relatively recent and accelerating human development. By 3000 BCE agriculture was rapidly spreading to uncultivated lands. Agriculture both speeded and slowed migration. Larger populations resulting from the development of agriculture were better able to move in directions they chose, through force of numbers. Yet the work of farming caused families to become tied to land they knew well, and made movement risky and often unwarranted. Other important developments of this period included wider use of metals, the expansion of commerce, and development of large-scale, organized religion.

The most common way to tell the story of this accelerating pace of human development is by emphasizing the rise of civilizational centers. The leading early civilizations included Sumer, the Nubian and Egyptian kingdoms, the Achaemenid Empire of Persia, the Greek and Hellenistic states, the Qin and Han states in China, the Roman Empire surrounding all the Mediterranean, and the Mauryan and Gupta states of north India. Based on the experience of these early states, the period of time from about 3000 BCE to 500 CE is often taken as a sort of base line for world history. This period, known as "the ancient world" or "ancient and classical times," consisted of the earliest times for which we have written records. The histories of "ancient" times reaffirmed the experience and the outlook of the social elites dominating early literate civilizations. These histories narrated the achievements of civilizational centers and expressed the anxieties felt in these centers about the "barbarians" from outside the city walls, who sometimes sought to seize the wealth and power of the cities. Such history privileges cities over countryside, empires and emperors over farmers and herders, the priests and their temples over the spirituality of families, and the accumulations of wealth and artistic creativity in imperial courts over village dances and the designs of domestic implements.

Another way to tell the story of accelerating change is to focus on the expanded connections among groups of humans. In adopting this approach, I intend in this chapter to emphasize two sorts of connections in ancient and classical times. The first is migratory connections, for both rural and urban regions: connections including the great centers of the ancient and classical world, and connections far from those centers but still significant to human change. For instance, I will emphasize the ties of Sumeria to lands far away from its cities, the ties between Egypt and India or Rome and Han China, and the connections among Indonesia, East Africa, and the South Pacific. I will concentrate on the interdependence of imperial city and distant hinterland, the innovations in the countryside as well as the city, and the beliefs of those far from imperial centers as well as those at the great temples.

The second type of connection I will emphasize is in the rise of commerce. The ancient and classical era was equally unique for its creation of the formal institutions of trade, which have developed since then with a success that perhaps exceeds that of institutions of government. Arguably, the benefits of commerce to human society were greater than those of kingdoms. Kingdoms brought benefits to their rulers in the short run, although the royal accumulation of wealth and creativity may have brought benefits to broader strata of society in the longer run. Commerce, too, served particularly the needs of elite strata, but it was more likely to bring benefits to common people in the short run, and its connections shared benefits rather widely over the long run.

The opening and closing sections of this chapter describe the creation of formal systems of *commerce* out of earlier systems of *exchange*. Exchange among communities can be traced far back in human history. Archaeologists have demonstrated the existence of long-distance exchange in the lives of many of the sites they have investigated within the past 10,000 years, and perhaps further back. Minerals and manufactures of interest have been carried, in one way or another, over great distances from their sources to those desiring to use them for a purpose of importance. By 3000 BCE, such patterns of exchange had begun to develop into organized and specialized systems of trade, most prominently to link major centers of population, but also linking less populous sources of valuable goods and destinations where goods were in demand.

In the era beginning 1000 BCE, long-distance commerce became institutionalized, with the development of money, banking, large-scale shipping and caravans, major marketplaces, and ports and caravanserai. This was also a time of the emergence of major states and the rise of major religions. But emphasizing commerce rather than empire or religion gives us a closer look at patterns of migration and regional interconnection, so it is the theme on which I will focus for this period of 3,500 years.

Exchange among communities

For rare or desirable goods, people have long been willing to travel great distances or to pay unusual prices. In times before the smelting of metals provided a new medium for tools, the sharp blades made from the black stone of obsidian were exchanged over long distances in the Americas and in the Eastern Hemisphere. For thousands of years, those with a desire to sharpen the taste of bland foods have sought out peppers from Southeast Asia, West Africa, and the Caribbean coast, and carried them to consumers far away. Eye-catching decorative items, such as the deep blue lapis lazuli stone from Afghanistan, have traveled extraordinary distances. Perfumes such as frankincense from Arabia gained a reputation and a steady demand from early times. Materials known or reputed to bring healing or improvements in one's capacities, from herbs to parrots' feathers, have been exchanged as far back in time as a need was expressed for their benefits. These things from far away that make a difference have made exchange an element of human society from earliest times.

Given the importance of these goods to communities far away from the points of origin, it has been equally important to develop techniques for conveying them and exchanging them appropriately for other goods. For some goods light in weight and compact in size, it may have been sufficient for an individual to put them in a bag and carry them on foot, over a shoulder, or in a package carried by head. But carrying larger quantities began to depend on beasts of burden. Donkeys had been domesticated thousands of years earlier in northeastern Africa, and proved useful as pack animals. Cattle, water buffalo, and later horses were able to pull heavy loads. Camels and llamas, while domesticated rather late, in their turn served effectively as pack animals.

Transport by water similarly facilitated exchange of goods, and especially for goods that were heavy. Rivers in every part of the world were traveled, in the areas where their waters were calm, by small craft which might nevertheless still carry significant quantities of goods. These craft were made of reeds, rafts of wood or bamboo, canoes hollowed out from great logs, and wooden frameworks covered with watertight skins or bark. In the major seas and at the edge of great oceans, larger vessels carried goods from one shore to another. By 3000 BCE there existed vessels that relied on sail as well as oars, and sailed the Mediterranean, Red Sea, Persian Gulf, the north shores of the Indian Ocean, the South China Sea, and the western Pacific. Caribbean mariners, lacking sails, nevertheless developed large canoes for the voyages among islands. Of these, perhaps the most remarkable set of techniques for traveling the seas was that of the Austronesian-speaking mariners and their outrigger vessels. They began to venture beyond the sight of land, and began to learn the winds, the currents, and the patterns of birds that enabled them to connect areas previously left isolated. On sea as on land, those who traveled began to develop and to pass on information about geography.

Moving goods from one place to another involved more than identifying the desirable goods and developing means of transporting them. In addition, the people who transported the goods had to be able to sustain themselves, to establish cordial relations with those along the way, and to communicate in detail. The social systems needed to provide food and housing for those on the move, and needed to protect them against the bandits who would surely arise to seize valuable goods. Language specialists, in order to communicate with people at each step along the way, needed to develop their skills. Among the topics of their conversation were ways to estimate the value of goods and to exchange them along the way.

In areas where exchange became relatively dense, there grew up systems for housing travelers, along with fairs and marketplaces for the display of goods. Local centers at which people exchanged foodstuffs could include sections where a smaller quantity of goods brought from long distance could be displayed. Opportunities arose occasionally for certain groups to become specialized in exchange – to become merchants. The Phoenician mariners, who sailed from what is now Lebanon along the Mediterranean coast as early as the third millennium BCE, are perhaps the best-known early commercial specialists. These early merchants did not invent exchange, but expanded existing networks of exchange. Out of seaside villages they created ports, and out of the complex system of Sumerian cuneiform they developed a simplified and highly functional system of writing to assist in the record-keeping of merchants. Two thousand years later, their commercial beginnings would be followed by the emergence of a hemispheric web of commerce.

Rural migratory connections

The human habit of migration, by small and large groups, made itself felt in this era as in previous times. The difference is that after 3000 BCE migrations are easier to document in detail because of the availability of written records. Still, some of the most significant migratory movements of this era are documented by linguistic and archaeological evidence rather than through written records. In this section I will describe migrations that linked rural areas to each other, and which in so doing led to significant change in world population distribution, and to opening of new linkages among populations.

Migrations in Southeast Asia, in this period as in earlier times, set trends affecting much of the Eastern Hemisphere. Sino-Tibetan-speakers, with an ancestral homeland in the deep valleys to the east of the Himalayas, had periodically sent migrants out in various directions. In Chapter 4 we discussed their movement, in the early days of agricultural domestication, to the lower Yangzi Valley and to what is now North China. In the period leading up to 3000 BCE, the Tibetan plateau yielded to new technology, including domestication of the yak (a high-altitude relative of cattle), and the Tibetan population and language took shape. In the same period, Burmese-speakers moved south along the Salween and Irrawaddy valleys and occupied lands up to the shores of the Indian Ocean.

Meanwhile the neighboring Austric family of languages, with an ancestral homeland only slightly further lower in the same valleys, also spread from Yunnan in various directions, especially to the south and the east. The Austric languages, spoken in an area overlapping Sino-Tibetan languages, were nonetheless distinct. Most speakers of these languages remained on the Southeast

Asian mainland, where today they predominate in the nations of Vietnam, Thailand, Laos, and Cambodia. The northern range of the Austric homeland, over time, came to be shared with southward-moving groups of Chinese-speakers.

Best documented, however, are the migrations of those among the speakers of Austric languages who left the mainland and populated the islands of Southeast Asia and the Pacific. The ancestors of Austronesian-speakers had developed a homeland downriver from Yunnan, with advanced rice production, but also with boats. These canoes with outriggers for stability may have been developed in the inland rivers, but when fitted with sails they proved to have special benefits for oceanic travel. After crossing the strait of over 100 kilometers to Taiwan, the developing Austronesian populations were then able to sail with shorter crossings north along the chain of islands leading to Okinawa and toward Japan, and south to the Philippines. This migration began in about 3000 BCE, or perhaps somewhat before that time. Setting up farms of rice, yams, chickens, and pigs as well as harvesting the sea, Austronesian-speakers settled throughout the Indonesian archipelago and even moved northwest to the Malayan mainland.

Some of the Austronesians headed further west, and their languages survive in Madagascar — where languages are most closely related to languages of Borneo. These mariners appear to have made their travels at the beginning of the Common Era or perhaps even earlier. They thus appear to have been sailing the Indian Ocean at the same time as Greek, Roman, Indian, and Persian ships were sailing the same waters. This is also the era that Lynda Shaffer has called "Southernization," in which Indonesian and Indian mariners knit together the whole Indian Ocean.

Austronesian-speakers spreading into Taiwan, the Philippines, and the Indonesian archipelago encountered local populations who, presumably, spoke Indo-Pacific languages and lived by fishing, hunting, and gathering. (Language-distribution studies indicate that the Indo-Pacific languages once covered a huge area, including most of Indonesia and areas of the eastern Indian Ocean, as well as islands surrounding New Guinea, and Tasmania as well.) The Austronesian-speakers, with their economy relying on rice and yams, became more populous and absorbed the Indo-Pacific-speakers until they got to Papua New Guinea and the Bismarck Archipelago, where Indo-Pacific-speakers had long since developed agriculture relying on taro, bananas, sugar cane, and other crops. The Papuans were too numerous to be absorbed by the visitors. The incoming Austronesian-speakers, however, were able to establish a firm presence in the coastal areas of New Guinea and neighboring islands. The stage was set for intermarriage, an exchange of traditions, and development of a new tradition.

Out of this social crucible came populations that occupied lands across the far reaches of the Pacific. These populations were the sole groups to inhabit the area now known as Polynesia, and they shared with other groups the lands of

Micronesia and Melanesia. They speak Austronesian languages, but their culture and their genetic composition rely substantially on the Indo-Pacific-speaking peoples of New Guinea. This culture thrived beginning about 3000 BCE along the northern coast of New Guinea and the neighboring Bismarck Islands. By 1000 BCE these settlers had reached Tonga and Samoa, thousands of kilometers to the southeast. Rice lost its importance among these farmers, but Southeast Asian yams, chickens, and pigs combined with Papuan taro and bananas and with seafood to provide a varied cuisine. The development of a characteristic style of pottery known as Lapita marks the archaeological remains of these peoples. Equally important was the double-hulled sailing craft developed by the Lapita peoples, which eased the sailing of the high seas. The Polynesian double-hulled vessels had stability, speed, maneuverability, and the capacity to hold large numbers of sailors and supplies for long voyages. With these vessels, navigation skills could be developed to a high level. Without writing or instruments, but with intensive observation of stars, winds, the currents, and the patterns of birds, mariners of the Pacific were able to develop pinpoint navigation.

From their homeland, Polynesian mariners reached the Marquesas Islands, from which they were able to carry out voyages of discovery north to Hawaii, east to Easter Island, and south to New Zealand. It is likely even that these mariners reached and settled on the coast of South America. The evidence is indirect but, I find, convincing. There they learned to cultivate sweet potatoes from the peoples of the Peruvian coast, and brought cuttings with them to the islands. Ultimately, the sweet potato made possible the development of a large Polynesian population on the islands of New Zealand – a region where the normal Polynesian crops, especially taro, could not thrive. These Lapita societies maintained an active trade network until about 500 CE, then allowed it to decline. In the western Pacific, however, the network of rapid connection among islands through double-hulled and outrigger canoes continued to the nineteenth century.

Meanwhile, at the opposite, western fringe of the Austronesian diaspora, the occupation of Madagascar and the Comoros may have been parallel to that of Polynesia and Micronesia in two fashions. First, Austronesian-speaking mariners led in the settlement. Second, it may be that Austronesian connection with East African populations led to a social and biological synthesis that distinguished this stage of migration from those before it. That is, we may seek an East African equivalent to the Lapita homeland of the Pacific. In each case, the argument is that cross-community exchanges may have been important even in migrations that appear from a distance to be a massive colonization effort.

At about the time when the Austronesian mariners began their voyages, Indo-European-speakers in the steppes north of the Black Sea took steps beyond their practice of hunting horses and were able to domesticate them. The result soon led to horse-drawn chariots and then to mounted warriors, especially among Indo-European-speakers but also among neighboring groups speaking Altaic or Semitic languages. Horses, harnessed to two wheeled chariots, became a potent military force, and were associated with the expansion of several Indo-European-speaking groups, including the Hittites of the Anatolian Peninsula. Among the eastern groups of Indo-European languages were the Indo-Iranian languages.

This expansion of Indo-European horse-keepers was a development subsequent to the spread of agriculture throughout Eurasia, which had begun several thousand years earlier. The Indo-Iranian subgroup of Indo-Europeans filtered into Iran and, in a related movement, into north India. Those in Iran gave rise to the religious tradition of Zoroaster and then to the Achaemenid dynasty that created the first large empire. Those in India brought the religious poetry known as the Vedas.

Horses spread beyond Indo-European-speakers soon enough. Speakers of Altaic languages, also reliant on horses (and, in the opinion of some, the first to domesticate them), moved periodically from the East and Central Asian homelands far to the west and somewhat to the south. The Avars and Scythians were such groups in the first millennium BCE, and were followed in the fifth century CE by the Xiongnu in the east and the Huns in the west. Domestication of camels – both in Central Asia and in Arabia – took place in the first millennium CE.

At much the same time as the Aryan migrations into Iran and India, another set of movements remade the map of a similarly sized region of Africa. This was the dispersal of Bantu-speakers into Central and eastern Africa. Their style of movement, however, was on foot rather than by chariot, and warfare appears to have been less important than farming in their expansion. They were farmers like the Aryans, but lacked horses. They slowly advanced into the forests that are now Cameroon and Congo, displacing and absorbing previous inhabitants in a fashion parallel to that of the Austronesians and the Aryans. When Bantu migrants reached the highland areas of East Africa late in the first millennium BCE, they encountered other farming groups. There, as had been the case in Melanesia, a more complex set of interactions and a new set of innovations developed. Through combination with peoples from Afroasiatic and perhaps Nilo-Saharan language groups, the Bantu-speakers adopted cattle, sheep, and millet, and expanded more rapidly into eastern and southern Africa.

To show that these three stories of rural migration were not only similar but connected, we need only return to the Austronesian voyages to the western Indian Ocean. On the eastern coast of Africa, Austronesian-speakers introduced bananas, Asian yams, the music of xylophones, and outrigger canoes. The first three of these innovations spread across the African continent from hand to hand; bananas were of particular importance in the valleys and highlands of Bantu-speaking Central Africa, where they became a crop of first importance.

By the same token, the Austronesian migrants had to pass through Indian waters on their way to East Africa, and surely camped and settled at several points along the coast, probably as merchants. Along the coasts of north India and Iran, they would therefore have encountered Indo-Iranian-speakers whose ancestors had entered the region over a thousand years earlier.

I have selected certain rural migrations of this era to show something of their character. But one could just as well have told the story of movements by populations in other parts of the world. The Celtic-speakers, the westernmost group of Indo-European languages, found reason to expand their settlements far to the east in roughly 3000 BCE. Later they found their area of settlement restricted by other groups, until they were limited again to the northwestern shores of Europe. Among those who expanded at the expense of the Celtic-speakers were the Germanic-speaking peoples of central and northern Europe. The Berbers of the North African mountains, the westernmost of the Afroasiatic-speakers, adopted camels in the first millennium BCE and expanded their range to the south, ultimately spreading their populations throughout the western and central Sahara. Similar movements took place in the Americas in the same period, though they are not yet known in much detail: for instance, successive migrations from northern South America led to repopulation of Caribbean islands, but also led to expanded population in the southern Amazon basin and the savanna areas further south beyond it.

Urban connections

Early centers of urban civilization, which in many general texts are each given separate chapters, are here summarized as a group. While this approach loses much of the detail for each society, it allows greater attention to the similarities and especially the connections they had with each other and with other regions. Early cities developed especially along waterways where agriculture had become productive in relatively narrow territories. The large populations of cities, while bringing the benefits of combining many social functions in a compact zone, also presented problems of supply and organization. Sometimes these problems were resolved by peaceable organization of complementary functions; such was the case for the early cities of the Indus Valley and West Africa. At other times organization was enforced by the establishment of social hierarchy with coercive power, as in Mesopotamia. The development of urban administrative techniques relying both on cooperation and hierarchy served to lay the groundwork for creation of wider empires. Cities, further, brought association with several sorts of migration: migration from rural to urban areas, movement of elites and artisans from city to city, the reliance of urban areas on produce from rural areas near and far, and changes in rural areas because of developments in urban centers.

Cities of the Nile Valley arose before 3000 BCE. Indeed, a recently discovered city of the Nilo-Saharan-speaking Nubians arose thousands of years earlier. The rulers of cities of the Afroasiatic-speaking lower Nile, in Egypt, went upriver to Nubia for the ceremonies of their enthronement, indicating that the Nubian states were in some sense ancestral to those of Egypt. Egypt became unified in about 3100 BCE, and the Egyptian kingdom was reorganized every few hundred years thereafter, with new dynasties replacing the old in a system that otherwise showed great continuity.

Also before 3000 BCE, the Sumerian city states arose in Mesopotamia, along the Tigris and Euphrates rivers. The epic tale of Gilgamesh, king of the Sumerian city of Uruk, recounted not only his construction of the city walls and his search for immortality but his travels to distant regions. The time of Sumeria as a collection of independent city states was interrupted as one of their leaders, Sargon, formed an effective army and, by the time of his death in 2334 BCE, had conquered one after another of the Sumerian cities. Sargon's successors were later displaced by Babylonian rulers including Hammurabi, best known for his code of law.

Meanwhile the domestication of horses led to big changes in politics and society, first in Asia and eventually in most world regions. Indo-European-speaking hunters north of the Black Sea turned from hunting horses to capturing and training them in the third or fourth millennium BCE, and the use of horses spread rapidly to neighboring areas. The Hittites, an Indo-European group in Anatolia, relied on horses as they entered into combat with the Babylonian state. The Hittites developed or adopted horse-drawn chariots, using light-weight wheels with spokes rather than the heavy wooden wheels of Babylonian ox carts. With their chariots, the Hittites destroyed the Babylonian state in 1595 BCE. The rapid spread of horses beyond their initial trainers is demonstrated by the example of the Hyksos, a Semitic-speaking group that had adopted horses centuries before the Hittite destruction of Babylon: the Hyksos took control of the Nile Delta before 2000 BCE, and it was some time before the Egyptian state could get rid of them.

The Indus River Valley gave rise to another set of cities, also by 3000 BCE, of which the largest were Harappa and Mohenjo-Dara. These large cities, presumed to be populated by Dravidian-speaking inhabitants, were marvels of urban design, including advanced sewerage systems. It is also of interest that they did not develop centralized political structures. Their trade with Sumeria has been documented. Indo-European-speaking migrants with horses came to the Indus Valley as well. The Harappan cities declined by 1700 BCE, apparently before many Aryan migrants arrived. The incoming Aryans settled, and their languages gradually became dominant in northern India.

In East Asia, along the Huang He Valley, cities grew up in the third millennium BCE. By 2200 BCE the Xia state had gained control of a large proportion of this fertile but irregularly watered valley; some four hundred years later the Xia state was replaced by the Shang state.

For the thousand years from 1500 BCE to 500 BCE, the historical record shows struggles for power within the framework of small but powerful states.

Babylonians enslaved Israelites; the Zhou kingdom achieved dominance in the Huang He Valley from 1122 BCE. The Nubian kingdom of Kush conquered Egypt in 750 BCE; then the Assyrians created the largest empire yet, conquering Mesopotamia, Syria, and Egypt by 664 BCE. Yet Phoenician ships traveled all the Mediterranean, and Egyptian ships traveled the Red Sea with connections to India. And while cities appeared increasingly to come under the power of strong rulers, the emerging cities of the West African savanna, along the Niger River, seem to have owed more to the complementary activities of different economic specialists than to subordination to a central authority.

From about 500 BCE, the scale of social organization expanded again as the Achaemenids, Indo-European-speaking warriors from Iran, gained control of the Assyrian Empire and added Iran and Anatolia, creating the largest empire to that date. Their techniques of warfare gained them the empire, but their techniques of administration were necessary to sustain it. Interestingly, the Achaemenids did not rely heavily on written records, though their system of rule gave great emphasis to ceremony and public spectacle. Later empires, however, have all relied on the written word for administration. Thereafter, other empires of similar scale arose. Alexander of Macedon conquered the Achaemenid state by the time of his death in 323 BCE. He did not expand its borders significantly, but his administration placed Greek language and culture in a leading position throughout his empire and its successors for several hundred years. In the time just after Alexander's conquests, the Mauryan state arose to control much of northern India. The Mauryan king Asoka came to control most of the subcontinent, and then shifted sharply from an early life of conquest to a later life in search of peace and justice: he was the first major monarch to convert to Buddhism. After a few hundred years, the Gupta state replaced the Mauryan state in north India.

In northern China, the era of the Warring States broke out in 404 BCE and lasted for two hundred years. At the end of that time the Qin emperor briefly united North China and some areas in the south, following a policy of ruthless military takeover. Following the Qin collapse, the Han state arose to gain control of much of the territory ruled briefly by the Qin, and China's first full-scale dynasty began its period of rule. The Han governed from the city of Chang'an (now Xian); the capital later moved eastward to Luoyang.

Meanwhile, in the same era that the Han state arose, the regional state of Rome expanded from its Italian base to gain control of most of the Mediterranean. The capital city of Rome had up to a million inhabitants, supplied with water from long aqueducts and grain from Egypt and northwest Africa. With its many other cities, the empire had the most vigorous urban life of the ancient world. Even as Rome weakened and collapsed in the fifth century CE, migration from rural areas fed the cities of the Mediterranean region.

An important connection to urban life grew out of rural migrations that began beyond the northeastern frontiers of the Roman Empire. In the first century CE the Goths – peoples from the Baltic coast of what is now Poland, speaking Germanic languages – began to spread southeast along the Vistula River and eventually to the coast of the Black Sea, north of the Danube River. These farming and herding peoples gained dominance over local peoples, developed kingdoms, and gradually became Christian. Suddenly in the late fourth century CE a new force entered the region from the east: the Huns. These mounted warriors had fought their way across the grasslands from east of the Volga until they reached the Danube. The Huns destroyed some Gothic kingdoms and caused other Goths to escape by requesting permission to cross the Danube and settle within the Roman Empire. The continued arrival of Huns, settling especially in what is now Hungary, led eventually to the rise of a Hunnish Empire. Attila, the empire's last and most effective leader, controlled most of the land north of the Danube and east of the Rhine from 434 CE to 453 CE. Hunnish conquests caused many Germanic-speaking groups to flee—some to the west and others to the south. Moving to the south, across the Danube and into Roman territories, were groups of Goths who ultimately formed two great confederations. The Visigoths arose under the leadership of Alaric, who conquered the city of Rome in 410 CE. The Ostrogoths formed after 450 CE; Theodoric, their greatest leader, was actually born in Constantinople. Gothic and other Germanic-speaking groups fought sometimes for Rome and sometimes against Rome.

Cities all over the Roman Empire began to include Goths—either as free persons or in slavery, depending on the fortunes of war. Fleeing the Huns in another direction, across the Rhine to the west, were the Vandals, Franks, Angles, and Saxons. Attila's empire collapsed as soon as he died, but the migrations had started and were to continue for more than a century. With time, the invading armies founded kingdoms and settled in cities. Visigoths moved to Gaul and set up their capital in the city of Toulouse; Ostrogoths settled in northern Italy and made their capital at Ravenna. The Vandals moved through Iberia to North Africa, establishing their capital at Carthage. The Franks moved from the Rhine Valley and eventually based their kingdom in Paris. These migrating groups soon adopted local languages and lost their military dominance, but the memory of their powerful, mobile armies remained in written history and oral tradition.

Commerce, 1000 BCE to 500 CE

Christopher Ehret, in analyzing the history of East Africa in the era from 1000 BCE to 500 CE, concluded that the term "commercial revolution" was appropriate as a description of the Mediterranean, the Indian Ocean, and the adjoining lands. While "commercial revolution" is a term most commonly applied to Europe in medieval and early modern times, Ehret's new application of the term seems appropriate. This was the time of the invention and elaboration of the main institutions of commerce, so that informal exchange was transformed into formal commerce, with money, specialized merchants, and organized marketplaces, ports, and commercial taxes.

While exchanges of some sort probably linked almost every area of the world, one can also speak from this time of a web of direct commercial ties that linked a very large portion of the world, with active points in the eastern Mediterranean, South China, and India, and with connections to Europe, West Africa, East Africa, Indonesia, Central Asia, the North Pacific, and the western Pacific. The main elements for this new system of commerce and its changes from earlier systems of exchange included: an expanded set of commodities; the use of widely recognized systems of money; the development of new technology in shipping, accounting, and merchandising; the establishment of well-traveled commercial routes, with ports and caravanserai; the creation of social institutions of commerce such as trade diasporas; and the development of ideas and philosophies to address the problems of commerce. Among the commodities that entered formal commerce were metals, pottery, spices, precious stones, grain, religious artifacts, textiles, and leather.

The creation of metallic coins for money is an unmistakable hallmark of formal commerce. Mediterranean states began stamping coins in the first millennium BCE, and by the end of that millennium, Roman coins were scattered across much of Eurasia. At the same time, the various states of North China had circulated metallic coins, made of copper, bronze, silver, and gold. The spread of money facilitated the improvement of accounting practices and the beginning of banking. Loans and advances of goods to be sold became part of an expanding system of trust and obligations that built a network of personal ties to match the web of goods flowing from region to region.

Metallic coins coexisted with other sorts of money. Seashells in particular were popular as money over a wide area, especially the shells of cowries, which grow in the waters of the Indian Ocean and the western Pacific. From times before the rise of Rome, cowries from the Indian Ocean had spread to Etruscan Italy in the west and to central China in the east. Thus the system of multiple currencies (such as silver and gold) in later times may have got its start at the very beginning, as cowries and coins coexisted over much of the web of commerce. One may speculate that Austronesian-speaking merchants were important in the spread if not the invention of cowrie currency. The cowrie currency system thus spread not only throughout the Indian Ocean, but may have begun in the South China Sea, and spread through New Guinea and perhaps into Polynesian territory.

The technology of commerce consisted of many levels of tools, techniques, and knowledge. One may begin with the technology of transportation on land and sea. The vessels developed for commerce had to be appropriate to the riverain and oceanic waterways, but also benefited from developments enabling the carrying and preservation of steadily larger loads. Overland, goods could be carried by human porters but, where possible, pack animals and sometimes wagons were used. The development of camel transport was remarkable in that, once adequate saddles and packing gear were created, camels as pack animals displaced wheeled carts in the regions where camels thrived. Just as the techniques for loading and sailing at sea required a skilled workforce, so did the techniques for care and feeding of animals, loading, and unloading them. The rise of durable iron tools, eventually including nails, was of great use to merchants. Equally important, however, were the creation of leather goods, the assembly of boats and carts with wooden pegs, and the sewing of sails and tarpaulins. Navigation on land and sea required those who knew the routes, the seasons, and the obstacles to travel. Sailors in the eastern and western Indian Ocean learned to sail the open seas, following the annual rhythm of the monsoon winds, not long after Austronesian-speaking sailors in the western Pacific learned to cross the open seas.

Public works assisted in the development of travel: creation of roads, bridges, ferries, and fords to cross rivers, ports, and canals for boats. The canals of Ptolemaic Egypt linked the Mediterranean to the Red Sea in the early centuries CE. A more substantial and more enduring canal is the Grand Canal, created just after the Han regime to link the valleys of the Yangzi and the Huang He, and to facilitate the flow of rice from south to north.

By 500 CE, the routes of regular commerce extended by land and sea across the heartland of Afro-Eurasia, and into many of the peripheral zones. The most significant overland channel of long-distance trade, now known as the Silk Road, extended between the Black Sea and Mediterranean Sea in the west and the Huang He Valley in northern China, and linking all the desert and steppe lands in between. Other main overland routes linked Yunnan (southwest of China) with Bengal and the Indian Ocean; tied north India to Central Asia; and linked northern Europe and West Africa, respectively, with the western Mediterranean. The main sea routes were those of the Mediterranean and Black Seas; the Red Sea (reaching into Ethiopia and the Nile Valley); the Persian Gulf; the western Indian Ocean (reaching far down the East African coast); the eastern Indian Ocean; the South China Sea; the northern Pacific coast; and the archipelagoes of the western Pacific.

The social networks of the expanding network of trade were no less crucial than the technology or the economics of trade. Creating systems of trust and systems that effectively carried information was necessary to make long-distance trade a dependable activity. Certain languages became specialized for trade, and were spoken far from their home community for commercial purposes: Greek and Aramaic, in the early centuries CE, were two such languages. Another key social institution of commerce has come to be known as the "trade diaspora." Families of certain ethnic groups – including Armenians in western and Central Asia and, later, Mande-speaking West Africans known as Wangara – sent family members great distances to establish autonomous, self-governing communities, so that they could serve as hosts to traveling merchants from the homeland, and assist them in conducting their trade. Such trade diasporas were central to long-distance commerce until the modern period.

The era of the commercial revolution was also a time in which major new traditions developed in religion and ethical philosophy. Zoroaster and the Buddha, Confucius, Laotse, the Hebrew prophets, the Greek philosophers, Jesus, and others preached about the fundamental issues of life, death, community, and destiny, in ways that led to the organization of schools and of large-scale religious institutions. Of course both religion and the concern with ethics had been part of human society since the very earliest of times. But the prophets and philosophers of the first millennium BCE may have been addressing the new problems brought by the larger-scale organization of society, in addition to the age-old problems of small human communities. It may be that the increasingly successful search for wealth and the rise in inequality, both associated with the commercial revolution, gave importance and meaning to the new systems of religion and philosophy. Particularly in the case of Buddhism, religion and commerce became closely tied, particularly through the trade in religious paraphernalia. Religion traveled with trade, and religion was often about trade. Christianity was unusual among the new religions in that its ties to commerce were slow to grow. But for Islam, founded in the seventh century CE, the prophet Muhammad was seen as bringing the last and most complete revelation from God, and early Islamic religion focused particularly on resolving the conflicts among commercial profit and the pious support of the poor.

Conclusion

For the past two thousand years, migration has virtually ceased to consist of the occupation of empty spaces, though people may have spoken of the lands to which they moved as "empty." Almost every group of people found itself within reach of groups of "others" with whom to conduct exchanges or compete for resources. And there were always people who crossed the boundaries, willingly or not, whose experience centered significantly on learning new languages and customs.

Movement has been the focus of this chapter's interpretation of ancient and classical times, in contrast with interpretations focusing in a static fashion on centers, kingdoms, empires, temples, and great markets. In this chapter I have sought to show that wealth was created not only in centers of civilization, but through the commercial movements of both luxuries and basic commodities from place to place. Similarly, I have emphasized the ubiquity of innovation and the benefits of systems of exchanging ideas, rather than see innovations emerging only from isolated centers of excellence, surrounded by dangerous barbarians. New ideas came not only from geniuses and brilliant inventors, but also from the commerce of ideas and the linkage of innovations in the course of daily life.

Most migrations brought encounters between settlers and the established owners of the land (an exception was the colonization of new territories in

Polynesia). Established populations or immigrants prevailed depending on the circumstances, but in addition these encounters resulted in wider connections. Such wider connections included the spread of bananas and xylophones across Africa and the spread of Buddhism across Asia. Meanwhile, certain centers of migration periodically sent out new groups of migrants. The Sino-Tibetan homeland in the upper reaches of the Southeast Asian river valleys sent migrants to Tibet and Burma in this era as it had sent migrants to North China in earlier times. The Semitic-speaking coast of the eastern Mediterranean sent out migrants known as Phoenicians in the third century BCE, known as Aramaic-speakers in the late centuries BCE and early centuries CE, and known as Lebanese for the past two centuries. Greek-speakers from a nearby coast have migrated almost as consistently over the centuries.

The combination of rural and urban connections led to the development of commercial networks – webs of markets, merchants, money, commodities, and obligations that moved commodities and ideas short distances and long. In the period up to 500 CE, an impressive range of commercial institutions had been developed to facilitate the exchange of a growing range of useful commodities. Among the commodities were slaves who could be induced to provide services or produce more commodities. Thus the creation of commercial systems was more than a technical improvement of exchange: it also facilitated the growth of inequality in human society. As the differences grew between the wealthy and the poor, the free and the unfree, there developed a need for new ideas in religion and philosophy to address the meaning of inequality.

Further reading

Anthropologist Bruce Trigger has produced a concise and thoughtful comparison of the issues in early political systems, in *Early Civilizations: Ancient Egypt in Context* (Cairo, Egypt, 1993). For a recent analysis of the Phoenicians, highlighting their early leadership in systems of exchange, see Maris Eugenia Aubet (trans. Mary Turton), *The Phoenicians and the West: Politics, Colonies and Trade* (New York, 2001).

Rural migrations affected people throughout the world. For migrations of Austronesian-speakers, see Peter Bellwood, *Prehistory of the Indo-Malaysian Archipelago*, rev. edition (Honolulu, Hawaii, 1997). See also Lynda Shaffer, "Southernization," *Journal of World History* 5 (1994), 175–191. The effects of horses among Indo-European-speakers are discussed in Colin Renfrew, *Archaeology and Language: The Puzzle of Indo-European Origins* (London, 1987); and J. P. Mallory, *In Search of the Indo-Europeans: Language, Archaeology, and Myth* (London, 1989). Movements of Bantu-speaking peoples are analyzed in Jan Vansina, *Paths in the Rainforest: Toward a History of Political Tradition in Equatorial Africa* (Madison, Wis., 1990); James L. A. Webb, Jr., "Malaria and the Peopling of Early Tropical Africa," *Journal of World History* 16 (2005), 269–291; and Christopher Ehret, *The Civilizations of Africa: A History to 1800* (Charlottesville, Va., 2002).

For connections among urban areas, see Stanley Burstein, *Graeco-Africana: Studies in the History of Greek Relations with Egypt and Nubia* (New Rochelle, New York, 1995).

For interpretations of Sumeria emphasizing its long-distance connections, see Andre Gunder Frank and Barry K. Gills, eds., *The World System: Five Hundred Years or Five Thousand?* (New York, 1993). On the Achaemenid state, see Pierre Briant (trans. Peter T. Daniels), *From Cyrus to Alexander: A History of the Persian Empire* (Winona Lake, Ind., 2001).

For the notion of a commercial revolution in the first millennium BCE, see Christopher Ehret, *An African Classical Age: Eastern and Southern Africa in World History, 1000 B.C. to 400 A.D.* (Charlottesville, Va., 1998). On the contribution of the camel to commerce, see Richard Bulliet, *The Camel and the Wheel* (New York, 1990). On the links of commerce and religion, see Liu Xinru, *Ancient India and Ancient China: Trade and Religious Exchanges AD 1–600* (Oxford, 1995). On the Zoroastrian faith, see Mary Boyce, *Zoroastrianism: Its Antiquity and Constant Vigor* (Costa Mesa, Calif., 1992).

On the relation of declining Rome with surrounding and migrating peoples, see Peter Heather, *Empires and Barbarians: The Fall of Rome and the Birth of Europe* (Oxford, 2010); Ralph W. Mathisen, "Peregrini, Barbari, and Cives Romani: Concepts of Citizenship and the Legal Identity of Barbarians in the Later Roman Empire," *American Historical Review* 111 (2006), 1011–1040; and Verena Postel, *Die Ursprünge Europas. Migration und Integration im frühen Mittelalter* (Stuttgart, 2004).

Chapter 6

Modes of movement, 500 to 1400 CE

Within the past few chapters we have reviewed some remarkable achievements and inventions of our ancestors. Migrants from Africa settled new and different lands. Their distant descendants domesticated plants and animals, and created improvements in oceanic and land transport. Still later generations created metallurgy, writing, and states, and elaborated formal systems of philosophy, religion, and commerce. Along with these developments expanded that dubious but influential activity, warfare. All of these changes have drawn on migration, and all of them have generated new sorts of migration.

For the period of nine centuries to be considered in this chapter, I will emphasize not the opening of major new areas of human accomplishment, but patterns of exchange and advance within the framework of previous achievements. The tales of great states and major religious and intellectual developments – particularly in the lands of Islam and in the successive dynasties of the Middle Kingdom in China – have been told well in other works of world history. For the present analysis, these great states will be set into the background, so that we can get a closer look at the underlying human habits that sustained migration. As I argued in the opening chapter, habitual human patterns of cross-community migration linked regions to each other, spread earlier innovations, and brought new innovations. In this era, patterns of cross-community migration led groups of hundreds and sometimes thousands of migrants to expand the connections within the main continental areas. Similar movements brought expanded contact among each of the earth's main archipelagoes and oceanic basins.

The modes of movement across community lines included travel on foot, on horseback, and by boat. In one sense, such migration has changed little over the course of human history: people leave their home community, travel a distance, and learn to live among people of different language and culture. In another sense, the migrations of every period differ because of changes in environmental conditions, in technology, and in social conditions. Improved seacraft and better saddles eased travel by boat and by horse; accumulated knowledge of the routes eased travel on foot. Most migrants followed paths already opened. They relied on the institutional support provided by commercial networks or religious communities, and they encountered the support and restrictions brought by the existence of states.

An example of changes in modes of migration is in religious pilgrimage: the hajj, the Islamic pilgrimage to the holy sites of Mecca. From the time of Muhammad (who died in 632 CE), Muslims have followed the invocation of the Qur'an to come to Mecca at least once in their lives, if possible, to honor the sanctuary created there by the prophet Abraham. Within a century of the proclamation of the religion of Islam, pilgrims came from as far west as Morocco and Iberia, and as far east as Turkestan and India. By 1400, the hajj gathered pilgrims not just from the heartland of Islam, but from almost every corner of the Old World – as far as Siberia, West Africa, and the Philippines. Sometimes the voyage took years, and many who embarked upon it failed to return, yet the hajj stood as a testimony of the ability, in those centuries, of people of all social stations to travel a great distance for a religious duty, and then home again.

The beginning and end of this period are marked by two great waves of disease that swept across Afro-Eurasia. The microbes that brought such widespread death owed nothing to the good or evil of the persons and societies they infected; they simply took advantage of opportunities to reproduce. The epidemics are best known as Justinian's Plague of the sixth century CE and the Black Plague of the fourteenth century CE. Of the many factors underlying these disastrous epidemics, one at least was tied to the human social order: denser population and greater communication. As the routes of human contact opened ever more widely, opportunities arose for microbes to infect populations from which they had previously been isolated. In each case, however, after some decades with horrible loss of human life, populations began to recover and even to accelerate their growth for a time.

Most people, of course, did not travel very far. In every population most people lived out their lives in the region where they were born. All, however, were influenced by those who moved short distances or long. The focus here is on those who moved, and how they changed their own lives and the lives of those they encountered. The individual histories had remarkable parallels over time, but the accumulation of those histories changed the world, so that communications by 1400 were much advanced over communications in 500. The stories recounted here trace people who moved on horseback, on foot, and by boat: Figure 6.1 illustrates migratory paths for each of these means of travel. In the grasslands of Eurasia and Africa, horses (and, in the driest areas, camels) provided mobility for pastoral populations. During this era, horsemen and pastoralists gained control of new territories. Sometimes they challenged and even conquered major states; at other times they competed among themselves. On foot, meanwhile, migrant farmers and warriors brought political and cultural changes to Mesoamerica, and groups of farmers and pastoralists moved across sub-Saharan Africa to make changes of their own. By boat, Vikings in Europe, Arab mariners of the Indian Ocean, Austronesian-speaking voyagers

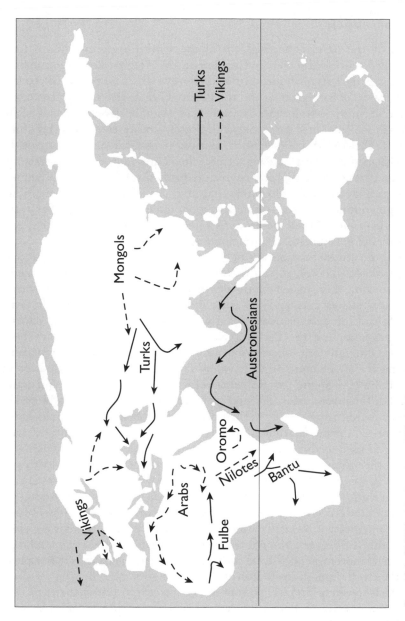

Figure 6.1 Old World migrations, 500–1400 CE

of Southeast Asia, and Amerindian navigators of the Mississippi and St. Lawrence valleys each built on existing water routes to expand their influence.

On horseback

In 500 CE the Arabs comprised one of the Semitic-speaking groups long established south of the Fertile Crescent in the Arabian Peninsula; mostly pastoralists, they also included farmers, city-dwellers, and people of the sea. Arab seafarers of South Arabia and the Persian Gulf carried part of the Indian Ocean trade from classical times forward. Then, with the development of Islam, Arab armies – mounted on camels and horses – conquered a vast territory, largely similar to that conquered by Alexander the Great and before him by the Achaemenid Persians. Newly formed Arab elites moved in and settled in the main cities of the Caliphate. Arabic gradually displaced the other Semitic languages of Syria and Mesopotamia, and more slowly displaced the Egyptian language. In Indo-European-speaking regions under Islamic rule (today's Iran and Afghanistan), Arabic became the language of religion, of justice, and sometimes of government, though not of daily discourse.

This great transformation was only one of several such equine migrations: Arab, Turkish, and Mongol pastoralists traveled great distances to new lands, and in so doing reorganized ethnic identity and political organization within the great stretch of grassland and arid zones running from the Atlantic coast of the Sahara through the deserts of Arabia and Central Asia to the Manchu territories adjoining the Pacific. Commonly these migrations have been explained through stories of overpopulation, dessication, and visions of nomadic heroism. It may be more productive, however, to search in addition for an explanation in changing relations between nomadic populations and states governed from urban areas. Pastoral societies encompassed various lifestyles, and they could change rapidly in their organization. Pastoral peoples included merchants and noble families as well as simple herders. Sometimes pastoral societies focused on quiet herding and on orderly trade with their neighbors, and at other times they formed great confederations to gather wealth and perhaps to conquer. As pastoral armies gained power over settled states, the divisions within pastoral societies grew even deeper. Among the Arabs, the difference between simple Bedouin herdsmen and the noble families of Mecca became a permanent hierarchy after the expansion of Islam. Similar divisions arose within Turkish and Mongol societies as they expanded, along with Arabs, in a general movement of pastoral peoples throughout the Eastern Hemisphere from the tenth through the fourteenth centuries.

Turkish-speaking peoples, pastoralists of the central Eurasian steppe who relied significantly on horses, united occasionally, as in the Gokturk state from 552 to 740. Others migrated westward periodically to the lands north of the Black Sea, at the fringes of grassland and forested areas. Turkish-speaking groups known as Avars and Bulgars moved into eastern Europe in the early centuries CE and warred with the Byzantines. Another group of Bulgars moved to the Volga Valley north of the Caspian Sea, and created the city of Bulgar as their capital. When the borders of the Islamic world reached the edge of Turkish territories at the beginning of the eighth century, Muslim missionaries entered Turkish lands to compete with the Buddhist and Christian missionaries who had preceded them. The Muslims had steady success: the Volga Bulgar state adopted Islam in the tenth century.

Quite a different sort of Turkish movement was that into the more popu-lous regions under the rule of Islamic states. Turkish migrants moved into Afghanistan and Iran partly as pastoralists looking for new grazing lands, and partly as groups of mounted warriors aiding one ally or another, occasionally establishing their own states. The Seljuk Turks began as a group of warriors fighting at the northeastern fringe of Iran. They continued as professional warriors defending the cause of Orthodox Islam, and in the eleventh century CE became the major military force supporting the Abbasid Caliphate, based in Baghdad. As such, their principal struggle was with the Shiite Fatimid state of Egypt.

The Fatimid Caliphate, which conquered Egypt from its Tunisian base in 969, supported the Shiite interpretation of Islam and sought to challenge the Abbasids for control of the whole Islamic heartland. But this Arab dynasty had its troubles with pastoralists: in particular, with the numerous and rest-less Arabian tribes that had taken up residence in the Nile Valley upstream from Cairo. From about 1050 the Fatimids urged the two major tribes, the Beni Hilal and Beni Sulaym, to move west, and to punish their disobedient provincial governors in Tunisia. In a migration that was part invasion and part settlement, the Bedouin tribes took control of Tunisia and extended their influence all the way to Morocco. As they arrived, the Beni Hilal and Beni Sulaym settled, married into local populations, turned agricultural land into grazing lands, and expanded the influence of their lifestyle so that within three centuries the population was principally Arab in identity and language rather than Berber. From Morocco, Arabs continued migrating into the desert, and what is now Mauritania became Arabic-speaking. The noted Tunisian-born scholar Ibn Khaldun, writing in the late fourteenth century CE, spoke bitterly of the Arab tribes as invaders and locusts. More generally, the transformation included an alternation of warfare, coexistence, and intermarriage.

The Seljuks in Baghdad found themselves with a dilemma similar to that of the Fatimids. Families of Turkoman migrants poured into the Iranian highlands, establishing a pastoral way of life and driving out farming popu-lations. The Seljuk rulers sought to restrain such disruptions: they were more interested in their struggle with the Fatimids. But the Seljuks were drawn into a struggle with another enemy, the Byzantine Empire, and won a great victory over the Byzantines at Manzikert in eastern Anatolia in 1071, with the help of other Turkish forces. Thereafter, the Seljuks allowed Turkish pastoralists to migrate into Anatolia. As with the Arab migrations, these immigrants intermarried with the local population, so that over time most of Anatolia became Turkish in language and identity, though genetically the previous populations (of Greek and Armenian ancestry) remained preponderant.

Over a century after the migration of Arab tribes from Upper Egypt to North Africa, a further expansion of Arabs departed also from Upper Egypt, and went south, up the Nile River and into the savanna. Arab settlers married into local populations, but since the Nubians followed matrilineal kinship rules, it enabled the Arab men to gain control of the lineages of their wives. So, as in North Africa, within a few centuries a moderate-sized group of Arab migrants had brought about a change in the identity of the population of Sudan, as language and identity became Arab and religion became Islamic. The population remained dark-skinned since, as with the other populations that became Arab, the genetic change was only partial, while the change in identity was nearly total.

The conquests of the Mongols in the thirteenth century were thus not the first expansion of mounted warriors. Instead they followed the paths and used some of the same techniques as earlier migrants, especially Turkish groups, but did so with deadly effectiveness. The development of Mongol military might is known in detail: it emerged out of a fight to the finish among competing Mongol principalities, each in contact with the Jurchen state in northern China. Chinggis Khan gained dominance in a Mongol confederacy by 1206. By 1220 mounted Mongol archers and their allies had conquered most of the Jurchen realm, and thereafter Mongol troops began conquering to the west as well as to the south. Many of the soldiers of the Mongol armies were Turkish, so that while Mongol conquest and administration dominated this vast region for a century, Mongol settlers were outnumbered by the Turks. Especially in the Khanate of the Golden Horde – the Mongol successor to the Volga Bulgar state – Turkish populations spread west across the steppes, encompassing many small ethnic groups of the Caucasus, and dominating or displacing the Slavic peoples. Once the Golden Horde adopted Islam, Arabic became the principal written language in its realm, as it had been under the Volga Bulgars. The Duchy of Muscovy, centered in Moscow, got its start as a client state of the Golden Horde, and slowly expanded its influence until it was able to renounce its tribute and later conquer the remains of the khanate in the sixteenth century.

Migrations of horse- and camel-keeping peoples, as armed forces and as settlers, thus influenced large portions of Africa and Eurasia. Aside from the cases described above, in this same period (sometimes known as the "feudal" era) horsemen came to dominate the armies of western Europe, West Africa, China, and parts of Southeast Asia. Even beyond the regions where horses were practically useful, their prestige was unmistakable: in the fifteenth century the kings of Benin, in a forested region of the West African coast, maintained several horses brought at great expense from the north.

On foot

There were few empty places left in the world in the first millennium CE. Most migration, therefore, consisted not of colonizing virgin lands but of settlers moving into established communities. When settlers were pleased enough with their new situation they invited family members to join them. Often the settlers adopted the language and the identity of their new home. At other times, what began as cross-community migration by a small number of settlers could become a larger movement of colonization. Groups of migrants from a home population joined another society, but formed enclaves that grew steadily, with the immigrants maintaining their distinct identity and perhaps displacing or absorbing the original population.

The patterns of language distribution in North America and Mesoamerica show that groups have migrated back and forth over the ages. One pattern of migration is that of speakers of Central Amerind languages who have moved from valley to valley in the mountainous areas between Utah in the northwest and Oaxaca in the southeast of Mexico. Dense populations arose periodically in certain valleys, forming centers that gained influence over surrounding areas: the Hopi in modern Arizona created one such center from about 500 CE. The greatest early center of population was Teotihuacán, at the northern end of the Valley of Mexico, which reached an estimated 200,000 inhabitants in the sixth century. Yet Teotihuacán collapsed rapidly and was virtually abandoned by 750 CE. At much the same time, the great Maya states of the lowland forests of Yucatán and Guatemala experienced similar collapse: the timing of these changes has led some scholars to suggest a disastrous epidemic as the common cause.

Into the aftermath of this collapse of states came a small group of migrants now known as the Toltec. The story of their influence confirms the significance of migrations across community lines in Mesoamerica. Bands of young warriors left the region of Zacatecas, five hundred kilometers to the northwest, and traveled to a valley north of Teotihuacán. There they settled, took wives, built up their influence, and created their capital at Tula. They were joined by another group of migrants coming from the opposite direction: the Nonoalca, who had lived five hundred kilometers to the east along the Caribbean coast, in the region where the Olmecs had earlier thrived, and who had sustained some of the traditions of Teotihuacán. The Toltecs and the Nonoalca joined forces, and by the mid-tenth century had built a state at Tula that combined the martial qualities of the Toltecs and the ritual powers of the Nonoalca.

Meanwhile, as the Nonoalca moved west, others of their countrymen moved to the east, into Mayan territories. There they became influential in the founding of Chichén Itzá, the most substantial Mayan state to arise after the eighth-century collapse. With time, Chichén Itzá came to have clear links to Tula, though the cities were separated by a thousand kilometers and existed in very different cultural and ecological zones. It appears that Toltec migrants came to Chichén Itzá, perhaps settling and then seizing the city, and imposed their traditions on it. Chichén Itzá remained a Maya-speaking area, but its architecture and sculpture show very close ties to Tula. The Toltec "empire" was thus not a great territory administered by a central power, but a series of widely separated urban centers, some as far north as New Mexico, linked by ties of trade, migration, and political tradition.

Centuries later, after the Toltec regime in the highlands of Mexico had fractured, another group of migrants filtered into the region, apparently from the region of Nayarit to the northwest. Known as the Mexica, they succeeded in maintaining their identity, and gradually built up an urban center on a lake in the Valley of Mexico at Tenochtitlán. From this center they launched war on neighboring cities in the fifteenth century, and collected enough tribute to constitute the Aztec Empire.

A Central African example of such regional migration brought a slightly different result. The Congo River basin had been settled by farmers early in the process of Bantu expansion, and divergent social systems gradually emerged. In the region where the Congo River gradually bends to the south, villages with large populations resulting perhaps from trade developed strong male leaders and gradually changed their descent system from emphasizing all relatives to focusing on descent through the male line. In one region, patrilineal societies developed a military organization based on lances, and lance-carrying warriors moved south and west, spreading their regime as they went. After a spread of some 400 kilometers southwest, however, the lancers met a resistant organization. Oral traditions recall this struggle as the Battle of Bolongo Itoko, and it is estimated to have taken place early in the fourteenth century CE. The advancing lancers encountered peoples with an effective countervailing organization – a military organization based on archers and swordsmen rather than spearmen, and a matrilineal social organization led by *nkumu* titleholders who had gained titles and won adherents through great feasts and displays of wealth. The struggle went on for some time, and ended up as a draw: the battle line remains defined by the ethnic boundaries of today. The expansion of lance-carriers was halted, and the *nkumu* organization survived and expanded.

Pastoralist people, whether relying uniquely on their herds or relying significantly on farming as well, are relatively mobile. Three African examples of cattle-keeping people in movement show how they were able to move substantial distances and maintain their identity, yet make significant adjustments in their lifestyle. First, Nilotic-speaking peoples of the middle Nile Valley began migrating with their cattle upstream (to the south) early in the first millennium CE. Most were farmers as well as pastoralists, but some groups specialized in keeping cattle. Some of these Nilotic-speakers crossed into what is today Uganda and established rule over Bantu-speaking peoples, leaving archaeological remains of great enclosures of the Bito dynasty, created in about the twelfth century, in what became the kingdom of Bunyoro. Dynasties emphasizing Nilotic ancestry created or gained control of the states of Buganda,

Busoga, and Ankole (in modern Uganda), plus Rwanda and Burundi. The immigrant elite maintained its power, but lost its language to the Bantu-speaking majority. Other Nilotic immigrant groups moved further into East Africa and maintained their language, but did not create large states: these include the Luo of Kenya, for whom farming came to predominate, and the pastoralist Maasai of Kenya and Tanzania.

A second long-term pastoral migration was that of the Fulbe of the desert edge near the Atlantic. They were both farmers and cattle-keepers in their Senegal Valley homeland, but some of the pastoralists began searching for greener pastures. Fulbe specialists in cattle-keeping began a movement, beginning perhaps early in the first millennium CE, that led them ultimately into all the areas that fit their ecological niche across the African continent. As they moved their cattle north and south each year with the rains, balancing the search for good pasture and avoidance of the tsetse fly which brought sleeping sickness to their herds, groups of Fulbe families moved gradually eastward. This movement too may have been affected by the growing power of states of the savanna. Over the centuries Fulbe cattle-keepers built up significant populations in Futa Jallon (the highlands of modern Guinea), the inner delta of the Niger (in Mali), interspersed among Hausa communities of what is now Nigeria, in northern Cameroon, and even the Nile Valley. The Fulbe language became the language of cattle-keeping throughout West Africa. Their expansion along the paths of expanding commerce led them ultimately to overlap with Arab cattle-keepers between Lake Chad and the Nile.

A third example of pastoral migration relied on a distinctive social organization: age grades, prominent in eastern Africa. With age grades, periodic initiations are held (often every four or eight years), and the boys and girls of several villages and of a certain age (say, eight to twelve) are initiated together. Out of the initiation, the youths gain knowledge for the next stage in life and form a corporate organization that will hold their cohort together for life. Succeeding initiations move the cohorts (and especially the males) forward to succeeding roles in life: together they take up the task of herding, hunting, fighting, forming families, governing, and eventually providing counsel as elders. It is not known when age grades were developed, but similar institutions are shared among groups speaking Cushitic, Nilotic, and Bantu languages in the Horn and East Africa. Age grades were convenient institutions for warfare and migration. The Oromo peoples of southern Ethiopia, though lacking kingdoms, relied on age-grade organization to spread in the fifteenth century from their homeland in the highlands of southern Ethiopia to the east and into the lower altitudes in eastern Ethiopia, then north and up into the highlands of the Christian kingdom of Ethiopia.

Merchant specialists also spread over wide areas in the course of pursuing their profession. Merchants traveled not necessarily only on foot, for they also had pack animals for their caravans and traveled at times by water. In the West African savanna, Mande-speaking merchants known as Juula extended their range from Jenne-Jeno, the commercial center of the Niger Valley, forming settlements both to the east and the west. As longer-distance trade and Islamic religion grew in influence, Jenne-Jeno was abandoned beginning in the twelfth century in favor of the nearby Islamic city of Jenne. Linked by the Mande-speaking communities at each stop along the way and by the caravans of donkeys that carried the goods, these merchant communities facilitated the flow of goods over a wide region. The epic of Sundiata, the tale of the thirteenth-century creation of the empire of Mali, provides a rationalization of the importance of both statecraft and commerce among Mande-speaking peoples. It tells the story that, many generations before the time of Sundiata, two princes of the early Mali kingdom divided their efforts, one becoming a merchant, the other becoming a hunter and king, and each of them passing their vocation on to their descendants.

Along the trade routes of western Asia and the Mediterranean, more heavily traveled than those of sub-Saharan Africa, a greater degree of specialization developed. Jews and Armenians were among those who became specialists in commerce, participating in the trade of Mediterranean galleys and Silk Road caravans. With the rise of Islam, most Jews lived in Islamic territories from Afghanistan to Iberia. With time, a sizeable number moved into Christian Europe, again with many specializing as merchants. The Armenian territories southwest of the Caucasus, which had formed an independent state for part of the first millennium CE, were absorbed into the expanding Islamic realm. Thereafter the Armenians, distinctive in their Christian religion, set up commercial bases throughout the eastern lands of Islam, and conducted trading ventures as far as Tibet and Siberia.

By boat

By the first millennium CE, mariners sailed each of the world's main archipelagoes and seas: the archipelagoes of the Caribbean, Indonesia, the North Sea, the Mediterranean, the waters of Southeast and northeast Asia, plus the larger basins of the Indian Ocean and the South Pacific. (Only the near-empty stretches, far from shore, of the Atlantic, the Pacific, and the Antarctic went uncrossed by man-made craft.) The maritime voyages of the period 500–1400 CE did more to strengthen earlier connections among regions than to open new lines of communication.

The most spectacular of the maritime migrants of the first millennium CE were the Vikings – the Norse or Northmen who launched sudden raids on England in the late eighth century, and thereafter carried warfare, trade, and settlement to the east, west, and south of their Scandinavian homeland from the eighth through the eleventh centuries. Through archaeological remains and written documents, the Scandinavians are relatively well known in the period before their expansion. The peoples of what are today Denmark, Sweden, and Norway were early users of horses and iron. They lived in distant contact with the trade and culture of Rome: Scandinavian graves have revealed numerous Roman decorative goods and coins, gained through contact with the Mediterranean via the rivers of eastern Europe, notably via the Vistula and the Dnieper to the Black Sea. By the third century CE, Scandinavians began creating inscriptions in runic letters, using an eclectic alphabet whose precise origins are still debated. Their settlements and homes reveal a prosperous and productive society. The artistic works of Scandinavians went through three discernible periods in the first millennium, becoming more abstract at each stage; their religion centered on a pantheon of gods similar to those of other Indo-European peoples such as the Greeks, Romans, and Aryans. Their settlements were fortified, and it may be that a series of wars among Scandinavians preceded the era of their expansion. Scandinavians also voyaged in the early first millennium CE, as shown not only by their trade with the Mediterranean but by their settlement around the Baltic and the North Sea. The Angles, another Scandinavian group, moved from Denmark to Britain and gave their adopted home the name of England.

In the Viking age, from the eighth century forth, the technical skills of the Scandinavians became more evident. Among their creations were finely decorated drinking horns, coins made of silver, bronze scales for measuring silver, and gold jewelry. Sturdy and elegant iron helmets added to the swords and shields of warfare. The Viking seacraft, of course, were their great accomplishment. Planks for the hull were bent and secured to each other by iron nails, nailed to the keel and then lashed to the ribs to allow flexibility. The mast was placed at the center of the ship, but could be lowered. The ships ranged from 12 to 25 meters long and up to 5 meters wide, and the warships carried as many as sixty oarsmen. They could sail the open sea but generally beached at night, raising a tent over the hull as the sailors slept.

In the late eighth century, Norse parties suddenly landed on English coasts, raided briefly and then headed home to Denmark. As they returned in larger numbers, they began to leave settlements, claim land, and conduct trade at points all along the eastern English coast. From 800, Norse raiders attacked Ireland, and one of their settlements became Dublin. By the mid-ninth century, Scandinavian raiders, merchants, and settlers were prominent throughout the British Isles, along the North Sea coasts of France and the Netherlands, and along the rivers of what are now Poland and Russia. Viking merchants used portages leading them to the Black Sea via the Danube or the Dnieper. Further north, through the Gulf of Finland, Vikings entered rivers that enabled them (again with portages) to reach the headwaters of the Volga, which flowed all the way to the Caspian Sea. Halfway down the Volga the Vikings came to the commercial entrepot of Bulgar, where most of them halted to trade. Bulgar was the capital of the Volga Bulgars, who controlled connections eastward to the Silk Road. It was there that the Arab diplomat Ibn Fadlan wrote, in 921, a detailed comment on the trade and personal habits of these wild but hardy merchants. He noted the slaves, especially women, displayed for sale by the

Norsemen. (Ibn Fadlan's visit was to confirm the conversion of the Volga Bulgars to Islam.)

Closer to the Gulf of Finland, Rurik of Sweden settled at the town of Novgorod, and by 839 he had built it into a kingdom known as "the land of the Rus." His successor moved south to the Dnieper, establishing a state at Kiev. This pattern of Norse monarchy and state-building continued for over two centuries in most of the areas of Viking activity. Norse leaders seized half of England by 886, created a kingdom in Iceland soon after the island was discovered in 890, and formed the duchy of Normandy in 911. Knut, already King of Denmark and Norway, became King of England as well in 1016, and opened the possibility of creating an immense state in the north. Unity, however, was short-lived among the Vikings: another group of Vikings, the Normans, crossed from France and conquered England in 1066.

At the peak of Viking influence, fleets of hundreds of vessels carried out frightening but ultimately unsuccessful attacks on Constantinople, Paris, London, and Persian lands adjoining the Caspian Sea. Commerce, war, and statecraft seemed to go hand in hand: observers on the coast of France noted that the Vikings opened an emporium for trade almost as soon as they had finished the battle to establish their dominance. Despite the ferocity of their raids and the wealth they accumulated, the Vikings married into the local populations and soon lost their distinctiveness. The Scandinavian language expanded to previously uninhabited Iceland, but gained dominance nowhere else. The states of Novgorod and Kiev, created by Viking settlers, soon became Slavic-speaking, and developed into the political core of an emerging Russian identity. Viking settlers in Greenland and North America disappeared as distinctive groups, perhaps through the same process. The Norman invaders of England made French the governing language. They relied on the Flemish technique of creating huge tapestries to commission the Bayeux Tapestry to record their exploits; the illustrations of the tapestry, perhaps ironically, include the best-known images of Viking life. In addition, Scandinavian adoption of Christianity came even in the era of their expansion. The Norman dukes converted rapidly to Christianity, and the Christian religion was accepted in Denmark in the 960s, in Kiev in 989, in Iceland in 1008, and in Norway starting in 1014. (Sweden, however, turned to Christianity only in the twelfth century.) The eleventh century was the peak era of Viking prominence. Thereafter, Scandinavian migrations declined sharply.

In one last wave of Viking adventure, no longer as mysterious raiders but as Christian mercenaries, Norsemen joined to fight in many areas of Europe. Norman adventurers Roger and Robert Guiscard led groups that fought for years to create states in southern Italy. Roger's kingdom of Sicily, from 1090, became a cosmopolitan center of knowledge and of interchange across religious lines.

The exploits of Vikings depended heavily on the qualities of their boats, adapted at once to the environment (the cold oceans and rapid rivers they navigated) and to their objectives (a mix of warfare, commerce, and settlement). Similarly, for other densely populated marine regions or for other times, the boats reflect the environment and the purpose of the mariners. In the North Sea and the Baltic, after the decline of Viking adventures and the expansion of commerce, Norse ships were replaced by *cogs*, broad and stodgy merchant vessels that carried heavy cargoes through rough seas. The Mediterranean was crossed by updated *galleys*, with slaves as well as free sailors pulling at the oars. Some galleys ventured into the Atlantic, linking Italy and the Netherlands. Adventurous Basque sailors, with their small but seaworthy craft, may well have crossed the Atlantic to find the cod fisheries of the Grand Banks. Portuguese mariners, extending their voyages into the contrary winds of the South Atlantic, eventually came up with the design of the *caravel*, a light, broad-beamed ship with lateen (triangular) sails at back and square sails at front.

In the early centuries of the Islamic Caliphates, the commerce of the western Indian Ocean expanded greatly. Arab and Persian mariners sailed the routes earlier sailed by Hellenistic sailors, from the Red Sea and the Persian Gulf to Ceylon, with connections there to Malaya and China. But they developed different craft, new techniques of navigation, and new routes. The new vessels, widely known today by their East African name of *dhow*, used a similar design for a range of large and small craft. With hulls pointed both fore and aft, and built up of planks sewn to the ribbing, these vessels were propelled by triangular or lateen sails made of canvas or at times of coconut fiber. The large cargo ships had multiple masts. Navigators learned the workings of the monsoon winds, blowing from the southwest from April to October and from the northeast from October to April, and also adopted the magnetic compass of Chinese invention. With these advances, they were able to sail directly across the ocean rather than hugging the coast. For a time in the ninth century, these ships traveled regularly to South China.

The other area with large cargo ships was the coast of China. The ships known as *junks* were effective for the open seas as well as for rivers and canals, especially because of the development of waterproof compartments. Iron nails were used not only for attaching the planks of the hull, but also for bulkheads below decks. Multiple masts held sails of canvas or bamboo for the large vessels, rudders helped to set their direction, and the compass was used for navigation. Merchant craft and occasionally warships sailed both north and south from the coast of China.

The seacraft of Southeast Asia and the Indonesian archipelago were the most varied of any region, as they drew on many traditions. To begin, the outrigger craft of the ancient Austronesian tradition continued to be developed. These rapid and stable craft (known as *proa*, though that term is also the generic term for ships) were usually small, but could also be made large for the purposes of merchants, though they were limited to a single mast. In addition, the regular presence of junks and dhows in Southeast Asian waters provided incentive for eclectic shipbuilders to try mixes of the various traditions. The lateen sail and the compass spread west through this region, each finally reaching the waters of Europe.

East of the Philippines, the waterborne trade routes extended out into the Pacific. In Micronesia and Melanesia, the single-hulled proas maintained communication among the islands. The system of currency based on cowrie shells linked the seas from the western Pacific to the Mediterranean, and encompassed mainland regions at a distance from the shores. Further east, however, in the Polynesian region, the tradition of great inter-island voyages died down. The double-hulled ships continued to be built, but for shorter journeys: New Zealand and Hawaii were cut off from the rest of the world for several centuries.

Less spectacular than the ocean-going craft were the riverain vessels. They were smaller and they are more difficult to document, but they may have carried a greater tonnage of goods in the aggregate, if over shorter distances. The greatest riverain ships of this age were the junks of the Grand Canal in China, carrying rice from south to north. For the rest, a list of rivers will have to suffice to indicate the paths of connection by water. The major rivers of North America were plied especially by bark canoes; the rivers of South America were plied by dugouts – and expanded versions of these dugouts carried mariners among the Caribbean Islands. African water transport followed the Nile, the Niger, the Congo and its many tributaries, and the great lakes of East Africa. The Himalayas fed the Indus and Ganges of India and the rivers of Southeast Asia from the Irrawaddy to the Yangzi. In the rivers as in the seas, the steady use of water transport and the sharing of ideas led to greater capacity, greater safety, and improved knowledge of navigation.

Conclusion

The paths of migration were worn deep by the feet of the travelers and, in the Old World, by their livestock. The rivers and seas closed instantly over the paths of passing boats, but ports and supply points along the shores marked the stages of maritime travel. In every era, modest numbers of sojourners, settlers, warriors, and merchants moved along these old paths. In selecting among the many paths for their journeys, migrants relied on the communities they encountered at each stage, and on the linkages of their accumulated patterns of commerce and political alliance. The stages of migration introduced the travelers to new languages and new cultures; at the same time, the company of migrants became a culture unto itself.

Cross-community migration has been the basic pattern underlying most major movements of humanity. What appears from a distance as colonization – the systematic advance of one ethnic group at the expense of others – appears on closer examination to have been a range of cross-community migrations. These include, for the period discussed in this chapter, cases of immigrant males marrying into local communities, sojourners traveling as sailors or laborers and then returning home, and enslaved girls sent to become domestics. Networks conveying individual migrants included trade diasporas, religious communities, and slave markets. We have seen the repeated choices in what language to use and what customs to follow, reminding us that many people, as a result of their travels, could be at home in multiple communities. With an accumulation of enough such small changes, the ethnic preponderance of a region could change.

Further, there were cases of invaders who sought to seize control of societies rather than join them. The Mongols of the thirteenth and fourteenth centuries produced the best attempt yet to conquer the world. (The previous attempt by Alexander the Great was impressive but fell far short of the Mongols; the conquests of the Umayyad Caliphs gained less territory but held it far longer.) The Mongols conquered most of East Asia, half of the Islamic world, and virtually all of the Eurasian steppes, opening up interregional connections that shifted the balance decisively if impermanently from the seas toward the lands. The very success of the Mongol regime in opening contacts across Eurasia, linking the expanding societies of all the Eurasian regions, may help explain the disastrous epidemics of the Black Plague, which raged from China and Central Asia to Europe and northern Africa, and caused severe population declines in the mid-fourteenth century.

It was not only Eurasia under the Mongols that experienced closer regional interconnections and exchange of ideas in this period. Even in the distant Americas communications among regions expanded, through Aztec conquest of highland Mexico and Arawak invasions of Caribbean islands, but also through expanded contacts in the Mississippi Valley, linked to the ritual center of the great mounds at Cahokia, near the confluence of the Missouri and Mississippi Rivers. Migrations in every region of Africa reaffirmed old links and established new ones. In Oceania, while the longest voyages were discontinued, connections in the western Pacific were constantly reinforced by mariners. In Europe, Italian merchants in the south and German merchants in the north deepened their networks. No region was entirely isolated.

Further reading

The era from 500 to 1400 started and ended with catastrophic epidemics. For an imaginative reconstruction of the first of these, see David Keys, *Catastrophe: An Investigation into the Origins of the Modern World* (New York, 1999); on the latter, see Norman F. Cantor, *In the Wake of the Plague: The Black Death and the World it Made* (New York, 2001). Meanwhile, the Islamic pilgrimage brought believers across the world to Mecca: see F. E. Peters, *The Haj: The Muslim Pilgrimage to Mecca and the Holy Place* (Princeton, N.J., 1994).

Ibn Khaldun's fourteenth-century condemnation of pastoral Arab migration into North Africa is included in *An Introduction to History: The Muqaddimah* (trans. Franz Rosenthal, ed. N. J. Dawood; London, 1967). On the Turkish and Mongol peoples of

Central Asia and their migrations, see Richard N. Frye, *The Heritage of Central Asia: From Antiquity to the Turkish Expansion* (Princeton, N.J., 1996); and Thomas Barfield, *The Perilous Frontier: Nomadic Empires and China, 221 B.C. to A.D. 1757* (Cambridge, Mass., 1989). A classic account of the Mongol Empire is Bertold Spuler (trans. Helga and Stuart Drummond), *History of the Mongols: Based on Eastern and Western Accounts of the Thirteenth and Fourteenth Centuries* (New York, 1988). For a recent account, see Thomas T. Allsen, *Culture and Conquest in Mongol Eurasia* (New York, 2001). For an informative debate on the relative importance of warhorses and feudal social relations throughout Eurasia beginning in the tenth century, see R. J. Barendse, "The Feudal Mutation: Military and Economic Transformations of the Ethnosphere in the Tenth to Thirteenth Centuries," *Journal of World History* 14 (2003), 503–529; and Stephen Morillo, "A 'Feudal Mutation'? Conceptual Tools and Historical Patterns in World History," *Journal of World History* 14 (2003): 531–550. On horse trade in East Asia see Bin Yang, "Horses, Silver, and Cowries: Yunnan in Global Perspective," *Journal of World History* 15 (2004), 281–322.

For a recent study of the Toltecs and other Mesoamerican groups, see Alba Guadalupe Mastache de Escobar, *Ancient Tollan: Tula and the Toltec Heartland* (Boulder, Colo., 2002), and Alan Knight, *Mexico: From the Beginning to the Spanish Conquest* (Cambridge, Mass., 2002). On the "Battle of Bolongo Itoko" in Central Africa, see Jan Vansina, *Paths in the Rainforest: Towards a History of Political Tradition in Equatorial Africa* (Madison, N.Y., 1990). On Nilotic migrations, see Christopher Ehret, *Southern Nilotic History* (Evanston, Ill., 1971). On Jenne-Jeno and the middle Niger Valley, see Roderick J. McIntosh, *The Peoples of the Middle Niger: The Island of Gold* (Malden, Mass., 1998).

For a study of the Vikings in the time before their great migrations, see David M. Wilson, *The Vikings and their Origins: Scandinavia in the First Millennium* (New York, 1970). For the era of migration, see Peter Sawyer, ed., *The Oxford Illustrated History of the Vikings* (New York, 1996). On maritime life in the Indian Ocean, see George F. Hourani, *Arab Seafaring* (Princeton, N.J., 1995). For life among the riverain peoples of North America, see Lynda Shaffer, *Native Americans Before 1492: The Moundbuilding Centers of the Eastern Woodlands* (Armonk, N.Y., 1992).

Dirk Hoerder's extensive history of migration worldwide, focusing on cultural contacts, begins in the year 1000: see his *Cultures in Contact: World Migrations in the Second Millennium* (Durham, N.C., 2002).

Chapter 7

Spanning the oceans, 1400 to 1700

Over the course of human history, the shifts in available technology have sometimes favored life on dry land, and at other times life at water's edge. The period after 1400 brought a dramatic advance in maritime technology, and expanded human population and activities at the edge of the seas. All of the world's seagoing populations, but especially the Chinese, Arabs, and western Europeans, expanded their horizons and improved their navigational techniques. The result changed the paths of human contact permanently. While the land roads continued to bear most of the world's traffic, the sea lanes expanded greatly in importance.

Improved maritime technology enabled individual humans at last to succeed in spanning the globe. The opening of new routes brought exciting adventures and encounters, but it also brought disasters. Warfare and conquest brought the end to old regimes, and economic changes brought riches to some and despair to many more. Most significantly, the encounters were not only among people, but also included the diseases they bore and encountered along the newly opened routes. The spread of epidemic disease to unprotected populations brought massive loss of life and decline of population in the sixteenth and seventeenth centuries, especially throughout the Americas, where the population in 1650 had fallen to a scant five to ten million persons – as little as one-tenth of what it had been in 1500. Less disastrous but still serious population declines took place in parts of Europe, Africa, and Asia in this era. Mortality rates for every population rose in this age of encounter, and especially for travelers.

The character of life in each of the major ocean basins changed significantly, and the differences between them became more evident, as they entered into regular contact with each other. The Indian Ocean was the best traveled and most cosmopolitan of the oceans, as its long tradition of being criss-crossed by vessels launched from near and far was expanded into even denser trade. The Atlantic Ocean, where small numbers of vessels had hugged its shores, came to be crossed frequently, but with shipping dominated by Europe's maritime powers. The Pacific Ocean, by far the greatest watery expanse, continued to be traveled busily by large vessels along its western shore and small vessels in its southern archipelago, and also came to be linked to the Americas by the slender but significant thread of Spanish vessels.

The new shape of the world in this maritime age oriented West Africa toward the Atlantic and East Africa toward the Indian Ocean, while North Africa remained oriented toward the Mediterranean. The new sea routes put China and India in easier contact with each other and with Europe. By the same token, China and India entered into contact with the Americas and, indirectly, with the western shore of Africa. The numbers of people involved in these migrations rarely exceeded the several hundred people who could sail in a fleet of ships, yet the cumulative influence of maritime migrations over three centuries did much to change the world. After two or three centuries, the shocks brought by the global maritime connections died down, and a new system of intercontinental linkages entered a period of expansion.

The maps in this chapter show how language groups reveal the placement and migration of social groups. Figures 7.1 and 7.2 show three major language groups, from which there were significant migrations from 1400 to the present: Indo-European languages, and the various forms of Arabic and Chinese languages. (As a reminder, Figure 2.1 shows a map of the world's language groups, *c.* 1500.) Figure 7.1 shows the placement in *c.* 1500 of Indo-European languages—from Portuguese in the west to Russian in the northeast to Hindi in the southeast. Most of the Indo-European languages were written languages by this time. (For a more detailed version see Figure 2.3, which also shows two language groups that had disappeared before 1500.) Figure 7.2 shows the extent of Arabic and Chinese languages in spoken and literary versions, *c.* 1500. The Arabic language had expanded rapidly in the seventh century CE, and then changed into a series of distinct dialects. Standard written Arabic, however, united all the Arabic-speaking areas and extended to nearby regions where Arabic was not the principal spoken language. The Chinese system of writing extended well beyond the areas where various dialects of Chinese language were spoken.

This chapter explores four major issues in migration and in global equilibration from 1400 to 1700. First, is the pattern of exploration and conquest, which brought encounters both successful and disastrous among peoples, and set the terms of interactions long thereafter. Second, is the record of merchants and missionaries, whose travels and adventures opened important new connections even though their numbers were small. Third, I explore the social history of global migration through family life, showing how movements of migrants changed old families and created new ones. The concluding section, on carrying and borrowing culture, displays the types of cultural changes brought by maritime migration.

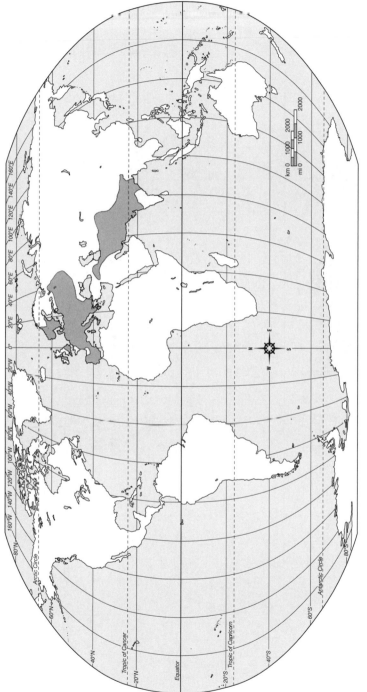

Figure 7.1 Indo-European languages, c. 1500

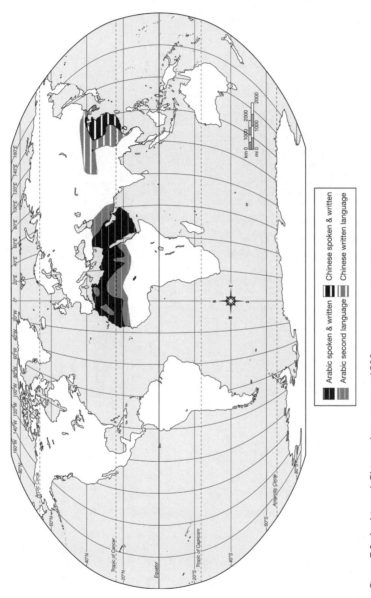

Figure 7.2 Arabic and Chinese languages, c. 1500

Explorations and conquest, 1400–1600

The pressures to open intercontinental connections had been growing before 1400. The Mongol Empire had reached from East Asia to Europe and to the doorstep of Africa, but the Black Plague swept through and beyond this realm in the mid-fourteenth century, weakening social structures everywhere. The decline of the Mongols set the stage for new empires. Regional and inter-continental migrations mixed with each other, and with the rise and fall of empires. Empires caused migration by conquest and expulsion; they also prevented migration by controlling populations. Regional migrations included the major conquests that took place on every continent – resulting in the creation and expansion of empires of the fifteenth century, such as the Inca Empire in South America, the Aztec Empire in North America, the empire of Songhai in West Africa, the Funj sultanate in northeast Africa, Vijayanagar in India, Majapahit in Indonesia, and Timur's immense but short-lived empire in Central Asia.

In the years from 1400 to 1600, a new system of global migration brought transoceanic movement of growing numbers of people and came to link the earlier patterns of regional migrations. The drawing of maps reflected and facilitated the increased mobility of people. This interaction of regional and global migrations in the fifteenth and sixteenth centuries led ultimately to a large-scale redistribution of the world's population. In this era, our globe also developed a worldwide system of plantations, mines, empires, and colonies that would lead to the exchange of goods and people. Yet as the continents and the oceans came into regular contact with one another, a great difference stood out, contrasting the suddenness and the extremes of encounters in the Atlantic world with the more gradual and complex interactions of the Indian Ocean basin.

New encounters

How does one encounter a person for the first time: as brother or as other? Is the person newly encountered to be treated as a friend and an equal, or as a person alien in nature and hostile in motive? Or are there yet other choices people can make? Does one person view another as friendly yet alien, or as equal yet hostile? The early modern age of new connections raised these questions repeatedly.

Voyagers, as they moved across the surface of the globe, sought adventure and achievement. Their thoughts turned to trade, exploration, escape, settle-ment, religious conversion, and conquest. Whatever their motives for traveling, they encountered other people, meeting new individuals and new groups that were distinct in stature, dress, skin color, language, religion, and customs. Each party decided how to act toward and how to view the other, choosing between emphasizing differences or similarities, unity or division. Sometimes these initial encounters resulted in mistakes that could be frozen over time, as when the peoples of the Americas came to be labeled as "Indians."

As might be expected, the evidence shows that people encountering each other for the first time reacted in a variety of ways, ranging from friendly to hostile. Attempts to communicate, even across a language barrier, emphasized the commonalities between peoples or at least attempted to articulate the differences. Instances of war, capture, and theft were common, but so also were efforts to trade with, communicate with, and assist each other. People of the East African port of Kilwa were surprised by the arrival of the Portuguese in 1498 but knew who they were; Kilwa had also received delegations from China earlier in the same century.

Migrant men, in settling down to start families with local women, gave emphasis to alliance and shared values. Yet in cases where these same men later denied rights or inheritance to their wives or children, they were emphasizing hierarchy and difference among groups of people, rather than commonality. Sexual relations can be a statement of dominance as much as of sharing. The impressions and the relationships created through these encounters have shaped society in the modern world.

Travel and exploration

The first large-scale intercontinental voyages linked the Pacific shore of China to the Indian Ocean basin. Between 1403 and 1435, the Chinese admiral Zheng He led seven voyages of Ming imperial fleets to the Indian Ocean. These voyages, commissioned by the Ming emperor, took Zheng He's fleets as far as India, Arabia, and East Africa. The expeditions included as many as 350 ships, with crews totaling thousands. The routes Zheng He followed had been charted by merchants of earlier centuries, and the web of ocean-going ties corresponded in large measure to the extent of the Islamic religion. The Chinese expeditions were in a sense part of this Muslim network: one of Zheng He's captains, a Muslim like Zheng He himself, completed the sacred duty of a pilgrimage to Mecca in the course of one voyage. Although the Ming imperial voyages ceased in 1435, private Chinese traders continued to ply the waters, sailing among merchants of numerous nations, many of whom shared the religion of Islam.

So when the Portuguese mariner Vasco da Gama rounded the Cape of Good Hope and entered the Indian Ocean in 1498, he was joining an existing network of trade and migration rather than creating a new one. The arrival of the Portuguese did make a difference, as they sought to challenge and dominate existing commercial and imperial powers. The Portuguese arrival initiated a century of war at sea in the Indian Ocean, which was paralleled by a century of war on the surrounding lands.

In the Atlantic, the pattern was different: intercontinental voyages in its waters were almost totally new, and they led to a rush for dominance among newly powerful European states. Connections to the gold trade with Mali encouraged Iberian and Italian mariners to push south. In 1420, Prince Henry of Portugal provided support for the first of many voyages along the African coast, hoping also to reach the Indian Ocean. (By this time, Zheng He had completed five of his voyages to the Indian Ocean.) The rough seas of the Pacific and the Atlantic had taught Chinese and Iberian shipbuilders to construct vessels that were seaworthy in any conditions. One difference was that some of the Chinese vessels were huge, with as many as nine masts, while the Portuguese and Spanish caravels had three masts at most. Nevertheless, the smaller Iberian vessels were to have more influence in connecting the world than the Chinese fleets.

Portuguese mariners discovered unoccupied Atlantic islands and made trade connections with densely populated areas of the African coast. The Portuguese created new sea lanes and kept them peaceful, because of their dominance, for most of the fourteenth and fifteenth centuries.

Then in 1492, Columbus traversed the Atlantic Ocean to the west on behalf of Spain, and added two more continents to the maritime connections recently opened between Europe and Africa. Spain dominated the West Atlantic as Portugal dominated the South Atlantic (including Brazil after 1500), establishing new trade routes, new ports, and new flows of labor. In the Atlantic, the Christian religion and people from the Iberian Peninsula dominated the connections across the ocean. The greatest change brought by the new Atlantic connections, however, was the exchange of diseases among the European, African, and American populations. The death rate in the Americas was horrendous, and by 1650 many American populations were only one-tenth of what they had been a century earlier. European and African populations encountered some new diseases, but did not undergo such catastrophic decline.

In the Pacific, the Spanish crossed the sea lanes earlier opened by Asian and Oceanic sailors, and extended them from shore to shore of the great ocean. Ferdinand Magellan's Spanish ship crossed the Atlantic and then the Pacific in 1532, reached Asia, and sailed on around the globe to Spain. When the Spanish later conquered the archipelago where Magellan reached Asia, they chose to name the islands after their king: the Philippines.

Figure 7.3 indicates some of the main transoceanic movements of population in the period from 1400 to 1700, showing the homelands of European, African, and Asian groups and some of the regions in which they settled in significant numbers. The movements of settlers tended to be from densely settled to sparsely populated regions, but the traffic of merchants tended to connect densely settled regions to each other.

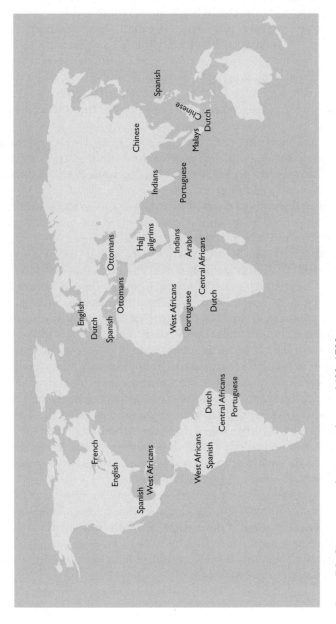

Figure 7.3 Commerce and migration by sea, 1400–1700

Conquest and empire

The years from 1400 to 1600 saw the rise of several new empires and the destruction of as many previous empires. Asian empires arose, among peoples who had previously been in contact, to remake the map from the Mediterranean to the Pacific. These empires caused migration. They did so by sending troops on missions of conquest and, when they were victorious, by expelling or chasing defeated armies and civilians into further territories, where they sometimes became conquerors themselves. The most powerful of these empires, the Ottoman Empire, had destroyed the Byzantine Empire and taken its capital of Constantinople in 1453. The Ottomans expanded again from 1512 and took control of most of the Mediterranean, southeastern Europe, and southwest Asia, where they were halted by the newly created Safavid Empire of Iran.

Migration also caused empires, as in the case of the Mughal Empire where Babur's army from Afghanistan created the new state. In 1526, Sultan Babur gathered his Turkish troops in Kabul and broke through the barriers to India, destroying the Delhi sultanate and forming the Mughal Empire. Once created, this empire caused migration by sending administrators, merchants, and settlers into newly conquered territories.

Other empires had varying effects on migration. The Ming Empire of China, formed in the mid-fifteenth century by rebellious armies that defeated the Yuan (Mongol) Empire, caused and halted migration. It encouraged overseas commerce for a time but then inhibited people from moving on the mainland. In contrast to this huge Ming Empire was the tiny yet important Portuguese Empire. The Portuguese Empire differed greatly from the others because it consisted mainly of islands, forts, and trading posts that drew on the wealth of the Indian Ocean and South China Sea. (The empire also included a large territory in Brazil and important bases in Angola.) The Portuguese Empire caused the migration of many Portuguese, as well as the migration of the workers and other people in its colonies.

In the Atlantic world, in which most of the connections were mediated through the religion and culture of Christianity, empires began uniting people who had not previously been in contact. Spain, a kingdom formed out of the union of the thrones of Aragon and Castile through the marriage of Ferdinand and Isabella in 1469, soon became the Spanish Empire. It conquered Granada and expelled Muslims and Jews from the Iberian Peninsula in 1492, the same year as the voyage of Columbus. The new empire expanded, not only through conquests in North Africa and the Americas – and the destruction of the Aztec and Inca empires – but also through fortunate marriages, which brought control of Austria, much of Italy, and the Netherlands. Though Spain ruled much of the world, it was only the fourth largest empire of its time in terms of area and population. (The Ming and Ottoman Empires were larger and more populous, and the Mughal Empire was more populous though perhaps smaller in area.)

By 1600, travelers from every region had reached the ends of the earth. They understood that they were limited to the surface of a sphere. The world was now known to be bigger than previously thought, and yet it was limited and finite. We might encounter strange peoples in distant lands, yet they are very much like us. For example, in China, one of the earliest modern novels, "Monkey" (also known as "Journey to the West"), was composed in the fifteenth century on just this theme. Its tale of an eighth-century trip by a Chinese monk to India and back, and of his encounters with many sorts of people (including himself), has remained popular in China and elsewhere. Also in about 1600, William Shakespeare and his partners named their theater "The Globe" to convey the worldly scope of Shakespeare's plays. Theatergoers in Peru, Java, Angola, and China (with the help of a translator) would probably have understood the reference.

Commerce and religion, 1500–1700

In the sixteenth and seventeenth centuries, merchants, missionaries, and would-be conquerors relied on the widening paths of intercontinental and regional travel to visit distant lands. They moved across the globe searching for new markets, populations, and territories. Some of these migrants were Muslim and Christian missionaries, while others were merchants from Africa, Asia, and Europe. Accompanying the contemporary waves of conquest and exploration, these merchants and missionaries transformed brief encounters into long-term relationships, and forged routes and links between the bases of their activity. In their travels, they developed pathways and beachheads for later migrants, setting in motion the dynamics of global interconnections that facilitated world migration and international trade.

The results of these movements included the rise of Christianity and Islam in new areas of the world, including the expansion of Islam in such areas of Southeast Asia as the Malayan Peninsula. Similarly, there were conversion efforts that looked promising but resulted in failure in other areas, as both Islam and Christianity expanded and then declined in China. Merchant contacts opened up, especially in such variable commodities as gold, silver, furs, spices, and expensive textiles. Networks of merchants and missionaries extended their contacts to ports and marketplaces all over the globe.

Migrant influences abroad and at home

Have migrations of small numbers of people sometimes had major results? Have merchants and missionaries, in their movements, had significant influence on the course of world history? Or should studies of migration in history be restricted instead to large-scale movements of people? I argue that small migrations did indeed have a major impact; the reader may agree or develop a different view.

One part of the argument for the importance of these small migrations focuses on the pathways of their movement: it emphasizes the stopping points and the allies of these migrants on the way to their destination, and the lines of communication with their homeland. Another part of the argument focuses on the beachheads of the migrants in the lands of their settlement.

For the merchants and missionaries who went abroad, it was certainly their intention to create new markets and to spread their religion, and in some of these cases their work bore fruit. In other instances, the efforts of merchants and missionaries led to little permanent change. The visitors were absorbed into the societies they visited, or simply expelled. Portuguese missionaries and merchants became influential in sixteenth-century eastern Africa, but by the end of the seventeenth century they had been displaced by Muslims from Oman. The work of Christian missionaries in China yielded an exchange of learning between Chinese and European scholars (and sent many Chinese ideas to Europe) but brought little expansion of Christianity in the long term.

The missionaries and merchants influenced their homelands even while they were abroad. Their accumulation of wealth and contacts was the most obvious change: the ports of Seville in Spain and Lisbon in Portugal gathered people and influences from every continent. As the Dutch rose to commercial prominence and became an independent state at the helm of a vast commercial empire in the seventeenth century, the port of Amsterdam came to be labeled as the "Queen of the Seas." The constituents of this queen were customers from around the world. The term was appropriate for another reason – many Dutch men went abroad as sailors, soldiers, and settlers, so the home population became predominantly female. In yet another step of transformation, the Dutch focus on world trade may also be a reason why industry in the Netherlands developed more slowly than in other areas of Europe.

In the Ottoman Empire, the cosmopolitan connections of trade and religion also transformed the home area. In one example of this, the trade in coffee (purchased from Ethiopia and South Arabia) created the phenomenon of the coffeehouse, which spread throughout the empire to create new centers for socializing and debate. In another example, the Ottoman Empire's dominance of the holy city of Mecca enabled the Ottoman sultan to claim leadership of the Muslim spiritual world, and to maintain a nexus of contact with Muslims from West Africa to the Philippines.

Pathways

Merchants were particularly important in charting new pathways. For instance, the family known as the House of Mendes moved by stages across Europe as its members escaped religious persecution. Their pathways took the form of a set of social links among commercial towns connected by roads, so that their relatives and friends could follow them more readily. Expelled from Spain with other Jews in 1492, the House of Mendes used business connections as they passed through Lisbon, Antwerp, Augsburg, and Venice before settling in the Ottoman capital of Constantinople in 1528. Doña Gracia Nasi, who had assumed leadership of the family and its international business activities while still in Portugal, contributed to a banking system that supported the spice and gem trade across Asia, Africa, and Europe. In this case, Doña Gracia Nasi brought important commercial contacts to her adopted homeland, while also clearing the path for Jewish families leaving an increasingly intolerant Christendom.

Another case is that of the Armenian merchant Hovannes Ter-Davtian, whose logbook shows that he left his home in Isfahan (capital of the Safavid Empire of Iran) in 1692. His pathway was a set of links among commercial centers. He traveled to the western and eastern coasts of India, then moved to Tibet to trade from 1686 to 1693. Then he left with a load of musk, plus gold and Chinese porcelain, to sell in Calcutta. Throughout his travels, he stayed with Armenian families resident in each town.

New mixtures of population and society emerged as the merchants and missionaries traveled and settled. In West and Central Africa, Christianity overlapped with local religion and symbolism: the crosses long used in Kongo helped encourage that region's conversion to Catholicism, while the gods of West Africa became saints in the regional version of Christianity. As the pathway of the Atlantic slave trade widened, African Christianity came to the Americas, but the Catholic population of Kongo declined as the slave trade expanded.

Beachheads

At the end of a pathway lay a beachhead – a small immigrant community able to sustain the connection between the home area and the area of settlement. The Mendes family developed a beachhead in Constantinople that became its new home base. Portuguese merchants and mariners set up beachheads through their Asian voyages. When the Portuguese seized Goa on the Indian subcontinent in 1511, they created a beachhead from which Portuguese and then Dutch merchants plied their trade among merchants speaking Arabic, Swahili, Gujarati, Malay, and Chinese. As the Portuguese expanded eastward, they used developing relations with local merchants along China's southern coast to establish a trading base at Macao in 1557, with the approval of the Qing imperial authorities. Hokkien merchants from China used Macao as a beachhead of their own, and also built beachheads in Manila (where they traded silk for silver with the Spanish), and in Batavia, the Dutch port on Java. While Macao as a beachhead was important in regional commerce, it was not a center of transformation of the regional system.

In North America, in contrast, French merchants and missionaries set up a beachhead that brought realignment of life among Amerindian groups. Populations declined through disease, as elsewhere in the Americas, and at the same time a fur-trading economy developed over a vast area centered on the Saint Lawrence River Valley. The lives of the Algonquians and other peoples of the region changed greatly as the fur trade and French settlement became more influential. Although French traders were widely scattered on the continent, by 1700 two major cities, Quebec and Montreal, had grown through local and overseas migration to populations of more than 10,000 each. The French beachhead in New France, though small, was sufficient to transform life for the surrounding Algonquin population.

Muslim missionaries established beachheads as they traveled by land and sea across Southeast Asia as early as the thirteenth century. Their efforts widened religious and commercial networks that opened pathways for Islam to spread into Malaya, Indonesia, and other islands of the East Indies in the fifteenth and sixteenth centuries. In their turn, the Jesuit Order of the Catholic Church sent energetic missionaries, with the identical intent as their Muslim counterparts, to the same areas of the Indian Ocean, the Americas, and Africa. Jesuits built a beachhead in the form of a mission complex within the Chinese commercial center of Nanjing and another among Amerindians in Paraguay.

Sometimes the initial success of merchants and missionaries met reverses and the beachheads disappeared. For example, in Japan, the military government of the shogun became uncomfortable with Christian proselytizing. After Christian participation in an anti-shogun uprising, the government crucified some priests and their followers, and eventually expelled Europeans and suppressed Christianity. Similarly, the large Muslim communities in coastal cities of China declined under the Ming and Qing Empires.

Throughout the years now known as the early modern period, commerce and religion drew traders and missionaries of diverse origins to every corner of the globe. Their journeys defined the outlines of a world system of conversion and commerce that overlapped with frustrated desires for world conquest. They widened the paths they inherited, and moved people, ideas, and commodities in all directions. In later times, migratory movements accelerated as a result of the earlier movements of merchants and missionaries. The evidence and arguments outlined in this narrative, and available in the field, provide ample proof that merchants and missionaries stimulated major changes in the world.

Figure 7.4 provides reminders of at least three types of migration on land: settlers, conquerors, and refugees. The colonists shown on the map were Chinese settlers who, under the Ming and Qing dynasties, moved to the west and the southwest to settle among peoples at the frontier of the empire. The conquerors shown on the map are the Mughals, warriors from the highlands of Afghanistan whose repeated attacks on India finally brought them success in 1526 and the creation of the Mughal state, which was to expand its control to almost the whole Indian subcontinent. The remaining groups shown are refugees. In North America and South America, some indigenous populations were driven from their lands by invaders from the Old World. They moved

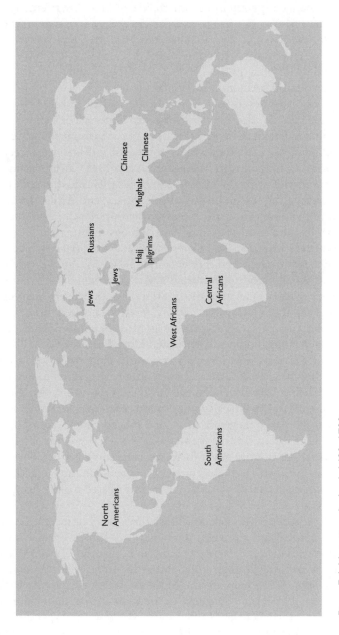

Figure 7.4 Migrations by land, 1400–1700

to new lands, often taking up new occupations, and in so doing often found themselves in conflict with their neighbors. In West and Central Africa, the wars and raids of the expanding slave trade caused some populations to migrate similarly in hope of security. In Europe, Jewish refugees expelled from Iberia and other parts of western Europe settled in Poland and the Ottoman Empire. In many though not all of these inland movements, one may argue that seaborne migrations helped to stimulate terrestrial migrations.

Families on the move, 1550–1750

Japan in 1550 experienced little migration. Consequently, families there grew multigenerational and complex. Numerous children and their cousins lived under the direction of patriarchs and perhaps matriarchs. Young people had to wait patiently before gaining the respect and power that went with age, and marriage was an alliance of families more than a union of individuals. The situation was similar in West Africa and in other areas with stable populations.

In the sixteenth and seventeenth centuries, as migration became more common, families changed in the lands of departure and the lands of destination. Migration stretched families over long distances, it broke apart existing families, and it formed nuclei for new families.

I propose to explore families in migration through three types of region. First were the regions where migrants dominated – regions where local populations were small or dispersed, and where settlers became numerous. In such regions, including parts of the Americas and on small islands of every ocean, new families took form. These populations became predominantly male, had many young adults, few children, and few old people. Young adults, little constrained by elders, could become heads of families. Migration to these lands brought new social distinctions. The differences in race, religion, and slave status left much room for hierarchy in these small, new families. Only after two or three generations could large families develop. When they did, complex racial mixes grew with them. If migrants continued to arrive, families tended to remain small.

Second, in regions where migrants formed a small but significant part of the population, they had a choice between joining existing families or starting new ones. This included a majority of migrants who moved from one part of the Old World to another from the sixteenth to the eighteenth centuries – from Europe to Africa or Asia, or from one part of Asia to another. These populations had a fairly even sex ratio but gained new types of families. Mixed populations, such as the Luso-Africans of Angola, the Indo-Portuguese of India, and the Chinese-descended mestizos of the Philippines, grew up during the sixteenth century.

Third, in regions from which migrants departed, the existing families changed in structure. These regions included parts of western Europe, West Africa, and South China. Families in these regions developed a relative scarcity of males. The role of long-distance migrant was most commonly a male role, as men and boys left home to take up new lives as sailors and merchants, or as captives. Women, left behind, had to take on the work of men, in the fields and in the household, and they lived with less of the companionship and less of the dictates of males. Sometimes the migrants were able to return or send fortunes to their families.

By 1750, families spawned by migration had emerged in a band of busy spots all over the world. In some areas, the new families had displaced the previous family order, as in the Caribbean. In other cases, the migrants had modified or complicated the previous family order, as in the Mediterranean and along the coasts of the Indian Ocean and Southeast Asia. In still other cases, a tradition of emigration, especially by males, changed society.

Forms of family migration

Every family is a unit, but it is also a mixture. The mixtures of male and female, and of contrasting genetic and social backgrounds, are just as important as the unity of the life shared by a husband and wife and the offspring they bring up. The family is created anew every generation, yet families can also live on for many generations. The family unit can be compressed to the minimum of a husband and wife or a mother and child, but it can be stretched to the size of lineages and clans of thousands. Every type of family has its own tension between its unity and its diversity.

Stories of families in migration are different from those of settled families. Questions of marriage, inheritance, and child rearing become different when migration is involved. For instance, among settled groups "family" usually meant "marriage," but among migrant populations, many families did not include marriage. For couples willing to marry, the formalities could sometimes not be performed. The institution of slavery complicated marriage. Some masters married slaves; more commonly, masters had children with slaves, yet remained the owners of the mothers and often of their children. The institution of marriage changed, as there emerged more families outside of marriage, and new kinds of marriage.

In all areas affected by migration, families changed. Families affected by migration usually became smaller and more varied. Their variety resulted from the mixes in race, religion, social status, and marital status of people who encountered each other through migration. Individuals arriving in a new territory became first-generation migrants, with adopted homelands. Their children, either with other migrants or with native-born people, became second-generation immigrants, living in the land of their birth, unless they too migrated.

The historian can clarify these changes by breaking the process of migration down into stages and exploring the relationship between stages of migration and family life. To begin, migration caused families in the home area to stretch geographically because they included relatives who went to distant regions. The feelings linking those who left and those who stayed behind often became an issue in family life.

While on the road, migrants formed strong bonds with each other that sometimes created new families. Once migrants reached the land of their destination, families formed in several ways. Many migrants – perhaps most – did not form new families but lived out their time as distant members of their home family. Others formed informal families, turning friends into "brothers" and "aunts." In still other cases, an immigrant man might marry an immigrant woman – the two settlers would have as relatives only their children and the adoptive relatives they chose. Alternatively, an immigrant man might marry the daughter of a local family.

After a generation or so, children of two local families might marry. Only in this case would family relations approximate those of a long-settled area, where new families form not so much as unions of individuals but as an alliance of existing families through the pairing of two of their young.

Thus, in the cities and colonies of the early modern world, where migrants were numerous, families took on a varied and nontraditional form. These areas may have had some great and powerful families that reproduced themselves with well-chosen marriages. The East African city of Mombasa provides an example of migrant minorities modifying a local population. Arab, Portuguese, and Indian migrants came to this port city, joining and forming families. The local ruling family, the Mazrui, intermarried with immigrants, yet retained its preeminence.

Most families were smaller groupings. These immigrant families resembled the nuclear families of today. For those who were slaves or otherwise indentured, marriage and family were all the more difficult to sustain except through individual arrangements. The families in zones of migration became models – the case of Melaka, where all of Asia's merchants met, stands out. Families of migrants, through the very fact of their contact with so much of the world, had influence on family values in all the areas they touched.

The term "creole," while defined in several ways, is important to understanding migrant families. I have adopted a broad meaning of "creole," including persons of all races born into societies dominated by the combination of migration and colonial rule. Creole families formed in many areas of the Americas, but they also appeared in the colonies, port towns, and plantations of Africa, Asia, and Europe. The growth of creoles as an element of human population represents one way that migration gave a new character to world history in the early modern period.

Creole societies experienced much cultural mixing, but they also developed new hierarchies based on race, religion, ethnicity, and legal status. Creole families defined as white sat near the top of this hierarchy, reaffirming their dominance with large and formal weddings. Creole families of "mixed" ancestry sat next in this hierarchy, subdivided into the first-generation mix of ancestries (without benefit of marriage) and the subsequent generations in which people of mixed ancestry married to formalize their intermediate role in society. Creole families born of slaves and other subordinate peoples maintained themselves without formal recognition of their marriages. At the peak of this complex social order were the officials from the European metropole, and at its margins were the "indigenous" people, displaced from their original lands and now playing a subordinate role in the new order.

Migration of men to Spanish and Portuguese America

Migrants to Spanish and Portuguese America, including the Caribbean, were mostly men. Females made up only one-third of the Africans and one-fifth of the Iberian migrants. Many of the men died without offspring. Female migrants were more likely to have children than males, though immigrant women had fewer children in the Americas than did native-born women.

Children born to immigrant men and local women populated the societies of the pathways and the beachheads. The Brazilian region known as Bahia became the most populous area of Brazil because of the arrival of free men from Portugal, who brought in larger numbers of African and Amerindian slaves. Their offspring were fluent in multiple languages and had complex identities. They could be identified by language, by birthplace, by nation or by color, yet none of these categories provided an absolute identity. Out of these distinctions came terms such as "settlers" and "natives" in the first generation, "creoles" and "mestizos" in the second generation, and more complex terms in later generations. Every family was mixed, and the terminology was equally varied.

The terms "creole" and "mestizo" reflect migration and generational descent. Locally born children of immigrants to the Americas were known as creoles. Children were "creoles" where migrants dominated, and "mestizos" where locals dominated. The term "creole" rapidly extended its meaning to account for this reality. Thus a Catholic priest, writing on the Portuguese colony of São Thorné in the 1580s, identified as "creole" the children of European and African immigrants to the island. In doing so, he referred not to the racial designation of the children but to their birthplace, and to his conclusion that their birth on the island brought both advantages and disadvantages to the Portuguese regime.

In the highlands of Mexico, the relatively healthy conditions enabled immigrants to survive longer and build larger families, including creoles, mestizos, mulattos, and Amerindians. The term "mulatto" emerged to describe children of European and African parents. The term "mestizo" referred to the children of Europeans and Amerindians in the Americas, but also to the children of Chinese and Filipinos in the Philippines. (The terms *mestizo* in Spanish, *mestiço* in Portuguese, and *métis* in French all translate as "mixed" in English.) Perhaps the biggest problem with defining these children as "mixed" was its implication that their parents were "pure." All these terms reflected efforts to both simplify and reinforce elite structures and the complex realities of life in these zones of interconnection.

In other cases, Portuguese and Spanish migrants encountered women in the areas where they settled. These relationships ranged from violations to loving and long-term marriages, and they produced a wide variety of families. These families often took on a culture and identity other than European, and they came to be known by such labels as mestizo, mulatto, Luso-African, or Indo-Portuguese. That is, they were mixed not only biologically, but also culturally and racially.

Migration of families to New England

The English migration to New England in the seventeenth century was unusual because it was made up of existing family units. Members of the Puritan religious community, unable to practice their faith in England, moved their families to Holland and then, beginning in 1620, to New England. The initial 20,000 migrants, including large proportions of women and children, grew rapidly in numbers and married formally within their community rather than created families with other groups they encountered. Therefore, a large and distinctive population emerged, so that, after 1700, New England sent out more people as emigrants than it received as immigrants. Emigrants from New England moved west and south on the North American mainland, to the Caribbean, and to the Eastern Hemisphere as well.

The Dutch settlements of New Netherlands and Cape of Good Hope, the French settlements in Canada, and the later English settlement in Pennsylvania shared some of the characteristics of this settlement of whole families. In all these cases, interaction with the original inhabitants remained an important dimension of regional life.

In British America outside of New England, very few families arrived as existing units. In the years before 1750, English, Irish, and Scottish migrants went in largest numbers to the Caribbean, then to Chesapeake Bay, and then to the northern American colonies; African migrants went to these areas in similar proportions. Both British and African migrants were overwhelmingly male, and the limits and problems involved in the creation of their families were severe. Two groups emphasized formal family life, sanctified by marriage and with written legacies to their children: whites with full legal rights at home, and free people of color reproducing their local community. However, the families bridging these communities – that is, mixes of whites and people of color – though numerous, tended not to be formalized by marriage and were often formally illegal. One exception to the rule was reported by Olaudah Equiano, who recounted the story of a white planter and free black woman of Monserrat who arranged for a wedding in a boat offshore to escape the prohibition of their marriage on the island.

The story of migration from the perspective of the family

Families, those fundamental institutions of human societies, have gained little attention from world historians. Perhaps these authors, in writing as they commonly do of empires and civilizations, have assumed that the history of families is included indirectly in their stories. Nevertheless, something is missing in an interpretation of world history that avoids placing families on center stage.

Has the character of family life changed for the world as a whole? For the period 1550–1750, one may respond by emphasizing two distinct trends. First, women predominated in short-distance migrations, while men predominated in long-distance migrations. The result reinforced the mix in families. Over the centuries, the reaffirmation of this pattern led to some significant developments in world population overall. Second, migration expanded the number of creoles in the world. It created new mixes in biological and cultural ancestry, and it brought new sorts of familial and social hierarchies into existence.

As constant as migrations have been to the human condition, and as much as migration has fostered the mingling of migrants with people they have encountered over the centuries, a new character to family life emerged from this early modern growth of creoles and their commingling, one that gradually worked its effect into societies everywhere.

Carrying and borrowing culture, 1650–1750

People who moved could not take everything with them. Migrants could carry some goods, but they had to recreate or reinvent others in their new homes. They kept hold of their ideas but often had to express them in different languages in the lands where they settled. The spread of culture, therefore, was not the same thing as the migration of people. Migrants both carried and borrowed their culture. And if goods and ideas sometimes moved slower than migrants, at other times the goods and ideas moved faster or farther than any migrant. Silk textiles, passed from hand to hand, often traveled much farther than individual merchants.

While no global culture had emerged to unite the world by the seventeenth century, waves of cultural change washed across the world's islands and onto the continents. These waves brought new traditions to the world by the eighteenth century. New food products had been adopted in every region – potatoes in Europe, maize in Africa, peppers in East Asia, peanuts in mainland and island Southeast Asia, yams in the Caribbean, and wheat in the Americas. Some textiles – Persian silks, Indian cottons, European woolens – spread everywhere, and with them spread new styles of dress. New connections arose in music, in religious tradition, and in styles of government. Through these connections, people in various regions developed new ways of organizing work, new ways of shipbuilding and home construction, and new ways of telling tales to children.

The exchange of goods and ideas took place everywhere, but especially at crossroads – intersections of the pathways of migration and trade. One major crossroad of the Eastern Hemisphere was Guangzhou, the southern Chinese port town through which merchants, sailors, and missionaries passed repeatedly. Muslims, Christians, Hindus, and Jews met with Buddhists in this metropolis with a Confucian government.

Crossroads did not always need to be in a great metropole such as Guangzhou. The small towns of Recife and New Amsterdam housed Amerindian, African, Portuguese, and Dutch settlers, including "New Christian" and Jewish migrants. Aside from ports, crossroads could be found at other junctures between differing geographies, such as Timbuktu on the frontier of the savanna and desert in West Africa, and Samarqand at a similar frontier in Central Asia. These meeting places accelerated social change.

Migration of cultural practices

The migration of individuals is relatively simple to describe. The migration of culture is more difficult to depict, in part because of differences of opinion as to what is meant by "culture" and what is meant by "cultural change." Culture includes the expressive culture of language and music, but also the material culture of tools and foodstuffs. It includes the elite culture of high priests and monarchs, but also the popular culture of village dances and folk tales. It includes the specifics of sculpture in wood, but also the totality of a civilizational tradition. Cultural change includes the migration of culture and its transformation through reinterpretation, translation, innovation, and combination. All these aspects of culture overlap and interact, of course, and migration has done much to facilitate the interactions.

Analyzing cultural change requires a terminology and some definitions. We need terms and concepts to explain the fascinating but complex patterns of cultural change. We need a terminology about culture that is as rich and textured as the cultural practices themselves. At the same time, we should be aware of the limits of any term in describing the complexity of cultural change. My proposed terminology distinguishes types of cultural production and types of cultural change or connection.

For cultural production, I distinguish material culture from expressive culture. The emphasis on these two areas provides a reminder that "culture" is not a unified tradition, but a range of cultural practices and products, each with its own patterns.

For analyzing cultural change, the terminology is somewhat more complex. Analysts often rely on simple terms such as "diffusion" and "spread" to describe the movements of foods, textiles, musical styles, and religious beliefs.

For music they might speak, for instance, of the "spread" of the guitar from the Mediterranean to every region of the world. But the terms "diffusion" and "spread" are too simple to provide a good explanation of cultural change. The music played on guitars depended not only on the instrument but also on the musical tradition already in the mind of each performer. Music changed in its instrumentation, and also in its rhythms and in the forms and purposes of musical performance.

The first step I offer to sharpen the analysis of cultural change is to distinguish between the carrying and the borrowing of culture. When French settlers in Canada planted wheat seeds, they were carrying their culture from their old home to their new one. But when people in West Africa and much of Asia learned to grow Caribbean chili peppers, they were borrowing culture. In both cases a product moved, but in the latter cases new groups adopted a product and developed new forms of cuisine.

The difference between carrying and borrowing culture is one of the many distinctions one can observe through paying attention to processes of cultural change. As an aid to identifying these processes, I propose a further list of types of connection. They range from simple diffusion to more complex patterns of innovation, fusion, and syncretism, interchange, inheritance, and improvisation.

Material culture: food, clothing, and housing

Food is always loaded with cultural meaning and value. The world trading system created a global agricultural revolution in taste, in processes for producing food, and in the commerce of food. Trades in tea, coffee, and sugar grew endlessly. Portuguese migrants introduced tempura to Japan, where it remains a popular food. The Chinese welcomed new foods like maize and peanuts. Africans made new use of those foods, as well as of cacao and squash. The coffee plant, native to northeast Africa, became important in the Americas and eventually spread to many of the warm parts of the world. Tomatoes, native to the Americas, became especially popular in lands of the Mediterranean basin as an addition to stews, sauces, and salads. Each one of these foodstuffs – the tomato, for instance – caused a small revolution in agriculture, economics, and taste. The crops themselves, as they moved, changed little. But the use to which they were put, and the meanings they came to have, varied greatly.

The cultivation of food, in turn, affected patterns of migration. The arrival of maize in China enabled farming on lands that had previously been marginal. The production of sugar in Brazil and the Caribbean led to the migration of millions of workers and brought other changes. In South Carolina, Africans from the rice-growing area of Sierra Leone were brought in to produce rice for workers on Caribbean sugar plantations.

Other examples of the migration of material culture show that cultural products could change as they moved. Calico cloth, a type of luxury white cotton from India, moved around the world through the work of merchants. Changing demand led to the painting of and then printing on calico. Indian producers found they had to change their patterns, sometimes rapidly, in response to shifts in demand among consumers as far away as West Africa or North America. Styles of housing also moved and changed. The bungalow, a simple house from Bengal that included a porch, appeared in varied but recognizable form all over the tropics.

Expressive culture: language and religion

Language is an example of expressive culture. Its changes reveal various types of cultural contact and change. As the Portuguese language came to be a major language for trade along the coasts of the Atlantic and Indian Oceans and the South China Sea, Portuguese terms worked their way into the other languages of these regions. For instance, the terms "cabess" (head) and "galinha" (chicken) came to be used in West African languages for quantities of cowrie shells used as money.

Languages could sometimes be imposed by dominant powers. The growing might of Spain, England, Russia, and China had much to do with the spread of their languages in the seventeenth and eighteenth centuries. At the same time, languages were governed by a sort of consensus among those who spoke them, so that even these expanding languages underwent sharp changes in each region where they were spoken. And it was not only the languages of the imperial courts that spread. Arabic, German, Hausa, and Armenian languages became widely spoken outside their homelands because of their importance in trade and religion. The poetry and literature in each of these languages drew heavily on the experience of migration. Sometimes individual words migrated rather than whole languages. Two Chinese terms for tea—"cha" and "te"—made their way into hundreds of other languages. The terms moved along with the trade in tea, which was long grown only in China. Terms based on "cha" dispersed across the Eurasian mainland ("shay" in Persian and "chay" in Russian), while terms based on "te" moved along the coasts of the Indian Ocean and the Atlantic ("teh" in Indonesia and "thé" in France). The Caribbean term "canoe" and the Arabic term "algebra" have spread almost as thoroughly.

Religion is a sort of expressive culture, though it is also a philosophy. The religion of Islam spread in early modern times, along with migration and commerce. As the Islamic religion and philosophy took hold in Southeast Asia and West Africa, the strict female dress code of the Middle East was somehow left behind. Are these cases of religious syncretism? "Syncretism" in religion refers to the combination of different traditions, where the two remain distinct. The Sikh religion, created in north India in an atmosphere of conflict between Islam and Hinduism, can be seen as syncretic, a compromise between two traditions. Followers of the Sikh religion, however, see it as a fusion, a new idea in which the different elements of the old ideas not only coexist, but are joined.

Many religious traditions overlapped in the African diaspora. Christianity competed with local religions in Africa, and Africans in the Americas who were led into Christianity often creatively engaged in it to make it their own. Vodun, a religion of the Bight of Benin in West Africa, contributed much to religions of the Americas, known as Vodun in Haiti, as Candomblé in Brazil, and as Santería in Cuba.

The concepts of syncretism and fusion can be applied to creole languages. Each creole language traces its origins to at least two languages, often with grammar from one and vocabulary from another. (If the term "creole" was sometimes applied to whites only in speaking of race or ethnicity, "creole" in language applied to all the speakers of that language, of whatever color.) Crioulo emerged as early as the fifteenth century on the Cape Verde Islands as a mix of Portuguese and West Atlantic languages, and remains the national language of Cape Verde. Similar creoles developed throughout the Atlantic. Indeed, both English and Swahili, widely spoken languages of regional and world significance, originated as syncretic languages in areas that were crossroads of migration.

Cultural connections

Connecting the patterns in development of global culture is a complex but fascinating exercise for the historian. To trace the connections among musical traditions, for instance, one can make distinctions among the instruments, the orchestration (the combinations of individual instruments), the rhythms of the music, the melodies, and the lyrics. The sounds of music in the past, of course, are what we would most like to hear and what is hardest to reproduce. But by paying attention to what is known of instrumentation and rhythm, we can mentally reconstruct a semblance of the past sounds and imagine how they were conveyed from group to group.

As people of different traditions moved and interacted, they tried out new ideas while holding on to their own. People in each cultural tradition made comments on others: for instance, musical compositions used melodies or orchestration to make references to other musical traditions. People also tried mixing and matching cultural materials. Not all the experiments were successful, but the attempts continued.

In a world of cultural change, some people chose to emphasize the purity of individual traditions, while others learned to value the techniques of cultural mixing. It was only with the flowering of jazz music in the early twentieth century that the notion of "improvisation" gained formal recognition as a strength in the cultural tradition of the African diaspora. It may be, however, that the act came long before the word. Migration has long combined people of widely different backgrounds, and it may be that the intensity of mixtures in the Americas has been developing styles of improvisation for a long time.

Conclusion

The maritime innovations that became evident in the fifteenth century continued throughout the period from 1400 to 1700: sailing techniques, ship construction, navigational skills, naval gunnery, and cargo handling all improved, for small vessels as well as large. The interconnections at the beginning of this period centered on spices and gold, and on movements of small numbers of mariners and missionaries. With time, the range of commodities broadened to include trade in silver, in furs, in silks and cottons, pottery and ivory, sugar and slaves. The crops that moved around the world began to be significant sources of nourishment in new regions by 1700.

Ports and shipping volume expanded in both new and old regions of maritime access. The expanding old coasts of maritime activity included the North Sea, the Mediterranean and Black Seas, the western and eastern Indian Ocean, the South China Sea, and the Indonesian archipelago. The regions where long-distance shipping was new included the western coast of Africa, the Caribbean, and other coasts of the Americas.

While populations living from the land remained much larger than those living from the waters, monarchs and merchants in land-based states turned their interest toward the sea. Although such earlier patterns of migration and social reorganization as those brought by the Mongol Empire continued into the period after 1400, they were connected to the seas: one of the reasons for the expeditions of Zheng He was to bring the flag of the Ming state into the region dominated by Timur.

The clearest cost of this expanded maritime contact was the effects of disease. The population of the world as a whole may have been smaller in 1650 than it was in 1500, especially because of declining population in the Americas, but also because of elevated mortality in Africa, Europe, and Asia. In addition, for those who traveled, death rates were always higher than for those who stayed at home. But the changes, both positive and negative, had come to stay. The new global connections brought by the expansion of maritime voyages led to permanent changes, in that all the oceans, continents, and islands were henceforth to remain in regular contact with one another.

Further reading

The expansion of maritime life from 1400 was led by the Ming voyages, which are summarized in a lively work of Louise Levathes, *When China Ruled the Seas* (New York, 1994). The Portuguese followed soon after, as described in A. J. R. Russell-Wood, *A World on the Move: The Portuguese in Africa, Asia, and America 1415–1808* (New York, 1993). Two more useful perspectives on maritime and littoral life of the Indian Ocean are Michael N. Pearson, "Littoral Society: The Concept and the Problems," *Journal of World History* 17 (2006), 353–373; and Craig A. Lockard, "'The Sea Common to All' Maritime Frontiers, Port Cities, and Chinese Traders in the Southeast Asian Age of Commerce, ca. 1400 – 1750," *Journal of World History* 21 (2010), 219–247. Alfred Crosby chronicles the interaction of Eastern and Western Hemispheres in *The Columbian Exchange: Biological and Cultural Consequences of 1492* (Westport, Conn., 1992); and Joseph E. Harris traces interactions between Africa and Asia in *The African Presence in Asia* (Evanston, Ill., 1971). For studies of the rise and fall of empires in this era, see Geoffrey W. Conrad and Arthur A. Demarest, *Religion and Empire: The Dynamics of Aztec and Inca Expansionism* (New York, 1984); James Forsyth, *A History of the Peoples of Siberia: Russia's North Asian Colony 1581–1990* (New York, 1992); and Jane S. Gerber, *The Jews of Spain: A History of the Sephardic Experience* (New York, 1992).

Stories of commercial networks in early modern times make up an important part of Philip Curtin's pathbreaking study, *Cross-cultural Trade in World History* (Cambridge, 1984). For a collection of studies treating commerce from an imperial point of view, see James Tracy, ed., *The Rise of Merchant Empires: Long-Distance Trade in the Early Modern World 1350–1750* (New York, 1990). Pilgrimage overlapped with commerce, as shown in M. N. Pearson, *Pilgrimage to Mecca: The Indian Experience 1500–1800* (Princeton, N.J., 1996); and in Mary Jane Maxwell, "Afanasii Nikitin: An Orthodox Russian's Spiritual Voyage in the *Dar al-Islam*, 1468–1475," *Journal of World History* 17 (2006), 243–266.

For the linkage of families and migration in early modern times, there are studies on many parts of the world. See Nicholas Canny, ed., *Europeans on the Move: Studies on European Migration, 1500–1800* (New York, 1994); David M. Crowe, *A History of the Gypsies of Eastern Europe and Russia* (New York, 1994); Richard Hellie, *Slavery in Russia, 1450–1725* (Chicago, Ill., 1982); John A. Larkin, *The Pampangans: Colonial Society in a Philippine Province* (Berkeley, Calif., 1972); Avigdor Levy, *The Sephardim in the Ottoman Empire* (Princeton, N.J., 1992); Muriel Nazzari, *Disappearance of Dowry – Women, Families & Social Change in São Paolo, Brazil 1600–1900* (Stanford, Calif., 1991); Robert Shell, *Children of Bondage: A Social History of the Slave Society at the Cape of Good Hope, 1652–1838* (Boston, Mass., 1994); and Cecil Roth, *The House of Nasi* (Westport, Conn., 1969). Perhaps in future analysis these regional studies will reveal global patterns in family life.

Cultural transfers and transformations are shown for the Americas in Jack D. Forbes, *Africans and Native Americans* (Urbana, Ill., 1993) and Frank Gilbert Roe, *The Indian and the Horse* (Norman, Okla., 1955). For Southeast Asian cultural change, see Anthony Reid, *Southeast Asia in the Early Modern Era* (Ithaca, N.Y., 1993).

The debate about globalization in history has mostly focused on recent times, so it is discussed in the concluding chapter of this book. Nevertheless, some works have considered whether the realities of globalization have played out over a longer time period, and among them are David Northrup, "Globalization and the Great Convergence: Rethinking World History in the Long Term," *Journal of World History* 16 (2005), 249–267; A. G. Hopkins, ed., *Globalization in World History* (New York, 2002); and Dirk Hoerder, *Cultures in Contact: World Migrations in the Second Millennium* (Durham, N.C., 2002).

Chapter 8

Labor for industry and empire, 1700 to 1900

The changing world economy of the eighteenth and nineteenth centuries brought an expansion in migration for economic purposes: first the forced migration of slaves, then the migration of agricultural and industrial workers with varying degrees of free will. Most of the migrating workers entered new language communities in the lands of their destination. Speakers of African languages learned each other's languages, the languages of their masters (such as English, Portuguese, or Arabic), and creole languages developed by communities of settlers. Chinese speakers of Cantonese learned Spanish in Peru and Thai in Thailand. Migrants from Scandinavia, Greece, and Lebanon learned languages of the Americas as they crossed the Atlantic. As so many times before, but now on a larger scale, people crossed community boundaries, and in so doing reinforced the creative energies of human society.

The pace of migration accelerated in these two centuries. In the early eighteenth century, tens of thousands of captives traveled each year in the sailing ships of the Atlantic slave trade. That number rose to nearly one hundred thousand transatlantic captives per year at the end of the eighteenth century, while tens of thousands of additional captives were forced to other African and Middle Eastern destinations. By the end of the nineteenth century, millions of free migrants sailed each year by steamship from Europe and Asia in search of work overseas. These long-distance, transoceanic voyages were supplemented by shorter-distance movements, increasingly by railway, to booming urban areas in Europe, Asia, and the Americas.

This acceleration in migration brought a further mixture in populations. In Southeast Asia, most of the Americas, parts of Africa, and in the Pacific, there gathered competing groups of immigrants numerous enough to rival or outnumber the native-born. These groups, placed in proximity and often in relations of hierarchy with each other, developed tense relations and stereotypical views of each other. The realities of cultural difference and the visual cues of physical distinctions each played a role in developing the notions of racial difference and racial hierarchy which grew to an unprecedented level by the end of the nineteenth century. These notions of racial difference spread along land and sea routes to reach people in every region of the world.

The expansion in the world economy thus brought migration and realloca-tion of productive labor, and also brought the spread of new ideas and new conflicts.

The four sections of the chapter address forced migration, the creation of national and racial identities, the migratory dimension of industrializa-tion, and the linked expansions in empire and voluntary migration. Forced migration led captives to the Americas but also to destinations in the Eastern Hemisphere, so that slavery became a building block of modern society in many regions. The remarkable extent of slavery and serfdom in the eighteenth and nineteenth centuries leads one to think of forced labor as a significant and painful step in the creation of the modern world economy. Second, as both unfree and free migrants settled in new lands, they and their descendants developed new identities and new relationships with other groups. From the eighteenth century these evolving relationships gave rise to a new terminology, identifying "nations," "races," and "tribes." Third, as industrial growth and transformation took place in European factories of the eighteenth and nine-teenth centuries, related growth also took place in farms, mines, workshops, and harbors around the world. Migrants in this era moved to take up work in factories or farms, cities or countryside, and temperate or tropical areas. Fourth, the turn of the twentieth century brought massive imperial conquests by the leading industrial nations, but also record-setting migrations from the most populous areas of the world. These two phenomena, usually treated as unrelated, are here shown to be connected in several significant ways.

Forced migration, 1700–1850

Many migrants moved against their will. Involuntary movements included expulsion of whole populations and the transportation of prisoners. Even the migration of children, as they left homes they did not wish to leave in the company of their parents, can be seen as involuntary. Nevertheless, the main type of involuntary migration centered on enslavement. Where expulsions were large movements in a short time period, enslavement involved smaller pro-portions of populations moving over a longer time and resulted in a larger total of displacements. Slavery provided a way to obtain and exploit labor when voluntary or paid labor was insufficient.

Systems of slavery grew in several parts of the world from about 1400 until 1850. The most profitable and most concentrated system of slavery was that of the New World. This system – focused on Brazil, the Caribbean, and North America – produced gold, silver, sugar, tobacco, cotton, and coffee for the world market. As late as 1600, Africans remained a minority of the world's slaves, since slavery at that time centered on the Mediterranean and most captives were drawn from Central Asia and Europe. By 1700, however, the largest slave populations were in the Americas, and they were overwhelmingly African (but included some Amerindians).

Why did slavery grow? The increasing European demand for slaves made the system expand. The ability of Portuguese, Spanish, Dutch, English, and French merchants to buy laborers for mines and plantations kept demand high and made slave prices rise. Captured Africans, taken to the Americas, built cities, cleared fields, hauled goods, grew crops, and ran the households of their owners.

The growing demand of European merchants drew steadily more Africans into capturing and selling laborers. African merchants kept some captives, and a West African system of slavery grew up in response to the New World system. Through contacts across the seas and across the continents, several other Old World systems of slavery arose in response to the expanding slave system of the Americas: in eastern Africa, the Middle East, the Black Sea region, the Indian Ocean, and Southeast Asia. Slavery in Russia, while different from the other systems of slavery, also had a role in the overall pattern.

Wherever there were waves of enslavement, waves of liberation ultimately followed. In New Spain and Peru, imports of slaves declined in the eighteenth century, and many children of slaves became free. In Haiti, slaves gained their freedom through an uprising, and in other areas, they gained freedom through legislation. In Russia, the large slave population was transformed into "serfs" during the eighteenth century. The number of slaves and serfs in the world peaked at perhaps as many as fifty million persons in about 1850. Thereafter, emancipation of bonded persons came more rapidly than new captures or births of slaves.

Forced migration, by gender and age

The example of the Atlantic slave trade shows how enslavement had different effects by age and gender. In the Americas, demand and prices were highest for males. The captives crossing the Atlantic were over 60 per cent male, and the slave system of the Americas therefore had a significant shortage of females as long as new captives were coming from Africa. Captives embarked on European ships had often been held for weeks or even months on the coast, and their captors had to pay for feeding and clothing them during that time. Once on board, as on the coast, men tended to be held separately from women and children. The transatlantic voyage lasted several weeks, and the captives, already weakened, lost, on average, 15 per cent of their number during the crossing. In another gender-based difference, the shipboard mortality rate for females seemed always lower than the rate for males.

On the African continent, demand and prices were highest for female slaves. Thus, the captives retained in Africa were well over 60 per cent female, and the result was the development of a sizeable African slave population, dominantly female, living in households dominated by free males. The men were able to use the female slaves as domestics and as concubines – any children belonged to the owner.

Africans were enslaved primarily through warfare and kidnapping, but also through court proceedings or witchcraft accusations. Once in captivity, some went to African purchasers and others went overseas. Prices were highest for male captives on the African coast, so male captives tended to be walked whatever distance it took to get them there. Females, on the other hand, had significant value as captives in many African societies, so female captives tended to be sold into slavery within Africa, near to their point of capture.

The other systems of slavery and instances of forced migration, which grew in large part as a reflection of New World slavery, also each had a particular composition by gender and age. The Middle East drew increasingly on slaves from North and East Africa and took mostly females for use in domestic service, leaving these parts of Africa with a shortage of females. The Russian system, in which the slaves were mainly male, was located near to that of the Ottoman Empire, in which slaves were mainly female.

African slavery in the New World

Some ten to twelve million Africans crossed the Atlantic in captivity. The oppression of slavery supported economic change through the expansion of plantation production of sugar, tobacco, indigo, and later cotton. Perhaps ironically, slavery also sustained economic progress because plantations contributed to the development of industrial organization. Cuban plantations expanded rapidly in the late eighteenth and nineteenth centuries, using steam engines, railroads, and other advanced industrial technology, and relying on an elaborate division of labor and the techniques of mass production – all with slave labor.

Few slaves gained their freedom, and few of their voices were heard in the societies that used their labor. The silence, however, was by no means complete. Perhaps the most forceful voice out of the African diaspora in that era was that of Olaudah Equiano, who purchased his freedom, lived a full life as a free man in England, traveled widely, and wrote a powerful plea against slavery in the form of an autobiography. That same autobiography provides one of the best available pictures of the territories and the issues of the eighteenth-century Atlantic basin.

Migration of slaves went beyond their initial capture and transportation. In two major cases, large populations of slaves were moved great distances in response to opportunities for their masters. In the American South, the slave populations of the Old South, working on tobacco plantations along the Atlantic coast, were sold or moved with their masters to the New South in the era from 1800 to 1860. In this time, roughly one million slaves were displaced, sometimes with their families broken as they moved. At the same time, the numerous slaves of Bahia in Brazil, caught in the decline of the sugar industry, found themselves moved piecemeal by a similar process to São Paulo and Rio de Janeiro, to become workers on the expanding coffee plantations there. As in the United States, roughly one million slaves were displaced by command of their owners, sometimes with their families split by the movement. In these cases, as with Cuban sugar, slavery was linked to growing industrial production.

Compulsion and gender in the Old World

In Africa, although European slavers occasionally came ashore to conduct raids, the only way they could get large numbers of captives was to buy them from African merchants. These merchants, in turn, set up arrangements with those that enslaved and transported people from coastal and interior areas of Africa. African populations suffered from the resulting warfare and kidnapping, and the fate of African kingdoms rose and fell with the slave trade. The Oyo Empire, a great state from the early seventeenth century, largely abstained from slave exports until the late eighteenth century. Then Oyo became an active participant in the slave trade for fifty years, which led to the collapse of the empire and abandonment of its capital circa 1830.

The demand for African slaves rose at the end of the eighteenth century in the Muslim Mediterranean and at the fringes of the Indian Ocean. Most of the Africans sent north and east were young women, who served mainly as domestics. African males were purchased for use as construction workers in the expansion of the holy city of Mecca, as pearl divers in the fisheries of the Persian Gulf, and as soldiers in Egypt. Texts and images from Istanbul show the importance of slaves as servants, as soldiers, as workers in mines and agriculture, and in other tasks.

Of captives taken into the Sahara, many did not complete the crossing. Some died in the course of the arduous journey, but many others were settled down as slaves in the desert – as miners digging for salt or as agricultural workers in the oases where dates and grains were produced for local use and for export. These Saharan oases were thus, in a sense, equivalent to the islands of the Atlantic and the Caribbean.

In Arabia, men expressed a particularly high demand for enslaved Oromo and Somali women from the Horn of Africa. These women became their wives and concubines. In Arabia as elsewhere in the Middle East, slave women tended to have children fathered by free men rather than by other slaves. The result, in contrast to the Americas, was the development of a slave-descended population that was assimilated, socially and biologically, into the free population. In the Americas, the maintenance of a separate black population was reinforced by racial discrimination and by prohibitions against the marriage of blacks and whites.

The shortages of women in the migrant populations of the Americas, and the shortages of men in Africa, were responsible for the small number of children born to slaves in the Americas and the relatively larger number of children born in Africa. Still, as calculations show, enough women left Africa in chains, or died in the process, that the African population declined in the eighteenth century, at a time when the populations of other world areas were growing.

Slavery expanded in Southeast Asia in the eighteenth and nineteenth centuries in much the same fashion as in the western Indian Ocean. The captive populations, however, came mainly from South Asia and from the islands that have since become Indonesia, rarely from Africa. Indonesian slavery expanded as local and Dutch planters in Java, Melaka, and Ceylon (now Sri Lanka) purchased slaves from those who would sell captives, and put them to work on plantations for coffee, spices, and sugar.

By the end of the eighteenth century, slavery had developed as a system of labor extending over much of the world, in which laborers were captured (mostly in Africa) and transported short or long distances to work, according to the needs and desires of their owners. African slaves worked on mines, on plantations, and as servants in the Americas; as servants and as laborers in Africa; as domestics and as artisans in North Africa, southwest Asia, and the Indian Ocean.

Not only was slavery a global system, but it helped change patterns in gender relations in every area it touched. The evidence available on the structure of enslaved populations provides insights into the lives of these populations. Ships' records indicate the age and sex composition of slave cargoes; plantation records indicate the age and sex structure of the slave work force. By combining these documents and other knowledge of the characteristic patterns of populations, it is possible to show the interactions and changes in the populations of Africa, of the captives in transition, and of the slaves in the Americas.

An unusual category of evidence is Portuguese censuses of Angola in the late eighteenth century, which show how slavery could skew the ratios of male and female. These censuses, summarizing various regions of the colony, show a serious shortage of adult men. The documents confirm what is otherwise clear from the pattern of transatlantic slave migration: Africa lost many more men than women, and therefore African populations included many fewer men than women. The shortage of males in western Africa, and the large number of enslaved women, encouraged the rise of a new sort of patriarchy. The men who remained in Africa were able to have multiple wives or slave concubines.

By distinct but related processes, systems of patriarchy grew up all around the eighteenth-century Atlantic, all of them linked to the expansion of slavery. In the Americas, male slave owners dominated their slaves, but also had great power over all women and over poorer free men. Free white men had children with black women, often with no social obligation to the women or children. The power of owner over slave, of white over black, and of male over female combined to define the New World system of patriarchy.

Still another change in patriarchy developed in eighteenth-century Europe. There the growth of factory production and with it the rise of the family wage (in which men were paid well and women poorly) led to a type of patriarchy in which men controlled the family income. The shared family income and responsibilities were replaced by a hierarchy in which family members were separated at work and men dominated.

The triangular routes of trade linking Europe, western Africa and the Americas reinforced the growth of these patriarchal norms. The precise meaning given to "patriarchy" in the three situations differs. Yet, all three social systems grew up at the same time, and in interaction with each other. The European system of factories grew in connection with slavery in the Americas and with slave trade in Africa. Goods from European factories went toward the purchase of African captives, and African slaves in the Americas produced raw materials for European markets. So the gender roles of the modern world have been defined in part by global connections, migration, and the experience of slavery.

Migration and identity, 1750–1850

Is one's identity determined by destiny or is it a matter of choice? One is born male or female and in a given place, and one grows up with a certain physical makeup, speaking the language (or languages) learned during one's childhood. Still, people can decide who they choose to follow and have control over at least some of their beliefs. Migration, whether voluntary or involuntary, provides more possibilities for identity. For instance, those settling in a new place can identify themselves as pioneers in a new home or as exiles from their old home. This section emphasizes the importance of migration for the definition of individual, ethnic, racial, and especially national identity.

If individuals can define themselves, so can groups. Individuals can learn new languages and become members of new communities. Whole communities can unify or divide themselves. These kinds of identity changes, individual and group, took place in the eighteenth and nineteenth centuries, where social and cultural conditions including migration fostered the development of some important new identities.

By the eighteenth century, after two centuries of accelerated migration and mixing, the world's population had been redistributed. Movements of people around the globe had fostered new relationships. Individual redefinitions of family and group identity – for example, settler, creole, and mestizo – propagated to a point where new social strata were created. It was a time, in short, for people to reconceptualize their identity. In response to this need, new definitions emerged for nation, race, and ethnicity.

One prominent example of an individual changing identity involves José Gabriel Condorcanqui of Peru, who grew up as a "creole." His Spanish ancestry put him on the second tier of the hierarchy of colonial Peru. However, his Peruvian ancestry linked him to the Inca royal family, and his practical experience linked him to other Peruvians. In his forties, as he became unhappy with Spanish administrative reforms, he changed loyalties and his identity. He maintained his creole connection but now subordinated it to his identity as a Peruvian. He became Túpac Amaru II, the heir to the Inca throne and leader of a powerful rebellion calling for a new social order in Peru.

Two great categories of group identity exist in today's world: "nation" and "race." These terms emerged at the turn of the nineteenth century and they appeared partly in response to migration. Early in the eighteenth century, "nation" meant (in European languages) a group of people sharing a language and culture. One spoke of the Iroquois, the Ibo, or the Bengali as nations, along with the French and Dutch. By 1850, after a century of revolution and political change, "nation" meant a people with a national government. The rise of the modern nation-state established new national identities and created a new hierarchy, one where people without nation-states were set at a lower level. Thus, the French, Dutch, and Brazilians were considered nations in 1850, but the Ibo and Bengali were no longer thought of that way: they were now labeled as "tribes." In the same period, the meaning of "race" changed, adding a hierarchy of physical type to the hierarchy of having or not having nationhood. The term "Caucasian" was developed in the late eighteenth century, and those labeled as not Caucasian were divided into from three to six racial groups.

Language, as always, served as an important marker of identity. The worldwide expansion of Europeans after 1500 brought their Indo-European languages into the areas where they settled. By 1750 the migrations of people and languages had already brought a modest but important change in the world's language map. As Figure 8.1 indicates, English, French, Spanish, Portuguese, and Russian were the languages that expanded most significantly (Dutch, Italian, German, and Danish also came to be spoken in regions far from their homelands). These languages came to be spoken in significant coastal areas of the Americas and in much smaller (but sometimes densely populated) regions of the Asian and African coasts. Russian came to be spoken by small numbers of settlers who extended all the way to the Pacific. With time, these languages came to be adopted as second languages by growing numbers of people in each region; in addition, European settlers to these regions also grew in number.

The interpretation of nation-building

Historians and politicians have debated the rise of the nation-state for over two centuries. In these debates, several interpretations, each with a different logic, have been used to explain the occurrence. This section introduces the various logics of nation-building, but its major point is to argue that patterns of migration must also be included in any thorough interpretation of nationalism and nationhood.

An early and still popular logic is the idea that today's nations are an inheritance from ancient communities. Scholars have applied the logic of inheritance

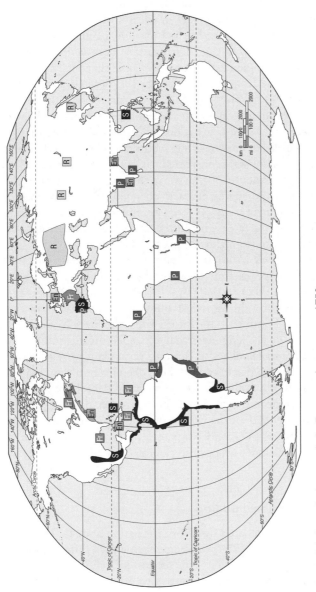

Figure 8.1 Spread of certain Indo-European languages, c. 1750

En = English; Fr = French; S = Spanish; P = Portuguese; R = Russian

in particular to countries such as France and England. In this view, centuries of political community and ethnic unity were "inherited," resulting in an "automatic" national identity. Those countries fortunate enough to inherit such a national identity were rewarded with the status of great nations.

The number of nations exploded in the twentieth century. It became clear that new nations such as Ghana and Indonesia could not be explained as the slow accumulation of national identity over the centuries. These countries had long histories, but their emergence as nations also depended on their experience with colonial rule and campaigns for independence. If the inheritance explanation is applied, then such countries were not legitimate nations – critics argued they could not claim ethnic unity or recognition as a state. If these countries were indeed nations, then the logic of their emergence needed to be re-examined.

One response to the need for rethinking the concept of nation was to interpret these countries through the logic of maturation. During the years of decolonization, scholars such as Hans Kohn argued that nationhood was a sign of political advance. The leading nations were mature communities, and other national communities could grow and evolve if conditions were right. The ex-colonies were labeled as "new nations" or "young nations" with this in mind.

In the 1970s, as nations around the world came closer to being treated as equals, scholars turned to interpretations relying on the logic of construction. They concluded that people constructed their nations actively and consciously, rather than inheriting them or nurturing their maturation. Benedict Anderson, Ernest Gellner, and Eric Hobsbawm are three leading proponents of the construction theory of nations, and they applied this logic as much to England and France as to Ghana and Indonesia.

The logic of constructing the nation makes one think of nation-building as a project and makes one ask who led in the project. The national project includes such objectives as gaining control of government, profiting from international trade, supporting domestic merchants, agriculture, and industry, and gaining recognition and prestige for one's national traditions. Benedict Anderson conceived of the nation as an "imagined community" that developed out of "print capitalism." Ernest Gellner, in a somewhat similar approach, emphasized the rise of governmental bureaucracies.

The debate on the logic of nation-building still goes on. While the recent interpretations are more realistic than the earlier justifications of nationalism, important issues still need to be clarified. Here are three. First, many of the interpretations of nation-building are still done on a case-by-case, nation-by-nation basis; in other words, they focus on a single country. In addition to these narrow interpretations of nationalism, one should also consider the ways in which one experience of nationalism influenced others. Second, what role has migration played in the rise of nations? The case-by-case approach to explaining national identity, downplaying the connections among cases, is one reason why scholars have tended to neglect migration as a factor encouraging the construction of nations. Third, what is the relationship between nationhood and race? Since the two sets of ideas emerged at the same time and in many of the same minds, the perceptions of "race" and "nation" are likely connected.

Migration and nation

Migration is usually left out of the debates on nationhood. Yet the migration of people was central to creating the need for new identities. European settlers in the Americas, even if loyal to their European roots, developed distinctive needs and alliances that created identities centered on the lands they occupied. So also did African slaves in the Americas, even if in slave status, develop new needs, new alliances, and a vision of community development on the lands they occupied. The Amerindian populations, too, developed new identities, whether they were conquered, displaced, or required to develop relationships with new neighbors. The Cherokee, for instance, were a "nation" in the old sense that attempted to become a "nation" in the new sense. Their project, launched in diplomacy, trade, and warfare from the 1740s, continued until they were expelled from their homeland in Georgia in the 1830s. Nevertheless, the Cherokee campaign for recognition as a nation does show how the impulse to create national units was shared by people of all origins who participated in the world economy, especially in its Atlantic zone.

Even in the Old World, migration played a significant part in the development of nationhood. The French emperor Napoleon played a role in nation-building, as his conquests accelerated the growth of national identity in Germany, elsewhere in Europe, and in Egypt. Napoleon's occupation of all Europe, under the banner of abolishing feudal restrictions, was welcomed in many German-speaking territories. Then it turned into a colonial system, exploiting central Europe with viceroys just as Spain had exploited the Americas with viceroys. In response, Germans began to focus on building their own nation and on developing German culture and commerce. In Egypt, following the conquest by Napoleon and the brief period of French rule from 1798 to 1801, a campaign of nation-building followed under the regime of Muhammad Ali, an Albanian-born Ottoman official whose rule lasted from 1805 until 1848. Until his military and diplomatic defeat by Britain in 1840, he built up agricultural and industrial output, education, and Egyptian national pride, though at the expense of war and enslavement.

Race and nation

While the term "race" was rarely used in the early eighteenth century, it had become common by the mid-nineteenth century, only then it had a new meaning. Where it earlier referred to individual ethnic groups (the "Danish race"), "race" had come to mean broad physical types labeled as Caucasian, Negroid,

Mongoloid, Malay, and American. Such racial categorization developed out of migrations in early modern times, which placed peoples of differing regional backgrounds in new and close dependence on each other.

The connections between race and nationhood can be seen most clearly through the case of Haiti. Haiti was created as a nation and as a state out of its revolution. The rebellion began not as an uprising against France, but as the participation of various social classes on the island in the revolutionary upheaval of France from the spring of 1789. Eventually the slaves too joined: they rose up in 1791, dispossessed their masters, and entered an uneasy alliance with free people of color – landowners who had to give up their slaves. Toussaint Louverture, who rapidly rose to leadership in the rebellion, served as governor of the island territory of Saint Domingue under revolutionary France. But when the leader of France, Napoleon, newly crowned as emperor, moved to reconquer the island and re-establish slavery, the stakes changed. Once the French were expelled at the end of 1803, Haiti proclaimed itself as a separate state.

While Haiti was defined as the first nation of black people, it is worth emphasizing that the racial definition of Haiti was determined from without. France, under Napoleon, revoked its recognition of the equality of all humans in its decision to reimpose slavery on blacks. The Haitian ex-slaves, having fought under the banner of liberty, equality, and fraternity, now faced making a categorical rejection of whites.

Meanwhile, the use of the term "race" did not immediately and fully shift to suggest that people within each racial group were considered equals. Consider the case of Ireland. The English, in speaking of "the Irish race," used terms as negative and deprecatory as any applied to other groups. Up until the end of the eighteenth century, the Irish were not permitted to celebrate any religion other than the Anglican and had no parliamentary representation. Irish workers were accepted on English lands and in English factories but at a price of constant degradation.

This new and more discriminatory use of the term "race" – that is, one that distinguished subgroups within specific racial definitions – was applied to Jews and Gypsies beginning in the nineteenth century. Those defined as being of an inferior race were assumed not to be worthy of recognition as a nation. In the rivalry for creation of nations, these groups were considered out of the competition. Discrimination by skin color, religion, and other criteria had long existed, but now the discrimination was being justified by "scientific" argument.

Crystallization of nationhood

The emergence of national units, in the fifty years from 1780 to 1830, proceeded so rapidly that one can speak of nations crystallizing out of previous political forms. The recognition of the United States as an independent nation in the 1780s showed that the process of crystallization was underway.

France reorganized itself as a nation in the 1790s, Haiti achieved national independence in 1804, and the mainland colonies in Spanish America gained national independence in the 1820s. Further, considering in addition the many national projects that failed helps to show how far the process of crystallization proceeded. Among the failed national projects were the Irish rebellion of 1798, the failed Polish constitution of 1793, the Peruvian rebellion of Túpac Amaru II in 1780–1781, the Brazilian "Tailors' Revolt" of 1798, and the long Cherokee campaign for national recognition.

The crystallization of nationhood was filled with debate and strife. National construction is a process of inclusion, in which people are induced to join the "imagined community" and accept a common identity. But it also involves exclusion: exclusion of foreign powers and of foreign national groups. In particular, slaves were generally defined outside national groups. The Declaration of Independence of the United States, for instance, emphasized the unity of the citizens of the thirteen states but avoided any reference to slaves. At the same time, it explicitly rejected any ties with the English king and with the Amerindians. Equivalent debates arose elsewhere. Should the French nation include all people who accept its universal declaration of principles? Should slaves be freed to become citizens of Venezuela and Mexico? The Haitian government of Alexandre Pétion gave shelter to Simon Bolívar, the Liberator of South America, when he was expelled from Venezuela in 1815, and supported his second expedition in return for Bolívar's agreement to free the slaves. Most of the ex-Spanish territories did abolish slavery but often did so slowly and only in part. In the rise of nationhood throughout the world, migration remained one of the key factors in the definition of national identity, and racial distinctions – distinctions influenced significantly by migration – were equally central to national identity.

Global economy, regional migration, 1800–1900

The term "factory" changed its meaning during the eighteenth century. From a commercial depot where goods were bought and sold, it became a productive center where goods were made using machinery. Factory production expanded during the nineteenth century. Factory-produced goods – textiles, soaps, shoes, agricultural implements, then steamships and railroads – were sold all over the world. Wage labor forces were concentrated in the large and small factory towns. Migrants from the surrounding areas reinforced the work forces of the growing factories, and migrants from greater distances joined them as well.

The factories were situated close to crucial resources such as water power or, later, coal for steam power. Further resources included a skilled labor force and the accumulation of previous investments: long after the decline of water power as the motive force for factory production, mill towns remained in the river valleys of Flanders, the English Midlands, and New England, where they drew on the work forces, the machinery, and the suppliers that had been gathered there.

Factories also relied on produce from the fields and on the transportation networks linking factory and field. The global wheat market, for instance, linked productive centers on every continent. Factory owners relied on consumers who might be anywhere in the world. The rise of Lever Brothers and the English soap industry, therefore, was more than a simple story of invention and investment in factory towns. It required raw materials from the Mediterranean, West Africa, and Southeast Asia, along with a global system of transport and marketing.

In the course of the nineteenth century, industrialization changed the world economy. Migrants flocked to growing industrial and commercial cities with steel foundries, commodity exchanges, and banks, especially in Europe and North America. Similar urban centers grew in Tokyo, Buenos Aires, Bombay, and Shanghai. But an equal number of migrants moved to rural areas, working in mines and on farms producing industrial raw materials: iron ore, coal, diamonds, rubber, guano, sugar, cacao, hides, wheat, and rice. Still others moved about as transport and construction workers, digging canals, serving as crew for steam and sailing ships, operating railroads, and directing teams of animals.

Industrial economy and migration

What was the key to the development of industrial production? Inventions have received most of the attention: new technology in textile machinery, steam engines, and iron foundries. But new technology was not enough. Production could not go forth without raw materials – in wool and cotton, in minerals, or in vegetable oils for soaps – and many of these came from areas far from the industrial heartland. Nor could production go forth without markets for the output – the buyers at home in England, France, and the US, but also the buyers in South America and South Asia. Technology, capital, raw materials, and markets were all essential to the new industrial economy.

Equally central was labor. This survey of industrialization focuses on the labor that performed each industrial task. Wherever labor was needed for industrial development, workers were recruited as wage workers, as settlers, as slaves, or as contract laborers. The movement of laborers around the world in the nineteenth century provides a map of those places where labor was most needed. The question is, which were the most important destinations of migrating workers? Was it the factories in nearby cities? Was it mines or plantations across the seas? Or was it the continual shifting of workers in construction and transportation?

Consider the experience of short-distance migrants in the industrial work force. These migrants went from rural areas in Europe to European cities, and from rural areas in North America to US and Canadian cities. Typically, a small peasant landowner or a village craftsman found that acreage was too little or manufactured goods too competitive to keep poverty at bay. Such migrants were predominantly young and intent on working hard and improving their situation in their new society. Migrants to the Rhine Valley helped create the great industrial center known as the Ruhr and expanded the commercial center of Amsterdam.

On the European continent, industrial and urban growth accelerated during the course of the century and developed a steadily growing and differentiating set of regional productive systems. Milan and Prague are examples of cities that drew on their hinterlands during the late nineteenth century to become major industrial centers. Similarly, Barcelona built on its strength as a commercial center to construct a substantial industrial base. The rise of Barcelona and its wealth, in turn, brought about a development in Catalonian nationalism. Catalan, the language of the several million people living in the hinterland of Barcelona, is distinct from the Castilian Spanish that had long been the official language of Spain. While Barcelona clearly participated as a regional metropolis in the global economy, its expansion in the industrial age was also very much a story of regional migration and the development of regional identity. A distinctive regional artistic and architectural tradition gained wide attention in this era.

Of the long-distance migrants, some went to distant cities for industrial work. Such was the case of the German and Irish migrants to Baltimore and Boston. More commonly, long-distance migrants of the nineteenth century went to fields, mines, and construction sites. Scandinavian migrants went as wage laborers to farmlands in the American Midwest. Indian migrants went as indentured workers to mines and plantations in Mauritius, South Africa, Malaya, Fiji, and the Caribbean.

Migrants to Malaya were attracted by the work in tin mines and plantations of rubber and palm oil. One common form of Asian migration involved a temporary sojourn in a new country, where the migrants went to earn money that would enable them to resettle in their home village in better circumstances. More than half of Chinese and Indian emigrants returned to their homeland. This return rate varied by destination. Over two-thirds of Indians who sojourned in nearby Asia or Africa returned home, such as railroad workers in the British colony of Uganda, but few indentured servants returned from Fiji or the West Indies.

Figure 8.2 summarizes global migration in the nineteenth and twentieth centuries, with boxes showing millions of departures between 1840 and 1940 for Europeans, Indians, and Chinese, and circles showing millions of arrivals at the main destinations. African migrants are shown for the main period of the slave trade, 1650–1880, a time when travel was slower and mortality was higher. These patterns combine to show the high level of human mobility.

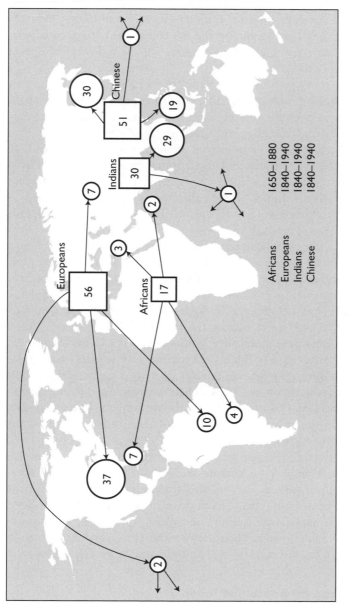

Figure 8.2 Migrations of Africans, Europeans, and Asians, 1650–1940

New technologies of transportation

Most labor migrants went to factories or fields, but a third category of laborers enabled the factories and fields to remain in contact. Of all the new technologies, the advances in transportation were among the most productive. Even where the technology of transport did not change, as with ox carts or transport by human portage, the growing commerce of the industrial age required an expanded work force.

The new transportation infrastructure included roads, bridges, wagons, canals, steamships, new port facilities, railroads, and stations. Creation of this transportation network brought demand for further industrial output for shipyards, railroad cars, digging equipment, and explosives.

In the early centers of industrial manufacturing in England, the Low Countries, and the northeastern United States, an active stage of canal building began at the opening of the nineteenth century. Canal building then accelerated on every continent. In China, the earlier centuries of canal construction laid the groundwork for a wave of expansion. The greatest engineering project of the nineteenth century was the construction of the Suez Canal, completed in 1869, which brought fundamental change to the shipping lanes linking Europe and Asia. In all these cases, canal construction required years of work by hundreds or thousands of laborers. Coming from near and far, they lived at the work site, and they had to move on when the work came to completion.

Railroad construction began in England in the 1830s, and then accelerated in region after region throughout the world until the network was virtually at its full extent by the outbreak of World War I. The United States and France were early in starting their railroad networks, but so also were Cuba and the Ottoman Empire. The Argentine railways were a particularly complete and successful regional network. Workers had to be recruited to build the railroads on every continent: Chinese workers in the western US, Indian workers in East Africa, Irish workers in South Africa, and Russian workers to build the Trans-Siberian railroad, which opened just after 1900.

Construction of these new transportation facilities and conveyances was the heroic stage; operating and maintaining them were long-term enterprises. Crews and dockworkers were needed for the steam and sail ships of every waterway. The crews of Indian Ocean steamships shuttled between Suez, Aden, Bombay, and Singapore, loading and unloading coal and commodities, and working the boiler rooms. These crews were African and Asian men, many of them slaves or ex-slaves; they were an industrial work force afloat.

New markets for goods and labor

Did the markets for industrially produced goods encourage migration over long or short distances? The markets for factory-produced textiles encouraged migration to the mills of the English Midlands and New England. However, the same markets encouraged migration of slaves to cotton-producing lands in the US, and migration of sheepherders to Australia and New Zealand.

The expanded demand for grains brought migration of farmers to the American Midwest, to Australia and Argentina, and to eastern Russia. The growing world market for rice encouraged migrations to rice-growing areas of Thailand and Java. The expanded demand for ivory – used in jewelry, billiards, and pianos – extended elephant hunting all over Africa. The demand for diamonds brought a wave of migration to South Africa. A steady rise in demand for coffee brought workers to Brazil from Italy and to northern Angola from surrounding areas.

The problem of allocating labor among all the competing demands for strong arms and accurate fingers grew steadily more complex. A world market for labor grew up, in which the differing conditions of peasants, wage workers, slaves, and serfs could hardly avoid encounters and discussions as to their relative benefits for worker and master.

Not only did the nature of each day's work change significantly, but there also was great change in the nature of relationships between workers and the others with whom they interacted. These "others" included employers, owners, landlords, governments, and still more. The struggles of wageworkers, as working classes formed in the industrializing cities, have been documented in considerable detail.

The story of the global economy

Telling a tale of world history is a complex task, perhaps particularly so for the world economy in the nineteenth century. Yet almost any product or any migration, if traced in detail, will reveal a narrative connecting factories and fields. Workers around the world faced complex changes in their conditions of employment. If heedless employers and dangerous machinery impoverished and shortened the lives of many, the rise of labor unions and community organizations gave workers new resources. Overall, while the era of industrialization brought waves of new discipline and oppression, it coincided with a sharp tendency toward emancipation of laborers. Slaves gained freedom in one country after another, serfs gained freedom to move, indentured servants gained more advantageous contracts, peasants struggled to reduce the amounts of their rent payments, and wage workers gained some recognition of their rights to organize. In all these cases, release from previous bondage made workers more likely to migrate.

The emancipation of labor was far from uncontested. Russian serfs, even after emancipation, had to apply for a passport to move. Former slaves in the Americas gained no compensation for their enslavement and encountered limits on their movement and difficulty in buying land. Chinese workers faced legal expulsion from the Americas after 1880. Trade unions were periodically outlawed or tested in long strikes. Slavery remained in force in many parts of Africa well into the twentieth century. Yet, for all these limits on the freedom of labor, migrants moved with more liberty and greater rapidity than before to every corner of the industrializing world.

New technology changed the links between factories and fields and the allocation of labor among them. The telegraph was the first technology to provide instantaneous contact among regions beyond visual contact. Governments and businesses, eager to obtain immediate news on decisions and prices in distant areas, invested heavily, and within a very few years there had been a great expansion in overland and undersea cables for telegraph communication. Those who controlled the information had new power over those without access to it. However, the lives of all were changed by the new speed of information. With quicker and (sometimes) more precise information, migrants could now undertake their voyages in more purposeful fashion, as they had a better idea of what would await them at their destination.

Empire and migration, 1850–1930

Atlantic migration in the second half of the nineteenth century took the form of millions of people leaving their European birthplaces in search of better opportunities. The size and the speed of these migratory movements were unprecedented. At the same time, a few powerful governments, mostly in these same European countries, invaded, annexed, and otherwise took control of lands in Asia, Africa, and the world's islands.

The resulting changes were demographic, political, and cultural. The distribution of world population changed, as Europeans filled many spaces in the Americas. The political map of the planet changed, as a small number of great powers took control of large territories. The patterns of the world's languages changed, as migrating families and conquering generals each took their languages to new lands.

This stream of migrants from Europe was not the only great migration of the era. Large numbers of Chinese, Indian, Japanese, and other Asian workers and settlers moved across the Asian landmass, the Indian Ocean, and the Pacific. The more than fifty million Chinese migrants equaled the number of European migrants, and the thirty million Indian migrants were not far behind. Similarly, there was large-scale labor migration within Africa and Latin America in the same period. Overall, the period from 1850 to 1930 was the most intensive era of migration in human history.

The British Empire, the dominant world power at this time, reflected the patterns of empire and emigration. Britain controlled areas known as "settler colonies" to which large numbers of migrants went from the home country: Canada, Australia, and New Zealand, as well as the West Indies. Britain also consolidated its hold on India and gained control of great new territories in the Middle East, in Southeast Asia, and in West, East, and South Africa.

Furthermore, millions of migrants moved from Britain beyond the boundaries of the empire, especially to the United States.

The cultural impact of empire and migration was manifested in, among other things, the languages of the world. English became the language of government for as much as one-fourth of the world's population. It was the native language in settler colonies and the language of government in conquest colonies. French became the official language in much of Africa, Southeast Asia, Syria, and Lebanon, and in several Pacific islands. Russian became the official language in newly conquered areas of Central Asia. Yet in the same era Chinese, Arabic, Gujarati, and Tagalog languages spread to new areas.

Empires of land, capital, and culture

This was the European era. Empire-building and migration were two major processes through which European societies – and societies based on European models – came to dominate the world of the nineteenth and twentieth centuries. What caused European migration? What caused the massive Asian migrations? What caused the new empires? Were these three phenomena connected? Tracing the answers to these questions requires thinking at different levels at once – especially at the levels of the individual and of society. Emigration is the story of millions of individuals, while empire is the story of a handful of great powers and their societies.

First, let me emphasize the empires of land, capital, and culture. Empires had risen and fallen for millennia, but this "new imperialism" brought the idea of empire to a new height. By 1920, a larger portion of the world was governed by empires than at any previous time in history. In each case, it is useful to think of the empire as consisting of a homeland and its colonies.

Empires of land were the immense new territories ruled by great powers. The German Empire came into existence in 1870 after the military defeat of France. It comprised a combination of many states in Europe. By 1885, Germany had added some overseas colonies to the empire. The British Empire, created in earlier centuries, expanded significantly from 1870 to 1905. The Second French Empire, created in 1852, was replaced in 1870 by the Third French Republic, but the term French Empire continued to be used for overseas territories. The Russian Empire conquered territories in Central Asia in the 1870s. Similarly, the United States conquered and annexed territories across North America and later took overseas territories. These were sometimes called the American Empire, but when territories were accepted into the union as states, as with California in 1850, they were no longer referred to as part of the empire.

Empires of capital consisted of home-country control of markets and productive resources in other countries. Numerous critics chose to explain territorial empire through what the English analyst John Hobson called (in 1903) its "economic taproot." According to this view, the essence of imperialism was not political conquest but the establishment of overseas economic control through export of investment funds and domination of commerce. According to this view, Latin America was part of the British Empire in the nineteenth century. By the same logic, Latin America became part of the American Empire in the twentieth century. In another example of this reasoning, Russia, with its great empire of land, was within the orbit of France, which controlled much Russian capital.

The interplay of industry and labor had much to do with the growth of empire. Debates on slavery and on economic freedom accompanied this era of rapid industrial change. Industrial growth generated a demand for labor and for migration. Industry provided improved steamships, telegraphs, and repeating rifles to imperial states. The increased advantage of the great powers in military and other technologies had much to do with the expansion of empire, and may also have had much to do with migration.

Empires of culture developed in association with the empires of land and capital. Those in the imperial heartland took on a sense of cultural superiority. They argued that the "West" and the "civilized world" were superior in accomplishment and in intellectual capacity to people of non-European countries or non-white races. In this case, culture referred not to the specifics of material or expressive culture but to an overall "way of life." The era of "new imperialism" was filled with comparisons of cultures categorized by race, religion, nationality, and language. The French spoke of their "civilizing mission" and gave great emphasis to the extension of the French language. Britain and the US, while at odds in many ways, gradually cooperated in extending the idea of "Anglo-Saxon" culture.

Emigration

Most European emigration or out-migration was voluntary, though some of it was impelled by harsh conditions at home. The crushing of European worker rebellions in 1848 and the pogroms in Russian villages in 1880–1881 each caused large streams of migration. Under these circumstances, migrants were probably motivated by a desire for political freedom, safety, and social and economic opportunity.

Migrants in mid-nineteenth-century Europe went first to nearby cities and then to areas beyond their borders. In the British Isles, migrants moved from rural Scotland to centers such as Edinburgh and especially Glasgow. Irish workers went in some numbers to Belfast and Dublin and in larger numbers to the growing industrial and commercial centers of Liverpool and Manchester. These were movements to build the family in part, but also (for those unhappy at home) movements to escape the family. When English-speaking migrants moved to Australia and Canada, they were in part migrating to build the empire. Those who moved to the United States might be seen as having left to escape the empire.

The rural population of France was comparatively slow to move, either to cities in France or to areas beyond the homeland. Perhaps the gains of the French peasantry during the revolution of the 1790s made them more content to remain on their lands. The French government was anxious to create a new empire, however: to that end, it invaded Algeria in 1830 and supported a move by Austrian Prince Maximilian to gain control of Mexico at the end of the 1850s. French settlers did move by the thousands to Algeria after 1850, but they migrated in relatively small numbers to other lands.

In 1850, what became the kingdom of Italy consisted of two major kingdoms (Sicily and Piedmont), a major republic (Venice), the Papal States, and some smaller units. An Italian consciousness had existed for centuries, but only in the mid-nineteenth century did the movement toward national unity gain real momentum. Giuseppe Mazzini and Giuseppe Garibaldi led in the early stages; King Victor Emmanuel of Piedmont was there to lead at the end, becoming King of Italy in 1861.

The movement toward national unity paralleled the industrialization and urbanization of Italy. Peasants streamed into Italian cities. At the same time, many moved beyond the newly unified Italy, to areas of North Africa conquered by France, then to Brazil, to Argentina, and later to the United States. Most of these migrants sought to build the family, in the sense that a very large proportion of the men going overseas were sojourners, who returned home once they had built up an income. Others sought to build new families as settlers in North Africa or the Americas. All of these could be said to have moved to escape the empire. In later years, a smaller number of migrants sought to build the empire, moving to Italian colonies established in Eritrea, Somalia, and later Libya. Spanish migrants, following similar patterns, traveled to the Caribbean and South America in numbers half as large as the Italians. In a different fashion, migration of Russians echoed the complexity of the migratory patterns of Italians. The emancipation of Russian serfs in 1861 gave peasants the right to move, though they had to apply for passports. Russians went first in largest numbers from their homes to other rural areas, from the Ukraine to Central Asia. Second, they moved to Russian cities, and third overseas, especially Jewish migrants to the US.

Conquests

At the same time as European migrants were changing the population of some regions, the empires of the world were redrawing the map of political power in other areas, particularly in Central Asia, South and Southeast Asia, and Africa. European empires took control of vast lands. In some cases, the conquests resulted from major battles, as in the Zulu kingdom in 1879–1880, Egypt in 1882, Madagascar in 1895–1896, and the Sokoto Caliphate in 1898. In other cases, Europeans annexed territories by treaty and later quashed rebellions to affirm their control. Small numbers of migrants from the European countries came to dominate the governments and economies of these territories. An unusual case of such imperial conquest was that of Congo, in which the King of Belgium was able to maintain his personal control over an immense territory for over twenty years.

For the Europeans, these conquests brought stories of exploration, annexation, and settlement. In part, Europeans conquered new lands in the hope of gaining control of economic resources. Sometimes it worked out – diamonds in South Africa, uranium in Congo, oil in Kuwait, tin and rubber in Malaya, and rice in Burma. In many other cases, no great wealth resulted.

For the African and Asian peoples concerned, the conquests brought episodes of resistance, assimilation, and expulsion. The conquerors seized the best lands and used taxation to force the inhabitants to work on their enterprises. As the French conquered the upper Niger Valley of West Africa in 1883, they required the slaves of the previous regime to stay in place and produce grain to supply the French army. In 1904, the slaves rose up and left, returning to their previous homes.

When the Ottoman Empire was defeated in World War I, its Arabic-speaking territories were divided among Britain and France. Britain established monarchies in Jordan and Iraq, while France ruled Syria and Lebanon directly. The establishment of British rule over Palestine, to which Jewish settlers had been coming from Russia and western Europe for decades, helped set the stage for a new conflict. In the Balfour Declaration of 1917, the British prime minister encouraged the flow of eastern European Jews intending to settle in Palestine.

In the case of the Japanese Empire, conquest and migration went in different directions. Japanese migrants moved to Pacific islands, notably Hawaii, as agricultural laborers, and then moved on to the United States, Brazil, and Peru. Meanwhile, Japan sought treaty rights in China, gained control of Taiwan in 1890, and seized control of Korea in 1910, five years after defeating Russia in a war for dominance in the western Pacific Ocean. After World War I, Japan was awarded control of some Pacific islands that had been under German rule.

For the United States, the path of migration and empire was longer and more complex. With purchases and treaties from other imperial powers, the US gained control of Louisiana, Florida, Oregon, and Alaska. Then through allying with settlers who sought to build the empire by rebellion and warfare, the US gained Texas and California from Mexico. The US also annexed Hawaii in 1893 and five years later launched its conquest of the Spanish territories of the Philippines, Puerto Rico, and Cuba. Of these, only Hawaii gained a large number of settlers from the US, and only Cuba was able to gain rapid independence.

Migrating to and from empire

Migration and conquest are two different phenomena. One is individually motivated and the other is the result of government policy – though governments can encourage or discourage migration. Why did European migration and imperial conquest take place at the same time? Industrialization – both in factories and in fields – was clearly an important factor in the timing of both movements.

But the full pattern of *causation* may be too complex to summarize in a simple statement. When that is the case, it may be easier to discuss the connections with regard to the *results* of migration and empire-building. One set of patterns is that of the movement of migrants to and from empire. People of Europe migrated, mostly, away from the empire of their own country. Migrants from Italy, Austria, Scandinavia, and Germany migrated overwhelmingly away from their empires. Migrants from Britain and Spain moved in large numbers to their colonies, but in larger numbers away from their empire. People of Asia, meanwhile, migrated mainly to empires of great powers: in particular across the Pacific or to British territories in the Indian Ocean.

The expansion of empires usually involved gaining control of lands overseas. But sometimes, as with the US and Russian conquests, the new lands adjoined the homeland. (Canada and Argentina had similar experiences.) In these cases, most settlers came from the national homeland. For example, even while Russian Jews moved away from the empire, most other Russians moved within the empire.

A second way to explore connections created by migration and empire-building is through culture. The combination of empire-building and migration created so many connections around the world that people started to generalize about culture. The nations of the West came to be distinguished from the peoples of the East. In the West, the industrial nations of Europe and North America were dominated by the white race and had parliamentary governments. In the East, the peoples of Asia and Africa were mostly dark-skinned and lived without industrial wealth, many of them under colonial rule. The Soviet Union, the workers' state that emerged from the ashes of the Russian Empire, was categorized along with the other peoples and states of the East. Latin America, while formally part of the West according to this hierarchy, tended to be neglected within it.

Thus, the combination of empire-building and migration set the scene for the divisions and conflicts of the twentieth century. It created the geographical and political categories of East and West, North and South. The two great movements of migration and imperial conquest reached a peak just after 1910 and then were nearly halted by the disaster of the Great War (later known as World War I) from 1914 through 1918.

Conclusion

Maritime connections continued to lead the process of human migration through the eighteenth and nineteenth centuries. The great migration of the eighteenth century was the forced movement of Africans in captivity, mainly to the Americas. This labor system, tied intimately to the beginnings of large-scale industry, spread through Africa and Asia in the nineteenth century as it contracted in the Americas.

British naval power, established in numerous wars with the French, Spanish, and Dutch through the eighteenth century, expanded to bring the British global preeminence in the nineteenth century. The rise of steamships and their dependence on coal, a resource then dominated by Britain, expanded both the availability of inexpensive, dependable travel and the British leadership of the sea lanes.

Already in the eighteenth century the world as a whole had overcome the shocks of initial intercontinental connections, and had begun to grow in population and economic output as human and material resources were put to work in new regions. But the migration, growth, and regional redefinition led to the creation of new identities. These included new regional and national identities for peoples – identities created in part by the nature of the regional connection to the rest of the world. And within each region, new identities in race, ethnicity, and nationhood were created out of the same process.

In the nineteenth century, all of these forces came to be arrayed together in two seemingly contradictory fashions. On one hand, this was the era of what Kenneth Pomeranz has called the "great divergence," in which the nations of western Europe and the North Atlantic came to hold aggregate and individual levels of wealth that far exceeded those of other regions, but especially the regions in South Asia and East Asia that had earlier equaled or exceeded the wealth and productivity of the Europeans. On the other hand, the industrialization of Europe, the most distinctive aspect of the great divergence, was not a matter of the growth of an isolated region: instead, the growth of industry required the movement of workers and the production of goods in every region of the world.

In the late nineteenth century, the rising power of the industrial nations enabled them to expand the territories they controlled with a series of military and political victories that left European powers governing almost half the world's population by 1920. Yet even more spectacular in the historical change of the era was the remarkable expansion of migratory movement in every corner of the world. Africans continued to migrate even with the gradual abolition of the slave trade, but their numbers came to be dwarfed by the millions of people from all over Europe, most regions of Asia, and most regions of the Americas.

As this unprecedented wave of voluntary migration expanded and peaked, a parallel move by bound laborers worked its way more slowly to completion.

This was the campaign for emancipation by slaves and serfs for freedom from their masters, for rights to move as they wished, and for citizenship in the nations and empires in which they had served. Emancipation of slaves and serfs in Europe and the Americas began in the eighteenth century and reached completion in the nineteenth century, and in those regions women and wage workers joined in emancipatory movements with claims for their own freedom. Meanwhile, the freeing of slaves and bound laborers in Africa and Asia was not complete until the mid-twentieth century.

Further reading

For a global overview of slavery and the slave trade, see Patrick Manning, *Slavery and African Life: Occidental, Oriental, and African Slave Trades* (Cambridge, 1990). On the largest single segment of the slave trade, see Joseph C. Miller, *Way of Death: Merchant Capitalism and the Angolan Slave Trade, 1730–1830* (Madison, N.Y., 1988). For slavery and the slave trade in other regions, see Herbert S. Klein, *African Slavery in Latin America and the Caribbean* (New York, 1986); Rosalind Shaw, *Memories of the Slave Trade: Ritual and the Historical Imagination in Sierra Leone* (Chicago, 2002); Hakan Erdem, *Slavery in the Ottoman Empire and its Demise, 1800–1909* (New York, 1996); Ian Hancock, *The Pariah Syndrome: An Account of Gypsy Slavery and Persecution* (Ann Arbor, Mich., 1987); Abdul Sheriff, *Slaves, Spices & Ivory in Zanzibar* (Athens, Ohio, 1987); Markus Vink, "'The World's Oldest Trade': Dutch Slavery and Slave Trade in the Indian Ocean in the Seventeenth Century," *Journal of World History* 14 (2003), 131–177; and James Watson, *Asian and African Systems of Slavery* (Berkeley, Calif., 1980). On the production and consumption of sugar, see Sidney Mintz, *Sweetness and Power: The Place of Sugar in Modern History* (Baltimore, Md., 1985). On the experience of indentured servants, see Peter Wilson Coldham, *Bonded Passengers to America* (Baltimore, Md., 1983); and Robert Hughes, *The Fatal Shore: The Epic of Australia's Founding* (New York, 1986).

The estimated rate of early modern migration from Europe is significantly higher in the work of Jan Lucassen and Leo Lucassen, "The Mobility Transition Revisited, 1500–1900: What the Case of Europe can Offer to Global History," *Journal of Global History* 4 (2009), 347–377. For further discussion of this and related issues, see the articles in the section on "Global Migration" in *Journal of Global History* 6 (2011), 299–344.

Migration refashioned the identity of migrants and those they encountered. For colonial areas, these changing identities can be traced in Carl A. Trocki, *Opium and Empire: Chinese Society in Colonial Singapore, 1800–1910* (Ithaca, N.Y., 1990); Merwyn S. Gabarino, *The Seminole* (New York, 1989); Ronald Wright, *Stolen Continents: The New World Through Indian Eyes* (Boston, Mass., 1992); I. C. Campbell, "The Culture of Culture Contact: Refractions from Polynesia," *Journal of World History* 14 (2003), 63–86; Anand Yang, "Indian Convict Workers in Southeast Asia in the Late Eighteenth and Early Nineteenth Centuries," *Journal of World History* 14 (2003), 179–208; and Peter Gray, *The Irish Famine* (London, 1995). Migration was significant in the creation of national as well as individual identities. The main studies of nationalism can thus be reconsidered through the optic of migration. See Eric Hobsbawm, *Nations and Nationalism Since 1780: Programme, Myth, Reality* (Cambridge,

1990); Benedict Anderson, *Imagined Communities: Reflections on the Origin and Spread of Nationalism* (London, 1991); and Ernest Gellner, *Nations and Nationalism* (Ithaca, N.Y., 1983). For an identity at once national and global, see Olaudah Equiano, *The Interesting Narrative of the Life of Olaudah Equiano* (Boston, Mass., 1995).

Industrial expansion transformed Europe, but the same processes brought transformation to most other regions. For regional and global migrations, and the accompanying economic changes, see Joseph Inikori, *Africans and the Industrial Revolution in England* (Cambridge, 2002); Timothy J. Hatton and Jeffrey G. Williamson, *Global Migration and the World Economy: Two Centuries of Policy and Performance* (Cambridge, Mass., 2005); Kevin H. O'Rourke and Jeffrey G. Williamson, *Globalization and History: The Evolution of a Nineteenth-Century Atlantic Economy* (Cambridge, Mass., 1999); Leslie Page Moch, *Moving Europeans* (Bloomington, Ind., 1992); Alfred W. Crosby, *Ecological Imperialism: The Biological Expansion of Europe, 900–1900* (New York, 1993); Jeffrey Burds, *Peasant Dreams and Market Politics: Labor Migration and the Russian Village, 1861–1905* (Pittsburgh, Penn., 1998); Kathleen Neils Conzen, *Immigrant Milwaukee, 1836–1860: Accommodation and Community in a Frontier City* (Cambridge, Mass., 1976); David Northrup, *Indentured Labor in the Age of Imperialism, 1834–1922* (Cambridge, 1995); Ehud R. Toledano, *The Ottoman Slave Trade and its Suppression: 1840–1890* (Princeton, N.J., 1982); and David Eltis, *Economic Growth and the Ending of the Transatlantic Slave Trade* (New York, 1987). For this era as for others, see Dirk Hoerder, *Cultures in Contact: World Migrations in the Second Millennium* (Durham, N.C., 2002).

The late nineteenth century brought the overlapping experiences of imperial expansion and expanded overseas migration. A key global summation of regional migration is Adam McKeown, "Global Migration, 1846–1940," *Journal of World History* 15 (2004), 155–189. For a major study of the British Empire, see P. J. Cain and A. G. Hopkins, *British Imperialism, 1688–1914*, 2 volumes (London, 1993). For studies of migration in the same era, see Donna R. Gabbaccia, *Italy's Many Diasporas* (London, 2000); Adam McKeown, "Chinese Emigration in Global Context, 1850–1940," *Journal of Global History* 5 (2010), 95–124; Walter Nugent, *Crossings: The Great Transatlantic Migrations, 1870–1914* (Bloomington, Ind., 1992); Oscar Handlin, *The Uprooted: The Epic Story of the Great Migrations that Made the American People*, second edition (Boston, Mass., 1973); Dirk Hoerder and Leslie Page Moch, *European Migrants: Global and Local Perspectives* (Boston, Mass., 1996); Philip D. Curtin, *Death by Migration: Europe's Encounter with the Tropical World in the Nineteenth Century* (Cambridge, 1989); Randall Packard, *White Plague, Black Labor* (Berkeley, Calif., 1989); Albert Hourani and Nadim Shehadi, eds., *The Lebanese in the World: A Century of Emigration* (London, 1992); and Wang Gungwu, ed., *Global History and Migrations* (Boulder, Colo., 1996).

Chapter 9

Bright lights of urbanization, 1900 to 2000

Human mobility, after accelerating in the nineteenth century, expanded even further in the twentieth, and shifted among types. Transnational labor migration reached a peak of three million migrants per year in the early twentieth century, fell to a lower level from the 1930s to the 1960s, and then rebounded from the 1970s. Meanwhile two great wars in the first half of the century and many smaller wars throughout the century caused millions more to flee the battlefields and seek refuge, sometimes in hurriedly constructed camps but preferably in cities. Both labor migration and refugee migration contributed to the third major type of migration of the twentieth century: urbanization. The leading human movements of the twentieth century included the expansion of existing cities, the formation of new cities, the creation of various types of suburbs within reach of the cities, and the creation of new relations with villages. By 1990, virtually half the human population – nearly three billion persons – had come to live in urban agglomerations of more than about 20,000 persons.

Even in the accelerating flows of twentieth-century movement, the underlying patterns of migration remained familiar. Diasporas, refugee flows, and urbanization each drew on the ancestral habits of humans, especially cross-community migration. Young adults were most numerous among those moving, voluntarily or not, to communities where they would have to learn new languages and customs, and where they would both learn and teach. Of course in the twentieth century the language-based communities among which migrants flowed took on new shapes. The very nature of language communities changed in that, by the end of the century, most adults could read or write some language and spoken language could be transmitted electronically almost without limit. At a larger scale and with new technology, however, the processes and results of modern migration retained a substantial commonality with earliest human movements.

This concluding chapter explores the migrations of the twentieth century through four thematic sections showing the various influences of urbanization on human life. The first section emphasizes the cultural side of urban life by focusing on diasporas – those communities of migrants around the world that retain an identity with their homeland and their common ancestry. Diasporas, and not just nations, are shown to be an important source of the flowering popular culture of the twentieth century. The second section identifies new types of political conflict, especially those known as genocide and ethnic cleansing, and shows the importance of migration in those phenomena. It provides a reminder that nations and nationalism have grown in the era of rapid urbanization, and that national identities have been expressed most strongly in the cities. The third section concentrates on the experience of urbanization for families, showing how family ties have enabled people to move from countryside to city and then from city to city. Yet while families remain strong, the very nature of family strategy is changed by the physical structure of cities and the expansion of such public institutions as schools. The fourth section offers reflections on migration's influence on identities in the present urban and global age. Not only have cities grown, but suburbs have been expanded just as rapidly and villages have gained new contact to the urban areas.

Diasporas and culture, 1880–1950

The nineteenth and twentieth centuries have been the era of nationhood and of national culture. National flags, anthems, governments, and educational systems have affirmed the integrity and destiny of one nation after another. The prominence of nations tempts us to explain the world and all its patterns in terms of what happens within these geopolitical units and the interactions between them. But the world is more than an accumulation of nations.

Diasporas, both old and new, have stretched across national boundaries, carrying their cultures with them, and consequently have conditioned the modern world deeply. Earlier diasporas from Europe and Africa did much to shape nations on both sides of the Atlantic. With the expanded migration of the nineteenth and twentieth centuries, new diasporas emerged as people left Scandinavia, India, China, and the Mediterranean countries. These diaspora communities were primarily urban, and their urban concentration enabled them to maintain their identity and the vibrancy of their culture, for instance through music, community associations, or newspapers.

In this section I will compare the influence of nations and diasporas on the emergence of cosmopolitan popular culture. During the past two centuries, culture has become more cosmopolitan – that is, it has reached across the usual boundaries of nationhood and ethnicity, expanding at both elite and popular levels. For example, the music of symphony orchestras and popular bands has crossed many national and social boundaries. With the help of translation, works of literature have spread all over the world. Motion pictures have appeared on screens nearly everywhere, transcending all limits of language and literacy. Individual architects have constructed great buildings on every continent, and Chinese, French, and Indian cuisine has come to every region.

The early twentieth century is an excellent era for exploring cosmopolitan culture, and for explaining its origins in nations and diasporas. The symphony orchestra mentioned above is a good example – it is a European form of elite culture that has spread to every area of the world. Its skilled performers move with apparent ease from city to city and from language to language. Universities, too, are European-based elite institutions that have appeared all over the world. In the nineteenth century, German, British, and French models competed for dominance. The German form, remodeled in the United States, became the most influential, and has brought about the refashioning of the older university systems in South America, the Muslim world, and China.

Cosmopolitan popular culture has created a longer list of influences than the symphonies, universities, and high fashion of the elite. From 1880 to 1950, popular culture expanded to include photographs, magazines, recorded music, films, radio, dress, sports, bicycles, automobiles, cigarettes, and various types of food and drink. The sudden adoption of cigarette smoking all over the world from 1920 to 1950 is a powerful if unhealthy example of a cosmopolitan trend.

Where does cosmopolitan culture come from? I argue that diasporas, as much as nations, have created and disseminated the innovations underlying the cross-cultural trends of the past two hundred years.

As countries coalesced in the nineteenth and twentieth centuries, leaders described their nations as the heroic unit of history, as if nations rather than individuals were the principal actors. Many citizens agreed and came to celebrate national culture in music, literature, and dress. For example, Bedrich Smetana of the Czech nation, Richard Wagner of Germany, Peter Tchaikovsky of Russia, and Edvard Grieg of Norway provided musical statements of national pride. The marches of John Philip Sousa in the United States, the mariachi bands of revolutionary Mexico, and the theatrical music of Japan also reaffirmed national identities. Nations tended to treat their national culture as having sprung from within their own boundaries. By the same logic, people saw cosmopolitan culture as having national origins: French cuisine, jazz from the US.

A broader view, however, reveals that these "national" cultural forms overlapped with each other and with diasporic traditions to create cosmopolitan cultures. Take Canada, for example. The Canadian nation developed from a precarious mix of old diasporas and new, first from the British and French and then from a wider variety of cultures. By 1950, the country had developed a vibrant cultural tradition that was more cosmopolitan than national. Diasporas contributed actively to the creation and expansion of cosmopolitan culture in other times and places as well, even when the "nation" of origin had little or no official standing in the world's eyes. For example, the people of Lebanon had little recognition of their nationhood under the Ottoman Empire or under the French Empire that succeeded it. Yet the Lebanese diaspora sustained small shops along the coast of Africa, on Indian Ocean shores, and throughout the Americas. The essayist Kahlil Gibran came as an adolescent to Boston, and then in New York he wrote *The Prophet*, a Lebanese condensation of modern wisdom, in Arabic. The book, a tangible example of diasporic culture, has since been translated into many languages and published all over the world.

Identifying evidence of cultural change

Nations are defined by present homelands, while diasporas are delimited by homelands of the past. Nations, as defined in the twentieth century, include a central government, clear borders, and citizens with a sense of national unity. Modern nations require international recognition in order to function. Ethnic groups and diasporas, in contrast, can sustain and transport their traditions without formal political recognition of their existence. A diaspora is a community that maintains contact with its various elements and that keeps its identity across great distances. Diasporas generally have no army and no government – they are held together by shared customs. Diasporas can be large or small. For example, the associations of Ibo settlers from southeast Nigeria, though parallel to the diaspora of Chinese all around the world, appeared only in cities of northern or western Nigeria during the 1930s and 1940s.

As noted earlier, nations are commonly seen as both the repository of culture and the source of cultural change. But diasporic communities also preserve old cultural practices and develop new ones – from religion and philosophy to dress and cuisine. Sometimes the migration creates mutations, so that the culture of the diaspora becomes distinct from (though related to) the national culture of the old homeland. For instance, Mexican song, Sikh religion, Polish cuisine, and Filipino dress each spread to new areas of the world in the early twentieth century, and each of these practices changed somewhat as it moved.

New diasporas: contacts with the homeland

The social and cultural structure of a diaspora originates in the homeland from which people departed, either recently or long ago. Connections with the original culture across the diaspora can be retained through oral and written history, literature, and song. The linkages sustaining diasporas include family, religion, language, occupation, and traditions in dress, music, art, and cuisine.

Recent, or "new," diasporas can easily keep in touch with their homelands through direct communication, first through travel and the mails, and later via telephones and the Internet. Families in the diaspora can also expect to receive new, young migrants from time to time, just as families in the homeland can expect to see returnees. Those who move back and forth are charged with carrying news and gifts.

Chinese migration began centuries ago, but the number of migrants after 1850 grew so large that the Chinese diaspora is best seen as new. Since 1859, Chinese governments have tried to take responsibility for Chinese expatriates, and those in the diaspora have kept their interest in the nation at home. The interaction of the Chinese homeland and diaspora is made especially clear by their twentieth-century language reform. This change, which began in earnest in the 1920s, made Mandarin the leading version of the Chinese language.

Diasporic culture can also evolve through unexpected innovations. For example, new and varied versions of Italian pizza developed in the US. Pizza pies, carried to Italy through the interplay of Italian migrants and their families at home, contributed to a cosmopolitan Italian culture. As this case illustrates, changes in the diaspora can lead to changes in the homeland when the two remain in contact.

The Chinese and Italian diasporas above underscore the importance of "sojourning," or short-term migration. The back and forth movement of people and cultural practices affects the original homeland and the diaspora. The experience of Turkish migrants to Germany, on the other hand, shows how sojourning can also create a permanent stigma. In Germany, the economic growth after World War II attracted industrial workers from other countries, particularly from Turkey. Since many of these workers returned to their home countries after a time, they came to be called "Gastarbeiter" or guest workers. As a result of this development, people born in Germany of Turkish ancestry, in part because of that label, did not qualify for German citizenship.

Old diasporas: nostalgia for the homeland

If a migration took place long ago, the tie of diasporic community to the homeland is conceptual rather than practical. The links are maintained not so much by the movements of young people as by the memories and traditions of older people. In the case of the Jewish diaspora, religious identity provided the ideal for a single community. The Jewish diaspora began with ancient dispersions to Babylon, Egypt, and Rome, followed by later prohibitions and expulsions. While family movements could keep different parts of the diaspora in contact, the only way to stay in touch with the homeland was through the imagination.

Migrants and their descendants commonly intermarried with people from outside the ancestral group. Lacking the reinforcement of new migrants, the diasporic community might fear dilution through intermarriage. Consequently, the question of membership in the diaspora was posed to each generation descending from mixed marriages: would the children adopt the identity of their mother's family or their father's? In answering this question, the conscious badges of group membership took on great importance – names, dress, religion, and even cuisine become ways to express one's identification with a diaspora. These emblems of identity also preserved the memory of the homeland. The bagel is one such emblem. It was developed by immigrants in New York but came to affirm Jewish identity so well that it was adopted by Jewish communities everywhere. With time, the bagel even became a Jewish contribution to cosmopolitan culture.

The African diaspora was another in which migrants were cut off from their homeland. Young migrants were moved in chains. Few of them could ever return home or send letters or earnings. Preserving their tie with home was a matter of memory and of unconscious preservation of tradition – for instance, through the retention of vocabulary and gestures from the homeland. Another way to preserve memories was telling stories. This tradition is well documented throughout the African diaspora. Even without new migrants from Africa, the Anansi stories from the Gold Coast remained alive in Jamaica and the Bre'er Rabbit stories of the American South preserved motifs from Senegal.

Because of the nature of their existence (as slaves for the most part in the early years of this period), segments of the African diaspora fell out of contact with one another and interacted strongly with the developing national traditions of the Americas. The ancestral African focus on popular dance contributed to many local innovations, such as the tango in Argentina, the samba in Brazil, the merengue in the Dominican Republic, and swing and the cakewalk in the US.

Two further characteristics of old diasporas are the occasional pilgrimage to the ancestral homeland and the effort to create a new homeland. For example, the movement to create a Jewish homeland succeeded when the state of Israel was formed in 1948. Of the various attempts in the African diaspora to create a new homeland, the Universal Negro Improvement Association of Marcus Garvey, which peaked around the Atlantic in the 1920s, gained the most support.

Sources of cosmopolitan culture

Culture has become more cosmopolitan with time. Yet cosmopolitan culture is necessarily more difficult to define and categorize than national or diasporic culture because it involves sharing across boundaries. As cosmopolitan culture has spread, an overlapping set of broad cultural identities has also been disseminated. The notions of "the West" and "Western Civilization" comprise a cosmopolitan culture expressed in the languages of western Europe and the traditions of Catholic and Protestant Christianity. These are both old and new identities. A cosmopolitan Muslim culture has existed for over a millennium, and a Chinese cosmopolitan culture has existed for longer. Pan-Arab, Pan-African, Pan-American, and Pan-Slav identities, however, have only developed in the nineteenth and twentieth centuries. A person from Ghana or Barbados might have both national and Pan-African identities and might also consider him or herself a part of Western Civilization.

How can one distinguish among national, diasporic, and cosmopolitan culture? The differences are clearer for specific cultural practices or products than for general cultural identities. For any cultural innovation, one may ask whether it originated in the homeland or the diaspora. In music, for instance, jazz is most easily explained as a product of a diaspora. Jazz, a range of musical forms for a small band, began most clearly as an improvisational style among African-American musicians in New Orleans. It dispersed and developed through African-American networks in the US and beyond, and its popularity spread it to musicians and audiences of every ancestry. Jazz is music of the African diaspora, but it also became music of a cosmopolitan, Atlantic audience.

For the cinema, in contrast, the national background was strongest. Motion picture cameras spread all over the world once they were invented but, particularly when sound developed, movies focused on audiences within a national framework. The film industry in the United States took off most fully, with German, French, and British industries creating their own approaches. In addition, immense film audiences developed in Russia, Mexico, and India, with smaller industries in China, Japan, and Brazil.

One of the great celebrations in popular culture is that of Carnival, which exists throughout the Catholic world as the feast before the beginning of Lent. Carnival developed most strongly in Brazil, and Carnival in Rio de Janeiro has become a centerpiece of Brazilian national culture. The celebration includes dance, costume, music, cuisine, and religious devotion. Its origin lies in the overlay of Catholic and African diasporas, and its evolution has benefited from the contributions of many other migrants to Brazil. In this and other instances, nation and diaspora intertwine in creating modern culture.

Nations and refugees, 1900–1980

Up until the advent of the twentieth century, empires continued to expand their control of the world. At the same time, nations inside and outside these empires grew in strength. World War I turned this trend around, however. Its chaos and destruction burst some empires asunder, revealing the nations within them. For example, the Ottoman Empire was reduced to Turkey, and its Arab territories became British and French colonies first and nations later. The Austro-Hungarian Empire shattered to become Austria, Hungary, Czechoslovakia, and parts of Yugoslavia. Meanwhile China, Germany, and Russia became republics, losing some of their imperial realms in the process. In all these cases, urbanization served as both a cause and a result of the transformation of empires into nations.

The people of countries proclaiming nationhood emphasized national solidarity – they displayed flags and sang anthems to celebrate their unity and claim their destiny. Unfortunately, some leaders chose to focus on the "threats" posed by peoples who lived within the nation but did not fit their ideal definition of citizen. These nationalists preached the uniqueness and the purity of their nation. As they gained power in governments, they strove to preserve and enhance this uniqueness by expelling or eliminating anyone who did not fit the mold. Sometimes the "threats" were identified as ethnic groups, sometimes as religious groups. The idea of "race" – a set of biologically distinct subgroups of humans – was widely advanced in the early twentieth century, and some leaders and national movements called for racial purification of the nation.

The era from 1900 to 1980 saw the creation of many new national governments and with it the creation of many new flows of refugees. Setting national boundaries – be they geographical, ethnic, ideological, or religious – could and did go beyond unification to become an act of exclusion, sometimes even leading to persecution. What happened in South Africa is indicative of these twentieth-century growing pains of nations. That country gained recognition at the beginning of the century, yet its policy of segregation excluded so many inhabitants from citizenship that it created streams of exiles. It failed to create a secure national unity until its dramatic effort at reconciliation in the 1990s. The South African case did not result in genocide, but similar pressures in other nations did lead to mass murder.

World War I served as a sort of turning point where movement as migrants changed to movement as refugees – people fleeing their homes for political and economic reasons. In the years before the war, most migrants made individual decisions to move for personal advantage; during and after the war, most migrants moved as members of groups identified for expulsion or oppression. At the conclusion of World War I and again after World War II, the national boundaries in Europe and Asia were redrawn to fit more closely with the nationalities. However, people were also moved, in one way or another, to suit the boundaries.

Conditions in South Africa and in every other area of the world during the twentieth century created flows of refugees. Time and again, the overriding desire for national unity led to the expulsion of minorities or dissident groups. The occasional assassinations that accompanied almost every campaign for national unity periodically turned into genocide. While the number of people executed is sometimes exaggerated, what is underestimated is how many cases of such massacres took place in the twentieth century.

The most systematic campaign of murder was the Holocaust under Nazi Germany during World War II. After the war's end brought the full realization of the horror, many observers vowed "Never again!" But mass murder in the name of the nations was not yet over. Incidents in 1965 in Indonesia, in the same year in Burundi, and in 1972–1973 in Cambodia showed that genocide still happens. When one looks at these genocidal outbursts individually, they seem so extreme as to be unique and unrepresentative. Yet the larger historical pattern ties refugee movements and genocide time after time to nationalism.

Interpreting nationalism, expulsion, and genocide

The world of the early twentieth century, like the preceding centuries, had many social divisions and cultural conflicts. These included class conflicts between workers and employers and between peasants and landowners.

Differences in race, nationality, religion, and gender were debated and sometimes fought over. Of all these differences and divisions, those driven by
nationality and race somehow gained the most attention. In the ideology of
the early twentieth century, national and ethnic divisions were seen to be the
most fundamental.

In the twentieth century, attempts were made to eliminate divisions within
countries. The techniques for unifying nations varied greatly. One strategy
for creating unity was known as "the melting pot," which suggested an
approach of mutual accommodation where the various ethnic groups would
gradually change to resemble each other. Another, somewhat different strategy
was assimilation, which required minority groups to give up their traditions
and adopt a dominant culture – this was known as "Americanization" and
"Russification" in those two countries.

The remaining approaches to ending national disunity all created refugees.
One approach was partition – splitting the state into two, as Norway split from
Denmark in 1905 and Ireland split from Great Britain in 1922. Another
approach was expulsion of unwanted ethnic or other groups – as with the Soviet
expulsion of the Volga Germans to Central Asia in the 1930s. The most
extreme approach was large-scale killing to eliminate and/or frighten off and
expel unwanted ethnic groups – in other words, genocide.

Massacres of people have taken place all too often over the course of human
history, but butchery in the service of nation-building is a recent phenomenon.
In the genocides of the twentieth century, long-time neighboring groups
turned suddenly to murder as a means to achieving national purity. The first
large-scale case linking expulsion and genocide centered on the Armenian
people under Turkish rule. In the previous century the Ottoman Empire had
experienced many conflicts as independence movements and foreign conquests
removed territory after territory from its control. As World War I began to go
badly for the Turks, who were allied with Germany and Austria, the Turkish
administration began to treat Armenians as a threat to the empire's security.
Beginning in 1915, Turkish officials began removing Armenians from their
homes and shipping them to southern areas of the empire. In the course of this
expulsion, their relocations turned suddenly and repeatedly into executions.

Holocaust

Whether led by the state, political parties, or social groups, the advocacy of
racial, religious, and national discrimination reached a kind of peak in the early
twentieth century. In the Armenian case as in anti-black racism, there were
publicity campaigns to humiliate and vilify the objects of the attacks.

None of these campaigns was so direct, however, as the campaign of
Nazi Germany against Jews. In the regime led by the National Socialist Party,
the emphasis was on constructing a nation of "pure" Germans of "Aryan" stock.
When the National Socialist Party came to power in Germany in 1933, much

of its campaign was based on removing Jews from positions of influence and from the nation. Jews were purported to be inferior, polluting the nation. The threat from the Nazis was clear, and consequently, a stream of Jewish refugees fled Germany until war broke out in 1939.

Thereafter, the millions of Jews in occupied territories were arrested and sent to concentration camps, where a campaign of genocide was carried out from 1942 into 1945. While the transportation and execution of millions was officially kept a secret, the removal of Jews from all positions of influence and their systematic persecution in the name of German nationalism was obvious to all.

Auschwitz, one of the earliest and largest of the concentration camps, became a prototype for them all. Auschwitz is the German name for a Polish village which, when taken over by Nazi forces in 1939, became the site of a concentration camp with the ironic sign, "Arbeit macht frei" ("Work makes for freedom"), over the main gate. In 1942, the gas chambers and crematoriums there were put into action.

In addition to eliminating Jews, the Nazi regime labeled other groups as unworthy of survival and executed them systematically. Gypsies, or Romani people, who had suffered expulsion and slavery in earlier centuries, lost the majority of their population in concentration camps. Homosexuals and the physically disabled suffered methodical execution, and Communists, labeled as unworthy because of their beliefs, were also sent to the camps.

The revelation of these executions, as the camps were liberated in 1945, led to outraged discussion around the world and, later, to the adoption of the term "Holocaust" to describe the events. After the war, the Allies created a war crimes tribunal at Nuremberg, which formalized the notion of crimes against humanity. The newly formed United Nations adopted a declaration of human rights. Thus, the wartime excesses of nationalism and national purification led directly to the creation of new international organizations and to ideas of human rights that challenged the sovereignty of the nation.

The horror of these and other cases of wartime executions made it easier to condemn the acts and their perpetrators than to think about how these incidents are linked to the rest of history. Hannah Arendt, herself a refugee from Nazi Germany, was one of a few to consider genocide in a broader political context. She wrote of the "banality of evil" as genocide became a routine occurrence, linking it to "totalitarianism," which she explained as nationalism gone astray. Other analysts have written of the role of rape and gendered violence in genocide.

Decolonization and mass murder

In the large area of the world under colonial rule, the era after World War II brought growing demands for self-government. The struggles to create national identities brought new levels of national solidarity, but also new divisions violence, streams of refugees, and occasional genocide. Frantz Fanon, the Martinique-born psychiatrist who became the leading theoretical proponent of anti-colonial revolution in Africa, argued that the colonial order was maintained by violent and sometimes genocidal rule, and that the overthrow of the colonizer would require a violent response. His analysis explained the French repression in Algeria and Madagascar in the late 1940s and justified the wars of national liberation in Algeria in the 1950s and in southern Africa from the 1960s. He also offered warnings about potential civil conflict in post-colonial regimes.

Fanon's analysis, though insightful, did not account for the refugee crises that accompanied decolonization. Perhaps the largest such refugee movement came with the formation of two new nations, India and Pakistan, where millions of people gave up their homes in 1947 to move across a new national border created according to religious criteria.

Thereafter, decolonization led to refugee movements all over the world. Post-colonial political struggles brought refugees from Sudan, from West Irian and East Timor in Indonesia, and from Kurdish territories. Environmental crises compounded the political: African refugees included many driven off the land by droughts that swept the continent from the late 1960s to the mid-1980s. For most of these refugee movements, the United Nations and other international organizations sought to offer assistance.

But in some cases, mass killings and refugee movements received no international response. In Burundi, factional strife turned suddenly to murder, and the wave of killing played itself out before any intervention took place. In Indonesia, an abortive left-wing military revolt in 1965 resulted in a murderous retaliation against the Communist Party and the Chinese Indonesians who were its most visible supporters. Assimilated Indonesian citizens of Chinese ancestry and first-generation arrivals were killed. Roughly half a million people lost their lives in a year, some through elimination by the military, others in riots. The hostilities underlying this outburst arose from factional politics, ethnic differences, and desires for revenge from the civil war that accompanied the independence of Indonesia from 1945 to 1948.

In the Cold War atmosphere of the time, this massive killing was hushed up on all sides. The new Indonesian regime of General Suharto spoke simply of re-establishing order. The surviving Chinese and Communists in Indonesia, having no allies, laid low. And in the US, though all leaders knew the number of people killed, virtually none chose to speak out. In this critique of the interpretations of nationalism (including anti-colonial nationalism) and how it can lead to expulsion and genocide, we need also to ask why some campaigns of persecution gain international attention, while others are neglected.

Views of solidarity and exclusion

The successes and failures of national unity are mixed inextricably. At best, nationhood provides each national society with a secure space where it can develop as it wishes. At worst, nations enable powerful groups within them to act with impunity and to expel or eliminate other groups selected for whatever reason.

The aftermath of the Holocaust led to nation-building and then to national disputes and more refugees. Zionism – the movement to create a Jewish state in the ancestral homeland – collided with Arab nationalism. The Holocaust and postwar migration of Jews heightened the Jewish determination to create a state out of Palestine, with wide international support. Yet the same region was the center of a movement, also decades old, for recognition of Arab nations in place of Ottoman, British, and French imperial rule. The results were war, the partition of Palestine, recognition of the state of Israel, and creation of a refugee population of Palestinians. As this confrontation of national movements continued for the next half-century, the United Nations and other international organizations intervened at every stage, though never with real power.

The national catastrophe of Cambodia resulted from its participation in the great twentieth-century struggles of capitalism against socialism, pro-Communist against anti-Communist regimes. The long war in neighboring Vietnam eventually drew Cambodia into the struggle. Anti-Communist military figure Lon Nol seized power and was in turn overthrown by the nationalistic and pro-Communist Khmer Rouge party. The Khmer Rouge version of nationalism opposed city life and also opposed the Vietnamese population of Cambodia. From 1975 to 1979, under Pol Pot, the Khmer Rouge emptied the city of Phnom Penh and executed as many as a million people – urbanites, ethnic Vietnamese, and anti-Communists. In 1979, Vietnamese armies stormed the country and forced the Pol Pot regime to the borders of Thailand. In a curious twist of international politics, the United Nations, with US urging, continued to recognize the Khmer Rouge as the government of Cambodia for an additional decade.

Genocide is the most extreme and repellent means of reducing disunity, but it is related by stages to all the others. Past efforts at genocide have rarely reached completion, but they shattered the affected populations, caused floods of refugees, and provoked cascades of problems wherever the refugees settled. The brutality of the events, carried out by leaders of autonomous countries, calls into question the very principle of the sovereignty of nations. Consequently, the reaction against genocide might eventually cause changes to the rights and powers of nations.

Families in cities, 1920–1990

Urbanization reaches far back into human history. The bright lights of the city have long fascinated the young and old. In the twentieth century, however, urbanization proceeded at such a rate that, by 1990, over half of the world's population dwelled in cities. Figure 9.1 illustrates urban growth around the planet by comparing the size of the largest cities in 1900 with the largest cities in 2000. More than growth of a few centers, this was a change in the patterns of human population. Cities drained the villages of inhabitants and then sent swarms of settlers into suburbs. Villages, once the core of family life, gradually became service areas for families based in cities. The strategies of families to achieve security or to advance their position changed to meet the new conditions.

The ten largest cities in 1920 had an average population of three million; by 1990, the ten largest cities had an average population of fifteen million. Furthermore, the changing pace of urbanization transformed the hierarchy of cities in the world order. The 1990 list of the world's ten most populous cities

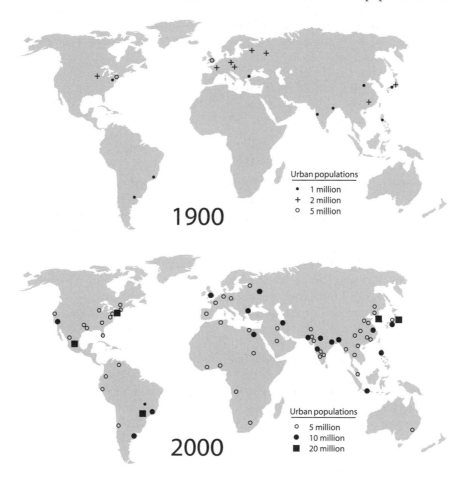

Figure 9.1 Urbanization

included only three from the same list in 1920 – London, New York, and Tokyo. The spectacular urban growth over this seventy-year period suggests that life may have changed in many ways in that time.

By the end of the twentieth century, every region had created its metropolis. The most populous cities, ranging from ten to twenty million inhabitants, were now Bombay, Mexico City, São Paulo, Jakarta, Istanbul, Shanghai, and Moscow – plus New York, Tokyo, and London. Mexico City, São Paulo, and Moscow were inland cities, while the others were seaports. Empires had largely passed and industry had decentralized, so the great cities of 1990 were centers of population, culture, and services. The cities were planned at their centers, but most were improvised at their rapidly growing fringes. Africa, though the least urban of the continents, had developed the massive cities of Cairo, Kinshasa, Lagos, Abidjan, Johannesburg, and Nairobi, ranging from two to ten million inhabitants.

Much as one may generalize about cities, each urban area developed its own character out of its environment, the character of its population, and the accidents of its history. In every case, most of the inhabitants of these cities were born in the city itself, or within a day's drive of the city. The character of each city, once established, tended to propagate itself, often in contradiction to the desires of the national government. When migrants came to a city, their first challenge was to come to terms with its personality.

Physical structure and social strategy in cities

Cities are endlessly being built and rebuilt. The physical sprawl of the cities that are wealthy and populous is daunting. New York, for example, has a population just over half that of Bombay, yet it covers four times the space of the Indian city. Though Bombay came to have an impressive center and a major concentration of wealth, its investment in roads, bridges, and buildings was greatly exceeded by that of New York. Paris, though dwarfed in population by Cairo, Istanbul, and Rio de Janeiro and equaled in population by Kinshasa, has a level of urban infrastructure that far exceeds its sister cities.

The social structure of the city is also endlessly being rebuilt. Urban society consists, first, of the familiar hierarchy of wealth and occupation: wealthy owners of enterprises are at the top, professionals in public and private service occupy the next level, followed by workers with regular employment, and then by those struggling to find work and those definitely without work. These groups can also be divided into those born in the city and migrants to the city, and into ethnic and religious groups.

I propose to explore family life in terms of strategy. Most people choose to hold on to the family they were born into and build on it. The choices on how to build the family include whether to have many children or few, whether to keep family members close together or encourage some to move, whether to invest heavily in education, and whether elders will play an important or minor role. Even those who choose to leave their family of birth by choice or through other circumstances must face the question of whether and how to build a family.

Anthropologists, who have long studied families in the village context, commonly segment their analysis of family strategies within five categories: residence, work, leisure, voluntary associations, and blood relations (meaning marriage, children, and inheritance). For life in the city, one must add at least two more categories to family life: the commute from home to work and the need for public services such as utilities and education.

Getting to the city

In the late twentieth century, many migratory paths led from the village to the city. Young males in particular moved from countryside to city to find work and bring home income. For those who established secure work in the city, and even for those who did not, the next stage of migration was to bring brothers, cousins, and wives to the city.

London, in the nineteenth century, had a large proportion of migrants, mostly from rural England and Ireland. With time, the number of births in London exceeded the number of new migrants. Yet each of the migrant communities has left its mark on the city. In the 1930s and 1940s, most migrants were from continental Europe. In the subsequent decades of decolonization, Indians, Pakistanis, and West Indians came to supplement earlier Irish and Scots. Consequently, London faced issues of racial and religious discrimination on an unprecedented scale but also gained a much more cosmopolitan dimension.

London grew at a modest rate, declined for a while after World War II, and then returned to growth. For the much smaller cities in the colonial world, the pattern was quite different. Cities such as Lagos in Nigeria and Hong Kong at the edge of China grew slowly in the interwar years, partly because governments limited access to them. Residential segregation was the norm, with separate quarters for Europeans and their servants, and modest elegance in their surroundings. During World War II, Hong Kong lived under Japanese administration for nearly four years. After the war, rapid economic growth enabled these two cities to expand at rates of 5 to 10 per cent per year, so that by 1960 each had reached several hundred thousand. The growth of cities such as these to populations of several million during the next thirty years took place at an even faster rate, in part because migration from the countryside was no longer limited.

The demographic growth of Kinshasa was even more spectacular. The city itself was an economic magnet, but in addition the difficult conditions of the Congolese countryside encouraged more people to take a chance on the city. Nouakchott, in Mauritania, grew during the 1980s to be a city of almost a million in the Sahara, with its back to the Atlantic, as cycles of drought removed people from the land. Children abandoned or alienated by their families chose to roam the streets, sometimes fitting in neatly with school children, otherwise working small trades or stealing to make a living. Through other processes not totally different from these, the other great cities of Africa and Asia reached populations of five, ten, and fifteen million inhabitants.

Living in the city

Each family, in setting its strategy for life in the city, faced the questions of whom to include in the family unit, whether to give priority to economic security or economic advance, and whether to allocate resources to parents, children, or grandparents. The examples below from Mexico City and Hiroshima show the choices made by some urban families.

Mexico City has been a great urban center for a thousand years or more, but its twentieth-century growth was nonetheless spectacular. Much of that growth came from people such as the children of Sanchez, a family from lowland Veracruz, that settled in a neighborhood known as Casa Grande in the 1930s. The strategy of this family focused on staying together and providing mutual support.

In the case of the Sanchez family, the strategy focused mostly on survival. They remained as renters, unable to buy a home, and provided basic rather than advanced education for the children. For the young adults, life centered as much on their associations with friends and groups from work as with their parents and cousins. Family members rarely visited the countryside.

The city of Hiroshima, the western Japanese port that suffered the first atomic bomb blast in 1945, presents a story of construction as well as destruction. Inhabitants of the city, after undergoing the disaster of the war and the tragedy of its long-term health consequences, resolved to take an optimistic approach to rebuilding the city and its future. Families came from the countryside to participate in the economic boom of the 1950s. The past was put in context but not forgotten: even as the city became a model of high technology, its citizens took time for public events in support of world peace.

City life requires work, including a great expense of energy in looking for employment. Work in the city is mostly for wages. The Japanese tradition of a strong state and social welfare system meant that many working inhabitants of Hiroshima had regular jobs with long-term contracts and good salaries. But even in Japan, many people were self-employed, finding incomes through providing services for those who earned wages.

Work in the city is rarely near home. The commute, then, has become a pervasive element of urban life. Whether people go to work on foot, by bicycle, by bus, train, or car, the phenomenon of the commute and of rush hour marks life in every city. On the technological side of this story are the many small changes in organization of the commute. For instance, in 1923 Tokyo's main avenue, the Ginza, became the first of any major city to have traffic lights set for automobile travel at a given speed. Another side of the story is the social – the alienation that can grow out of a long, daily commute, or the relationships that can develop in going to and from work.

Cities provided new opportunities for leisure and sport. Brazzaville, a small colonial capital in Central Africa, is an example of a city where leisure activities grew from modest beginnings to international importance. Games of football (soccer) were started up in the 1920s, played first by French officials and settlers. Young Congolese men picked up the game, and the best of them began to join the French teams and then set up their own. After hours, bars and music halls included a mix of musicians from the Caribbean with local musicians. Out of their alternations and improvisations grew the region's distinctive musical style, which by the 1960s had come to dominate record sales throughout West and Central Africa.

Changing family strategies

One way to picture the world is to treat it as an accumulation of families. Individual families grow and spread, units form within them, and new families form each generation. But family units also split, disperse, and die out. One can tell a story of the twentieth-century world through the strategies of families as they move among city, suburb, and village.

The conditions of family life have changed greatly during this century. Rates of infant mortality have declined so much that people can expect their children to live. The proportion of old people in the population has grown dramatically. And the rise in total population means that, at some level, people live in closer quarters than they used to.

The strategies of families respond to these changing demographic conditions. Migration usually makes families smaller, although a family that has lived in the city for three generations can build a multigenerational structure where older generations re-establish the control they once held in the village. If the family strategy focuses on gaining property or on building enterprises, it is likely to stay together. If the family focuses on schooling for the children, the children are likely to move away after their education.

Urban families must adjust their strategies to account for city government as well as demography. The public sector has grown greatly in the city, in comparison to villages. If people in villages follow the dictates of family leaders, people in cities have to follow the rules of public institutions as well as the rules of the family. A city requires a consensus or at least an acknowledgment among its inhabitants on how it is to function – for instance, deciding on conventions for street traffic and for the hours and nature of public service. City life requires literacy for most regular employment, so children have to undergo the socialization of the school as well as the socialization of their family. The city permits the anonymity enabling people to live their own lives, but the centrality of public services reminds people constantly of the norms of behavior.

One response is for families to seek out like-minded families: in this way, urban life encourages the formation of neighborhoods.

Those who want to distance themselves from the public norm must form private institutions. The wealthy do so by investing in private security systems at their dwellings and by sending their children to private schools. The poor do so by emphasizing mutual assistance within voluntary organizations, usually through religious groups: Catholic fraternal organizations and Muslim religious orders provide schools and self-help services in many cities.

Another way to gain distance from the public arena of the city is to sustain a link to a more private area beyond the city. This can mean reaffirming ties to families rooted in the countryside. Or, for families rooted in the city, it can mean going to the countryside for short or long visits. In an increasingly mobile world, family strategy focuses not only on how to live, but also on where to live.

Identities in a global age, 1970–2000

In the 1990s a new term, "globalization," came into use. Wherever people looked – at the economy, the environment, or their culture – they saw global interconnections, for both good and evil. On the good side, new technology has greatly speeded connections among us: telecommunications can connect almost any two voices on earth, and aircraft can move people or goods to any point within a day or two. In contrast, the shrinking tropical forest, which provides the largest portion of the world's oxygen, has become a concern to communities everywhere. Urbanization has obvious links to globalization, and so does the steady modification in relations among city, village, and suburb.

One aspect of the globalization taking place in the 1990s was corporate economic expansion. Take Coca-Cola, for example. Aggressive marketing, corporate organization, and attention to popular taste by the Coca-Cola Company sustained Coke as the world's leading soft drink. In the same era, another type of globalization, on a smaller scale, has also proved highly success-ful. Thai restaurants came on the scene in cities and suburbs everywhere. This collection of small but successful expatriate businesses reminds us that global economic growth can come without either corporate organization or a base in the US.

Is globalization new or not? Might it be true that global connections in earlier times were equally significant? This book demonstrates that there have been centuries of global connections, even if the earlier connections took place at a slower rate. The circumnavigation of the globe verified its shape; the prices of wheat, rice, and sugar have long allocated those products around the world. Even speed is not new: telegraph connections provided instant linkage to its users from the 1840s.

Arguably one can make the case that there was as much global activity in 1970 as in 2000. Student rebellions of 1968 on every continent revealed a restive young generation. The petroleum crisis of 1973–1974, as oil-producing countries cut off sales to most countries in retaliation for the attacks of Israel on its Arab neighbors, created a worldwide inflationary spiral in prices. The democratization movements of 1989–1992 were planet-wide, but so also were the networks of the 1970s aligning opposing sides of the conflicts in Vietnam and Angola. The world has changed, but one can argue that globalization is nothing new. Perhaps the difference is that, today, most people are conscious of globalization.

Forms of contemporary connection and identity

So, let us reformulate the issue. Rather than ask whether globalization is new, let us ask two questions: What changes are taking place in global connections? How do people identify their role in global connections? In discussing these questions, I emphasize two types of change in realities and in ideas about ourselves and the world. Global connections lead to convergence but also to divergence. In this investigation of connected patterns, I return to an earlier emphasis on convergence and divergence in patterns of human society – in this case in material connections and in ideas.

I have spoken in earlier chapters of various forms of connections in culture, noting that some connections are simple and one-directional, while others are complex. These categories of connections can be applied to the material world and to ideas.

In the material world, one side of global connection is the imposition of global trends on localities. Both technological advance and economic stagnation in recent times fit into this pattern. From 1970 to 2000, stereo equipment, computers of increasing power and decreasing size, and wireless communication devices spread from centers of manufacture to consumers. This growth was offset by decline elsewhere in the economy, so that working families earned no more in real terms in 2000 than in 1970, except perhaps in some Asian economies. For these types of changes, awareness of global interactions did not do much to either speed them up or slow them down.

Another side of globalization is that local populations have been able to take advantage of global trends. The Chechen people of the Caucasus seized the initiative and were able to make their local politics diverge from the global trend. Members of this small ethnic group, exiled to Kazakhstan in the 1940s, regained their homeland and reaffirmed their identity by the 1960s. As the Soviet Union crumbled after 1989, Chechen leaders relied on strong local organization, the Russian disarray, and the support of other Muslims to achieve virtual independence from Russia by 1996. Thereafter, Russian armies reconquered the region.

Similarly, ideas about oneself and about globalization are undergoing both convergence and divergence. I have also spoken in earlier chapters of alterations in identity for individuals and groups as their lives are transformed by migration and other social changes. What should one assume to be the basic source of identity? Is it one's national birthplace and citizenship? Is it religion, age, gender, economic status, work, or styles of cultural expression? Identity operates now on so many levels that it has become a matter of individual choice rather than something assigned according to national and cultural associations. Recent decades have been labeled a time of "identity politics" because of the many public assertions of and changes in self-identification.

In an unusual set of events, for example, the local population of Chiapas defined its own identity in a striking mix of local and global terms. This Amerindian population of southern Mexico supported a rebel group that followed up a brief military action in 1994 with a long political struggle against Mexico's central government. Here the small group demanded not independence but recognition within the larger nation. The Chiapas population relied on the growing consciousness of indigenous peoples throughout the Americas, in the Arctic, the Pacific, and parts of Africa. Their spokesperson, the masked and mysterious Subcommandante Marcos, relied equally on Internet communication with allies around the world. The people of Chiapas managed to avoid being labeled in local terms as a tribe or ethnic group, but spoke as citizens of Mexico and as participants in the broad movement of indigenous peoples.

Global connections and changing identities are reinforcing one another. In material connections, Coca-Cola becomes tied to the identities of its consumers everywhere, so that it is not seen as a foreign product. Yet worldwide processes bring local innovations such as Thai restaurants, Chechen independence, and the revolutionary movement in Chiapas. These successful divergences, contradicting the main global trends, then become part of globalization.

The peasants of Chiapas identified themselves not only as "Indians" or "Maya," but also as citizens of Mexico and as an indigenous people. In so doing they extended their recognition to other Mexicans and other indigenous peoples, and gained support from all over Mexico and all over the world. Groups and individuals have long asserted their own identities; what was different about the late twentieth century was that people were more willing to recognize each other's identity. While stereotyping of "the other" was still a common practice, toward the end of the century people became cautious about projecting labels such as "heathen," "native," and "uncivilized" on each other. Increased recognition of each other, much of it facilitated by migration, allowed for deeper interaction.

In grappling with the shifts in connections and identities that are commonly called "globalization," one can begin to see where these changes are taking us. Will we all become alike? Or are new differences growing among us? It seems that we will see some of each, particularly through the influence of migration. Migration brings the connections that spread innovations all across the planet, but it also brings the improvement in communications that enable people to resist or transform global influences.

One very big change is in the continued spread of a few major languages. English is the most commonly spoken language, though more people speak Mandarin (Chinese) and Spanish than English as a native language. Figure 9.2 shows Indo-European languages in c. 2000: comparison with Figure 8.1 shows how greatly these languages have expanded since 1750. English is shown separately for emphasis, with native speakers in the British Isles, North America, and Australia, and with second-language speakers in Africa and India. The other major Indo-European languages are Spanish, Russian, Portuguese, French, and Hindi. In one way or another, Indo-European languages are now spoken on most of the planet.

But other major language groups have been able to hold their own. Figure 9.3 shows Arabic, Hindi, and Mandarin, as first and supplementary languages. The regions they dominate have not changed much in the past five hundred years (compare with Figure 7.2), but their populations have grown greatly. Dialects of Arabic are spoken as native languages over a large area; Arabic is the main written language and an important spoken language in areas beyond. Hindi is the largest native language in India; it is very similar to Urdu, spoken in Pakistan. In addition, Hindi is the principal second language of India, spoken more widely than English. Mandarin, one of several closely related versions of the Chinese language, spread greatly in the twentieth century. Written Chinese is used in all of China, and functions for several spoken languages. Languages and populations continue to shift, but linguistic diversity is not likely to go away in the foreseeable future.

As global connections and new identities reinforce each other, how will the process of globalization change? For the period ahead, I believe, we can expect a mix of convergence and divergence – new similarities and new differences around the world. In the next two sections, I discuss each type of change.

A smaller world?

As communication improves, the world gets "smaller" and people in different situations find they share a common fate. Symbolic events can mark the fate that we share or that we fear. The catastrophic 1985 meltdown of the nuclear power plant at Chernobyl, Ukraine, became a symbol of a shrinking world. People everywhere, in learning of the disaster, identified with those affected by the breakdown. Nuclear power plants provided electricity but also the threat of radiation and death to all humanity. Chernobyl became a global symbol of the dangers of new technology and the ineffectiveness of big government. The Chernobyl disaster, recalling the previous generation's fear of nuclear war, pulled people together.

Another way in which the world has become smaller is in the resonant calls for democracy. In movements that surfaced in Iran in the 1970s, the Philippines and Haiti in the 1980s, and in China, plus all the world starting in 1989, masses of people have called for less governmental restriction, much more

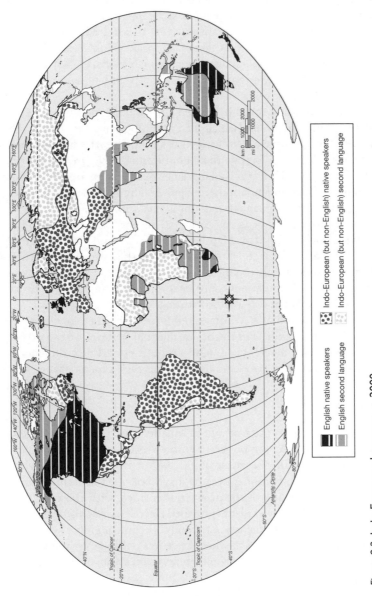

Legend:
- ■ English native speakers
- ▤ English second language
- ▨ Indo-European (but non-English) native speakers
- ⬚ Indo-European (but non-English) second language

Figure 9.2 Indo-European languages, c. 2000

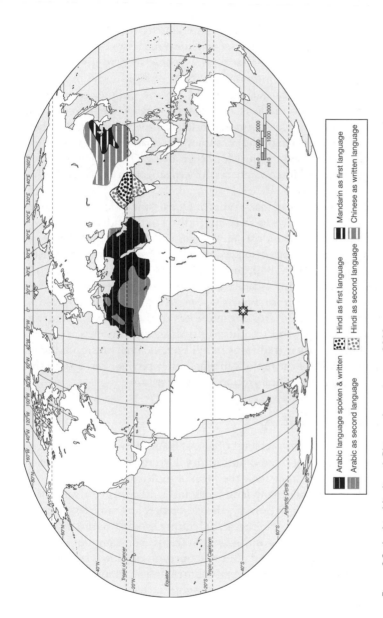

Figure 9.3 Arabic, Hindi and Chinese languages, c., 2000

Arabic language spoken & written
Arabic as second language
Hindi as first language
Hindi as second language
Mandarin as first language
Chinese as written language

freedom of speech, a voice in selecting their government, and recognition of the rights of minority groups. While at times the movements for democracy seemed to include all the people, in fact it became clear that the professional classes – students, people in the professions, and government workers – were the strongest supporters of this movement. (Of course, there also developed movements of backlash against the democracy movements.)

In interpreting this steadily smaller world, people tend to give national names to global phenomena. Commonly, instances of rapid social or cultural change are labeled as "Americanization," in the US and in other countries as well. For Americans, this term reflects a tendency to regard themselves, their lifestyle, and their culture as the norm and others as the exception. Furthermore, and more subtly, their reasoning presumes that change and development are natural for the US and exceptional for other areas. They conclude that a McDonald's restaurant in Moscow reflects Americanization of Russia rather than change for both societies.

Americanization is only one of many types of global connection. The changes of the late twentieth-century world were not limited to the radiation of power and influence from urban and industrial centers. The Caribbean diaspora, at once a new and an old movement, displayed the range of ways in which identity may be defined. From 1500 to 1850, this region received more migrants than almost any other area; by 1950, it had begun to send out more migrants than all but a few areas. People from English-, Spanish-, and French-speaking Caribbean islands migrated in growing numbers to the mainland countries of the Americas, to Europe, and to other continents, creating new diasporic connections, and linking their traditions in religion, cuisine, music, and work to each other and to those of the regions in which they settled. Perhaps, in this regard, there was also a "Caribbeanization" of the world.

The multicultural alternative

As the world grew smaller, the pressures of global connections tended to create differences as rapidly as they created uniformity. Divergence, which is always a part of global connection, now took the form of multiculturalism.

The realities of the world's many languages and cultures have always been there. But in the late twentieth century, the various groups came to celebrate their identity more publicly. For the many countries with nationally controlled press, electronic media, and school systems, the range of cultural choice available had been restricted. But the opening of global connections has led to more cultural choices in every country and in many families. As this trend developed, looking at a magazine stand or listening to a range of radio stations could give the observer an indication of the major subgroups in each region. The very ability to switch stations or to buy a different magazine helped clarify the degree to which cultural identity had become a matter of choice.

In popular music, some simple and uniform changes in technology led to a striking differentiation in musical performance. For example, the electric guitar, popularized in the 1940s in the US, spread rapidly to all the areas where guitars were in use — that is, to most of the world. Consequently, each local style of music developed an electrified version. Then the development of more accessible systems for recording and playing back music — 45 rpm records, reel-to-reel tapes, cassette tapes, and CDs — spread each of these types of popular music and promoted their interaction.

Music became specific to each community, though individuals now listened to music of several types. Musical preference became a statement of identity — by ethnicity, diasporic ties, and sexual preference — and especially by age group. Age groups became increasingly important in late twentieth-century identity, and they showed up with particular clarity in musical tastes.

The communities and the ideas of Buddhism provide another view of changing identities. Buddhism, being at once a set of organized religious communities and a tradition of philosophy, is free to expand both by the migration of its communities and by the work of its teachers. Migrations from Southeast Asia have spread the communities; the search for inner peace in an increasingly tense world has spread the philosophy even further.

In a rather different pattern, Pentecostal Christianity continues to spread all over the world. Its first churches emerged in the nineteenth-century US, drawing on both African and English traditions of Christianity, emphasizing a basic Biblical text, access to God through spiritual expression, and a conservative political agenda. Through the work of freelance preachers, it grew in many parts of the Americas, in Africa, and in Russia. With few corporate ties and no large organizations, this movement of religious faith gathered adherents across distances and language barriers.

Connecting identities

Who, then, adopts a global identity? If globalization and global consciousness are closely related, then perhaps a growing number of people identify themselves as "humans" or "people," or "citizens of the world." And if so, is that identity in addition to or a substitute for a national or ethnic identity?

The revolutionary activist Thomas Paine labeled himself a "citizen of the world" in the eighteenth century, though he traveled little further than Great Britain, the United States, and France. One may ask whether, after two more centuries, the term "citizen of the world" has become more meaningful. There exists no global government to convey citizenship or issue global passports, so becoming a citizen of the world still involves adopting an idea rather than assuming a legal status.

The answer to who adopts global identities seems to lead in two directions. On one side, many people adopt global and cosmopolitan identities, yet without cutting their local ties. On another side, many people acknowledge the growing global connections but focus on reaffirming their own, local identity. The expansion of global connections leads at once to greater toleration and to new types of intolerance.

Among the important changes in identity in recent times has been the assertion of rights by women and children. Women now have achieved formal citizenship and legal equality in most societies. Children, in various ways, now claim the rights of citizens: it is difficult to grant them full rights, but impossible to deny them recognition. Growing recognition of the rights of children is changing the functioning of many families.

One of the most striking ventures in changing identities during the 1990s was South Africa's Truth Commission, more fully known as the Truth and Reconciliation Commission (TRC). After South Africa's century of racial and ethnic exclusiveness, police repression, and war, the commission was an attempt to create a "new nation." The commission, in its public hearings, relied on fact-finding, confession, and forgiveness as a way to create emotional ties among the larger group. The work of the commission could not create uniformity: for instance, most South Africans had to listen to translations in order to understand parts of the proceedings. But the TRC acknowledged and renounced the hatreds of the past and offered a shared space for discussing them. In so doing, it created a new national accommodation within which the various communities could develop and overlap. Sharing the experience of their past, even from conflicting perspectives, tied South Africans together.

The TRC appears as a national institution working within a national context. But in reality, there is a great history of migration and connection behind it. It began with the migration of people of all backgrounds to South Africa as settlers and away from it as refugees. It continued with international connection among those calling for an end to the apartheid regime. The very idea of the Truth and Reconciliation Commission migrated from Chile and other countries, where it had been developed earlier.

Conclusion

Despite all that changed in the course of the twentieth century, some old patterns remain visible. Human populations, though overcrowded by unprecedented growth, still congregate along the waters. As lands and waters are each polluted by the intensity of occupation, we seek new resources in both directions. One difference is that we have gained access to the air. With the development of air transport and rapid ground transport, the rivers and seas are not much used for transporting people, but remain significant for moving goods.

Of the young people in each generation, some still leave their homes and settle, for short times or long, in communities where they must learn new customs and new languages to get along. For tiny communities these moves need not cover great distances. But some language communities have become so large – containing scores of millions of people – that the meanings of cross-community migration and home-community migration are changing. Still, even if the geographic scope of our movements has expanded, the basic nature of our habits remains unchanged. It is always of interest for some people to move to a different community, and the work of learning new languages and customs brings as a dependable by-product the development of new ideas.

In our long history, humans have relied on the habit of youthful, cross-cultural migration to serve many purposes. In an important and innovative application of an old pattern, young adult students travel for higher education. They leave home and settle for schooling at short or long distances away. They learn new cultures and new languages – spoken and written languages, but also the specialized languages of academic disciplines. In the course of their interactions with other migrants and with locals, they learn new ideas and convey their own ideas to others. Brand new ideas come out of these exchanges. After a time, the migrants choose among various paths: they can return home with new accomplishments, stay on to live in the environment in which they have settled, or migrate again to a further destination. Thus the institutions of higher education, perhaps the most productive source of knowledge in the modern world, rely heavily on one of the oldest and most basic human habits.

Cities have become the habitat of most of us, and the cities of the world resemble each other more and more. It has become logical and practical for us to think of ourselves, for many purposes, as part of a single, global community. Is globalization therefore causing convergences in human experience that overwhelm the forces that brought differentiation in the past? Are we all destined to become alike? One way to get an insight into this question is to look beyond the macro-changes of globalization and consider the micro-level interactions that compose the larger patterns. The migrations of individuals and groups across community lines have tended to bring about both: some innovations made communities differentiate from each other; other innovations make communities converge. Perhaps both trends will continue.

Language communities remain significant. Even accounting for the remarkable predominance of English today – the native language for nearly half a billion and a second language for millions more – the range of language communities remains significant. The differences of language remain, as they have always been, a strength as well as a limitation. If we all came to speak a common language and shared a single culture, we would lose what has been a fundamental source of human innovation: the effort and the results of learning new languages and new customs.

Further reading

The concept of diaspora can be applied to many times and places, but it is especially relevant to the migratory communities of the early twentieth century. The best general introduction is Robin Cohen, *Global Diasporas: An Introduction* (Seattle, Wash., 1997); other important studies are Stéphane Dufoix (trans. William Rodarmor), *Diasporas*

(Berkeley, Calif., 2008); Rainer Bauböck and Thomas Faist, eds., *Diaspora and Transnationalism: Concepts, Theories and Methods* (Amsterdam, 2010). Three exemplary diaspora studies are Donna Gabaccia, *Italy's Many Diasporas* (Seattle, Wash., 2000); Jack Chen, *The Chinese of America* (San Francisco, Calif., 1980); and Victor A. Mirelman, *Jewish Buenos Aires, 1890–1930: In Search of an Identity* (Detroit, Mich., 1990); see also Takeyuki Tsuda, ed., *Diasporic Homecomings: Ethnic Return Migration in Comparative Perspective* (Stanford, Calif., 2009). For the diasporic life of a widely read writer, see Robin Waterfield, *Prophet: The Life and Times of Kahlil Gibran* (New York, 1998).

The twentieth-century expansion of nationalism tended to bring claims to national purity, and then to creation of streams of refugees and, at worst, to genocide. A good overview of refugee life by a human rights activist is Judy A. Mayotte, *Disposable People – The Plight of Refugees* (Maryknoll, N.Y., 1992). Many Armenians experienced lives of exile after 1915, as documented in David Marshall Lang, *The Armenians: A People in Exile* (London, 1982). For people of Southeast Asia, conditions of migrants and minorities changed repeatedly, as shown in Mary F. Somers Heidhues, *Southeast Asia's Chinese Minorities* (Hawthorn, Australia, 1974). Danuta Czech provides details of Nazi Germany's most notorious extermination camp in *Auschwitz Chronicle, 1939–1945* (New York, 1990) and Hannah Arendt considers the wider implications of genocide in *Eichmann in Jerusalem: A Report on the Banality of Evil* (New York, 1963). See also Robin Cohen, *Migration and its Enemies: Global Capital, Migrant Labour, and the Nation-state* (Aldershot, UK: Ashgate, 2006), and Richard L. Florida, *The Rise of the Creative Class: And How It's Transforming Work, Leisure, Community and Everyday Life* (New York: Basic Books, 2004).

The movement of families to cities changed patterns of family life everywhere, but particularly in such immense and rapidly growing cities as São Paulo, Cairo, and Mexico City. For accounts of families in these cities, see David St. Clair, translator, *Child of the Dark: The Diary of Carolina Maria de Jesus* (New York, 1962); Homa Hoodfar, *Between Marriage and the Market: Intimate Politics and Survival in Cairo* (Berkeley, Calif., 1997); and Oscar Lewis, *The Children of Sanchez: Autobiography of a Mexican Family* (New York, 1979). For a critical and insightful view of Los Angeles at the end of the century, see Mike Davis, *City of Quartz* (New York, 1990). For contrasting views of urban life, see Anne Power, *City Survivors: Bringing up Children in Disadvantaged Neighbourhoods* (Bristol, 2007) and Edward L. Glaeser, *Triumph of the City: How our Greatest Invention Makes us Richer, Smarter, Freer, Healthier, and Happier* (New York, 2011); see also William J. Wilson, *When Work Disappears: The World of the New Urban Poor* (New York, 1996).

For two broad and useful statements on globalization, see Jürgen Osterhammel and Niels P. Peterson (trans. Dona Geyer), *Globalization: A Short History* (Princeton, N.J., 2005) and David Northrup, "Globalization and the Great Convergence: Rethinking World History in the Long Term," *Journal of World History* 16 (2005), 249–267. For a debate on the origins of globalization, see Kevin H. O'Rourke and Jeffrey G. Williamson, "When Did Globalization Begin?" *European Review of Economic History* 6 (2002), 23–50; and Dennis O. Flynn and Arturo Giráldez, "Path Dependence, Time Lags and the Birth of Globalisation: A Critique of O'Rourke and Williamson," *European Review of Economic History* 8 (2004), 81–108.

Appendix
Migration theory and debates

Patrick Manning and Tiffany Trimmer

What starts migration? What sustains it? What causes it to cease? Who migrates and who stays? What are the benefits of migration for those in the lands of departure, for those in the lands of destination, or overall? What problems does migration cause? These are the questions we review in this appendix.

This book has emphasized the continuity of human migration over our long history. It emphasizes the similarity of processes and functions of migration across time and space. While most of the theories of migration have focused on streams of migration within the past century, we seek in this appendix to show that migration theory can be applied to all of human history. For that purpose, migration must be described and defined in a way that is at once general and precise. The theories and debates discussed in this appendix address how to understand migration, how to research it, and how to write it up.

Descriptive framework and general theory for migration

The framework for the study of migration, as presented in this section, begins with a basic definition of migration and extends to identifying the elements of migration—the limits of the topic and the types of questions we should ask about it. In addition, this section briefly states a general theory of human migration. The next section discusses specific theories of migration, focusing on the dynamics of migration within the framework we define here.

Migration, in simplest terms, is movement from one place to another. Human migration shares some characteristics with that of other species, but it has its own character: it is determined less by biological necessity and more by social choice than for other species (Dingle 1996). More specifically, human migration is movement from one place to another and from one social context to another. By "social context" we usually mean community, where the limits of communities are defined especially by language but also by residence, ethnicity, and customs. Customs include cultural but also technological, social, and economic ways of living. A community, in turn, inhabits a certain habitat:

a habitat, for a human community, is a space in which people live with a given language and set of customs. Movement from one end of a habitat to another— for marriage or work – is best defined as mobility but not migration. Migration is movement from one human habitat to another (Manning 2006a). These definitions are intended to be valid for human societies of every type.

Migration may be seen as an event—the single step of movement from one place to another—but when it is scrutinized more closely it appears as a complex process, consisting of a sequence of smaller steps in the migratory process. The steps of migration include the selection of migrants, the preparation for their departure, the act of departure, the adjustment of the home community to the departure of migrants, the process of migrant travel (which may be eventful and may include several stages), the arrival in the region of settlement, initial reception of the arrivals, the more gradual process of incorporation of the migrants, and the adjustment of the destination community to the migrants. Still later stages can include successive displacement by the migrants or, if they remain in the region of settlement, generational change in the migrant community and its offspring.

Whether treated as event or process, migration includes several types of participants: not only individual migrants but a variety of social groups to which migrants belong or with whom they interact. The most notable groupings are by age and sex: that is, young adults are more likely to migrate than any other age group, while males and females commonly have sharply different migratory patterns. Whenever possible, studies of migration should pay attention to the age and sex of migrants. Other social groupings of importance in the study of migration include the community of departure, the migrants themselves, and people who facilitate or regulate migration (such as recruiters, transport workers, suppliers of resources, and border guards). Still other groups include the reception community, settlers, and the second generation or offspring of settlers and their local or migrant mates. Still more roles that one can identify among participants in the migratory process distinguish between movers, non-movers, former movers, future movers, return migrants, facilitators, employers, captors, sojourners, invaders, and colonists.

Migration must also be situated in space and time, and both space and time each have multiple dimensions. The spatial framework for study of migration includes such levels of aggregation as local, enclave, national, transnational, and comparative. Other spatial terms relevant to migration are colony, metropole, and zones of departure, transit, and arrival. Furthermore, the steps of the migratory spatial progress take place along trajectories. The simplest trajectory is one-way migration, in which the migrant moves from homeland to destination, although this movement may involve several stops along the way. In two-way migration, the migrant moves to a destination and, sooner or later, returns home—again with the possibility of stops along the way. In addition, migrants traveling from one point to another may proceed along several different paths, with resultant influence on the overall process.

The temporal framework includes several ways of looking at time. One may identify the absolute time of migrations, as with years of departure or periods of calendar years in which migration is studied. One may also consider the seasonal or generational variations and cycles in migration. Further, one may study the processual time for the unfolding of a single voyage or for a large-scale migratory movement, from start to finish. In world-historical terms, one can ask how the patterns of migration have changed over the millennia. On a slightly more localized scale, one may ask how long a certain social organization of migration may continue. That is, it seems that flows of migrants along a single trajectory rarely last more than half a century without undergoing some major revision.

When the analysis of migration gets more specific than basic definition and specification of time and space, it must address social institutions, social networks, and dynamics of social interaction. While some individuals may migrate as wanderers, moving unassisted, most migration takes place with the support of institutions and networks. Any large-scale migration requires organized social behavior to support it, in order to provide transportation services, nourishment, information, and more. Here we distinguish between relatively formal social institutions and informal social networks. Institutions include transportation firms, borders that separate political units, passports that assist individuals in crossing borders, mines and plantations relying on migrant laborers, and the military organizations which have tended to send young men away from home to prepare for warfare. These institutions may exist for other reasons, but they bring structure and regulation to migratory flows. Migrant networks, in contrast, are here defined as personal inter-connections that facilitate migration. Because migration fluctuates in volume and direction, the social structures that sustain it tend to be impermanent and *ad hoc*; their mutability makes them an integral part of the migration process. Families can sustain migration through "chain migration" of successive family members. Generalizing more broadly, we may say that networks of migration facilitate many human movements. In recent times these include employers, recruiters, transportation workers, regulatory officials, and suppliers of sustenance for travelers.

The dynamics of social interaction that cause and influence migration are of many types. The academic world has set up a disciplinary framework for study of such social interactions. The disciplines of history, economics, demography, sociology, political science and anthropology each focus in characteristic ways on aspects of migration. In fact the subject matter and approach to migration analysis in each of these disciplines vary widely. To give some idea of the range of disciplinary patterns, here are some characteristics and one arena of work for migration studies within each of these disciplines. For historians, migration data are collected widely. One of the important areas in which historians have led in migration studies is that of the Atlantic slave trade: since 1970, historians have scoured shipping records and coastal archives to trace the number of people enslaved in Africa and carried across the Atlantic to the Americas, as well as in other directions (Curtin 1969; Eltis *et al.* 2009). As they have done so, they have focused upon the age, sex, origins, destinations, occupations, and lifespans of the enslaved. Economists have worked especially on North Atlantic migration, tracing the rise and fall of migration in response to prices, wages, and incomes on both sides of the Atlantic (Thomas 1954; Hatton and Williamson 2005). They have emphasized wages, cost-benefit, risk, human capital, target income, remittance and occupation, and summarized these ideas through notions of push and pull. Demographers tended for a long time to avoid study of migration: their system of analyzing rates of birth and death was complicated when migrants changed the size of the base population. But the development of spreadsheets made calculations easier, so that from the 1980s demographers entered migration studies in a big way, especially in analysis of the largest migrant flow of the time, that of workers moving from Mexico to the United States (Massey *et al.* 1993). Demographic analysis focused on age and sex composition, birth and death rates, migrant flows, family size, gender balance, and life cycle. The "mobility transition" thesis of geographer Wilbur Zelinsky proposed a sharp nineteenth-century expansion in migration as central to the rise of modernity in Europe (Zelinsky 1971; Hochstadt 1999; Lucassen and Lucassen 2009). Sociologists have a long tradition of analyzing migration, focusing especially on studies of how immigrant communities are incorporated into the nations they migrate to (Portes and Böröcz 1989). Political scientists analyzed how national sovereignty shaped migrants' prospects for attaining political rights, especially in terms of acquiring citizenship or refugee status—or being labeled "illegal." Anthropologists have focused almost as much on emigrating communities as sociologists have focused on immigrants (Brettell and Hollifield 2000). One more important discipline is that of public administration. For reasons having to do with public policy rather than academic research, state officials collected migration statistics for administrative or political purposes, e.g. slave trade monitoring and abolition, labor recruitment, taxation and influx control (Willcox and Ferenczi 1929). In some cases these data were helpful in addressing the policy questions that elicited their collection. In any case, scholars may use these data for further review of the issues. In addition, such other disciplines as genetics, linguistics, and chemistry have value for study of migration, especially in situations without states or written documents.

Finally, the social scale of analysis must be considered for all the elements identified above—for migration's definition, stages, participants, its place in space and time, and its social dynamics. The social scale of analysis may range from the individual to the global. That is, the stages may be broken into sub-stages; the participants may be considered at individual, household, community, regional, or macro levels; the space and time of analysis may range from the localized to the large scale; and social dynamics may range from individual interactions to long-term social change. Commonly, quite different

Interestingly, it was study of the earliest migrations of our species, where detailed information is scarce, that led to development of the most general theory of migration now available. In a wide-ranging overview of early human history it became clear that migration was a recurring if highly variable phenomenon. At a species level, migration theory can address the reasons for human migration and the benefits and problems that arise from the practice of migration. The first chapter of this book develops a classification of four types of human migration (home-community migration, colonization, whole-community migration, and cross-community migration); it also develops a theory of cross-community migration based on movements among language communities. For further details on the latter, see Manning 2006a and Manning 2006b. This general framework for the study of migration emphasizes the underlying benefits of cross-community migration for human society. The particular forms of cross-community migration have changed significantly, especially in the last five centuries, as societies have grown and undergone transformation (Lucassen and Lucassen 2009; Lucassen and Lucassen 2011). This combination of general and specific analysis of migration suggests that there is more to be learned from comparing studies of migration in earlier times with analysis of current migration. Early migrations are important in the formulation of migration theory because they show that migration is recurrent and fundamental, if uneven. Stories of early migrations show that migration recurs not only because of the social or institutional specifics of a given society but also because of deep and underlying processes and motivations that make themselves felt in every human society. Analyses of migrations in the last couple of centuries, attentive to details and mechanisms, may in turn help us infer more of the specifics of early migration. We turn next to a review of specific theories of migration as they have developed over time. In some ways newer theories replaced the older ones; in other ways the new theories added to areas that had been neglected, addressing areas of the multidimensional migratory grid that had not yet been explored.

Specific theories and theorists

Formal theorization of migration rose as part of the broader emergence of social sciences in the late nineteenth century, and gradually expanded its range and its precision. The organized study of migration began especially with the work of E. G. Ravenstein, the German-born civil servant in Victorian Britain who collected British and European migration statistics and proposed several "laws of migration" in two influential articles (Ravenstein 1885, 1889). His "laws" included the following:

- most migrants only proceed a short distance, and toward centers of absorption
- each main current of migration produces a compensating counter-current

- the natives of towns are less migratory than those of the rural parts of the country
- females are more migratory than males.

Ravenstein's "laws" were limited in many ways to the specific conditions of nineteenth-century Europe, yet they showed insight into community patterns and processes of migration that later underwent more thorough analysis.

Social scientists in the early twentieth-century United States sought to understand the social and economic consequences of high-volume immigration, largely focusing on receiving societies. These scholars framed migration as a process that altered both the individual and the community. Examples included analyzing immigrant identity formation and the prospects for assimilation into white Protestant culture (Park and Miller 1925), the nature of connections between immigrants and their home communities (Thomas and Znaniecki 1918), and how the process of immigration shaped households' spending and saving habits (Breckenridge 1921). Sociologists in particular carved out a disciplinary niche by describing the ways that existing cultural fabrics might be altered by large-scale immigration (Brown 1933). This early theoretical work on how the cultural constraints of the receiving society could set parameters for immigrant identities and behavior would be expanded later in the twentieth century. In general, these studies focused on individuals within communities, especially within societies receiving migrants.

Other analysts sought answers at aggregate levels. In the United States, following a formal senate inquiry, the Dillingham Commission released forty-two volumes of immigration-related statistics and testimony in 1911–1912. Topics included immigrant working conditions in various industries, immigrant banking operations, investigations of conditions in steerage sections of transatlantic ships, the performance of immigrant children in public schools, comparative compilations of immigration statistics for other nations, and even a "Dictionary of Races or Peoples." A political scientist and an economist from the commission also published a survey text, *The Immigration Problem*, to make the data even more accessible to policy-makers and the general public (Jenks and Lauck 1911). Two decades later, the International Labor Organization and the US National Bureau of Economic Research co-published a compendium titled *International Migrations* (Willcox and Ferenczi 1929). It offered detailed statistical portraits of the nations and empires that had become sources of emigration in previous decades, as well as those that had become immigrant destinations. A second volume, *Interpretations*, collected nineteen essays by social scientists seeking to explain the broader socioeconomic and political dynamics driving early twentieth-century immigration and emigration "currents" linking the Americas, Europe, and Asia (Willcox 1931). Access to migration statistics in a concise, comparative format furthered discussion about which regions of the world were zones of emigration and which were zones of immigration. Sociologists and demographers turned their attention to theorizing how certain global "danger spots" of overpopulation and economic inequality—primarily China, India, and southeastern Europe—resulted in high levels of out-migration (Thompson 1930; Dennery 1931; Taft 1936; Davie 1936). These attempts to theorize causal relationships linking "sending" and "receiving" societies would again become prevalent with the advent of migration systems approaches in the late 1980s and 1990s.

Historians generally avoided explicit theorizing about migratory patterns, yet did express analytical priorities. In 1927 Marcus Hansen lamented how contemporary scholarship tended to treat migrants as "individual atoms" who broke away from one community and attached themselves to another. He advocated closer investigation of immigrant community organizations ranging from newspapers to parochial schools and farmers' cooperatives, which could be used to explain how individual migrants maintained ties to home and receiving societies (Hansen 1927). Historical studies periodically evaluated migrants' emotional and financial ties with home communities and the ties they built in their new homes. From the 1950s until after 2000, historians moved from categorizing immigrants as "uprooted" to "transplanted," then subsequently came to acknowledge the possibility that immigrants maintained links among multiple communities via seasonal and return migrations. Recent studies have also situated migrants' prospects for maintaining long-distance ties within the broader political and economic currents influencing both sending and receiving societies (Handlin 1951; Bodnar 1987; Wyman 1993; Gabaccia 2012).

From the 1950s economists fit migration into a macroeconomic analysis of economic growth (Thomas 1954). Neoclassical macroeconomic theorists posited that regions with less economic development and an oversupply of labor would become emigration zones; regions with a demand for labor and a developed economy would experience immigration. Wage differentials between regions of labor surplus (low wages) and labor demand (higher wages) drove migrants from sending to receiving societies. This "push-pull" relationship, initially centered on the relations among labor markets in an individual nation, was subsequently applied to international migrations (Lewis 1954; Todaro and Maruszko 1987). Building on the logic of the "pull" factor of labor demands in developed economies, but discounting the "push" of low wage rates and unemployment in regions of out-migration, Michael Piore introduced the theory of dual (or segmented) labor markets in 1979. In his theoretical model, the structural demand for low-skilled laborers generated by advanced, industrial economies is the exclusive cause of international migrations (Piore 1979).

Also firmly anchored in receiving societies were sociological theories on the formation of "ethnic enclaves" and "reception contexts." These theories concentrated more on localized communities than on receiving societies overall. In contrast to economic focus on wage rates and labor demands, these sociologists emphasized forms of cultural collaboration among co-ethnics in immigrant communities. Within these ethnic enclaves, established business owners employ recently arrived co-ethnics in an exchange that is theorized to be mutually beneficial (if not entirely egalitarian). In exchange for accepting the wages and employment terms set by enclave businesses, new immigrants benefit from the cultural protection of the enclave and the accumulated information about how to survive in the host community where prior waves of co-ethnic immigrants have already accumulated. Owners of businesses located in these enclaves gain access to a stream of cheap and relatively cooperative laborers which is assumed to give them an advantage over business competitors located outside the enclave (Portes and Bach 1985; Light and Bonacich 1988; Portes and Zhou 1992; Light and Bhachu 1993). In this light, successive waves of immigrants can benefit by drawing upon each other's physical, economic, and cultural capital.

A related theoretical notion, that of contexts of reception, embeds the ethnic enclave within broader dynamics of the receiving society (Portes and Rumbaut 1996). Reception context theorists argue that three interrelated dynamics shape an individual's prospects for incorporation into the society in which they settle. These are the political climate of the host nation (passively or actively in favor of immigration), the status of the labor market (open, neutral, or discriminatory), and the degree of economic diversity within their ethnic enclave (possible existence of entrepreneurs and professionals in addition to low-skill laborers).

Economists working at the micro level have tended to study individual behavior through an assumed rationality rather than through social context. Neoclassical microeconomic theory seeks to articulate the human-scale calculations that might shape migratory decisions. Microeconomic theorists, emphasizing rational-choice decision-making models rather than structural conditions of sending societies or labor markets more generally, argued that prospective migrants make cost-benefit calculations about potential earnings and productivity abroad based on their existing skill set and the costs of traveling abroad and finding work. Intellectual and emotional costs such as adapting to a new culture, learning a new language, and negotiating separation from their home communities are also theorized to be integral to the migrant's decision-making process (Todaro 1969; Todaro and Maruszko 1987). This theoretical approach, while affording some measure of human agency, leaves the individual migrant disconnected from his or her household or community contexts. In response to this concern, the "new economics of labor migration" approach addressed the issue of how migratory decisions intersect with wider family-level economic factors. Here, theorists posited that members of households collectively develop income-earning strategies which include the long-distance emigration of selected family members (Stark and Bloom 1985). Thus several related questions—who emigrates, who remains behind, how long emigration is expected to last, and how to allocate earnings from migration—are theorized to be determined within the wider cultural structure of the family and subject to its hierarchies of gender, age, and social status (Pessar 1999). Within the "new economics" approach, reasons for considering emigration can include minimizing risk during times of economic uncertainty or even perceptions that relative to other households in their community, not pursuing emigration would put a family at an economic disadvantage. This theoretical premise, known as relative deprivation, further grounds the prospective migrant and his or her family members within broader, community-wide socio-economic contexts (Stark 1992; Faist 1997). Similar questions have been investigated in the discipline of history through the construct of the "international family economy," which also employed the language of rational choice and analysis of wage rates and costs of living at home and abroad (Gabaccia 2000).

Theories developed in the 1990s sought, in various ways, to incorporate additional elements of migration. For instance, the emphasis on relationships between less-developed and more-developed regions of the world influenced sociologists' theorizing about why migration occurs. Extrapolating from the tenets of world-systems theory, in the 1980s–1990s scholars developed a set of assertions based on the argument that international migration results from core regions exerting influence over resources (including human labor) and land in peripheral regions (Sassen 1988; Massey 1999). A more concrete version of this relationship between sending and receiving regions (known as Migration Systems theory) also came to prominence in the 1990s, although it traced its origins back to the field of geography, rather than sociology (Mabogunje 1970). These theorists argued that relatively stable migration flows and counter-flows between sending and receiving regions resulted in identifiable geographic structures they labeled as "migration systems." Also helping to hold these systems intact were flows of information, capital, and material goods—the valuable commodities which permitted migrants to identify prospective destinations or were the tangible benefits of their sojourns abroad. They emphasize that "feedback and adjustments" within migration systems helped call attention to the ways in which local, regional, and global factors shaped the characteristics of migration flows and their consequences (Kritz, Lim, and Zlotnik 1992; Faist 1997). Another approach to migration systems, developed in the study of the slave trade, traced the demographic interplay of free and captive people by age and sex as they moved within continents (Manning 1990a, 1990b). The conceptualization of migration systems as responsive to local, regional, and world-scale dynamics has also been of interest to historians (Tilly 1978; Moch 1992; Lucassen and Lucassen 1997; Hoerder 2002).

Two theoretical developments of the 1990s—the transnationalist approach and the meso-level approach—made it easier to connect individual- and community-level migration decisions to the economic and demographic trends shaping migration systems. Both approaches offered additional avenues for foregrounding human agency in the study of long-distance migration. They also offered new vocabulary for describing the multifaceted layers of emotional and financial ties and obligations which shaped individuals' reasons for migrating, as well as their experiences of migration. Anthropologists theorizing that twentieth-century migrants had developed "transnational" identities based on the ways in which social networks connected them to two or more nation-states laid the foundation for analyses of migrant decision-making and identity formation that were simultaneously grounded in multiple locations within a migration system (Basch, Glick Schiller, and Szanton Blanc 1994). Employing transnationalist theoretical formulation made it easier to illustrate how migrants remained connected to the places they left behind, traveled through, and (temporarily or permanently) resettled in. For historians of migration, the underlying points of transnationalist arguments are attractive—especially their ability to highlight how migrant households were enmeshed in long-distance economic arrangements, and how migrants and their family members learned to conduct practical and emotional matters when separated for long time frames and across vast geographical distances. Yet historians have also had to acknowledge the limits of transnational vocabulary given the comparatively recent emergence of the nation-state as the dominant form of global political organization (McKeown 2001). Moreover, historians have rightly argued that transnationalism is much less new than most social scientists think (Foner 2000; Lucassen 2005).

By contrast, meso-level theorizations of migration sought to identify types of middle-level boundary-crossing socioeconomic settings where migrant identities were maintained (rather than identify multiple identities as in the transnational approach). In sociology, this took the form of theorization about "transnational social spaces" which existed on a kind of meso level defined by relationships among migrating and non-migrating individuals. These relationships conceptually existed on a "relational" mid-level somewhere between the individual and macro- or world-scale level. Thus meso-level approaches rejected the idea that ties between communities of origins and the migrants who left them were ruptured, instead asserting that migrant networks (discussed below) served as conduits for preserving and enhancing them (Faist 1997, 2000). In history, the meso level was defined as a "social arena" in which migrants and non-migrating family members gathered information, made decisions, received socialization to the ways of life in-transit, and worked to maintain family and community ties over time and space (Hoerder 2002). Meso-level theoretical formulations have helped migration analysts move beyond the dichotomy of micro (individual-scale) and macro (world-scale) analyses in two key ways. First, these theories articulate a framework for connecting the various pieces of the migration process (including decisions to migrate, leaving a "sending" region, being in transit, entering a "receiving" society, adjusting and being "incorporated"—or not, and possibly re-migrating, and returning "home"). Second, they posit specific types of social structures and social relationships that make migration possible by bringing migrants, non-migrants, former migrants, and potential future migrants into contact with each other in ways that can either promote or constrain migration (Faist 1997).

In an overlap with transnational and meso-level thinking, scholars developed three theoretical constructs in an attempt to illustrate the boundary-crossing identities and patterns of long-distance communication and decision-making associated with migration. These constructs are networks, institutions, and social capital. Anthropologists, historians, and sociologists all employed the vocabulary of "network" to convey a series of interconnected social, political, and economic relationships that individuals manage to maintain across space. In the context of transnational or meso-level approaches, networks have been seen as especially integral to explaining how individuals and households manage their affairs while pursuing long-distance migration strategies. Generally speaking, these networks have been described as sets of person-to-person ties among migrants, non-migrants, former migrants, and potential future migrants that in some way help individuals, families, and communities arrange migration strategies. Some formulations of "network" also explicitly foreground places and arenas where the above types of individuals might come into contact with each other. In this sense, communities of origin, transit centers, destinations, ethnic enclaves, workplaces, immigrant aid societies, government bureaucracies, and border crossings could be included in the definition of network (Kearney 1986; Boyd 1989; Fawcett 1989; Kritz, Lim, and Zlotnik 1992; Massey *et al.* 1993; Faist 1997). Theorizations which enmesh migrant decision-making, communication, remittance, and socialization strategies within networks helped scholars explain why particular links develop among communities of origin and destination, why migrants might defer individual short-term gain for longer-term family or community goals, and why the information available to them might be constrained by other people (Moch 1992; Moch 2012; Lesger and Lucassen 2002). This last factor highlights an especially vital component of network theories of migration – how these networks serve as channels for family members, communities, or co-ethnics to exercise power over one another (Faist 1997; Manning 2006a; McKeown 2001).

The relationships among network theory and its two co-related constructs, institutional theory and social capital theory – have been in flux since the 1990s. Douglas Massey, whose empirical work centered on large-scale migration from Mexico to the US, prepared two major theoretical overviews in association with his colleagues. In the first, published in 1993, he focused on social networks as the conceptual key to the migration process. In the 1999 review, however, social networks had given way to social capital theory, focusing on the investment in skills (Massey *et al.* 1993; Massey 1999). Both theories addressed types of resources assumed to exist within migrant networks. Institutions were theorized to develop as a result of desires to meet – or profit from – specific needs that arise as people in one part of the world arrange to emigrate to another (Massey *et al.* 1993). These institutions included government agencies, humanitarian relief providers, credit brokers, human smuggling rings, lodging houses, and so forth. The challenge for analyzing institutions separately from, or instead of, migrant networks is that it is often quite difficult to establish where the "institution" stops and the "network" begins (McKeown 2001). An alternative strategy was to focus on ways that migrant networks intersect with social capital. Broadly defined, social capital is theorized to be a resource created by personal interactions which may help people make better informed decisions, emotionally adjust in uncertain or unfamiliar situations, and channel promises of future assistance through common friends, family, or business associates (Coleman 1988; Bourdieu and Wacquant 1992; Faist 1997). In practice, social capital is used in two distinct types of explanations about the function of migrant networks. In one sense, social capital is theorized to be an individual migrant's ticket into a migrant network – their social connections allow them to make claims, ask for favors, and collect on promises made in the name of being part of a broader social collective (Portes and Sensenbrenner 1993). Yet social capital theories can also be used to explain what binds a migrant network together and keeps it running effectively.

This desire to theorize about the person-to-person, person-to-institution, and institution-to-institution dynamics that help make migration possible highlights both the strengths of network-related and meso-level migration theories, and their perceived limitation. While networks can be used to explain how migrations between particular regions of the world expand in volume and sustain themselves over time, network-based explanations require at least one earlier wave of migrations to have taken place without the network. Otherwise, there would be no network participants in the destinations those networks seek to direct migrants towards. Thus, networks, institutions, and social capital are most closely linked with "cumulatively caused" migration models which theorize that the ease of movement and the capacity for higher volumes of migration to a particular part of the world will increase over time, given that prior personal and institutional connections have paved the way for them (Massey 1999).

Overall, migration theories have developed and undergone transformation for over a century. To a certain extent, new theories have become more sophisticated and have displaced the old. In another pattern, new theories have largely replicated the old, but with updated terminology: thus the analyses of the 1990s, addressing the social issues of large-scale immigration into the US and Europe, clearly echo the theories of the early twentieth century and their attempt to develop policies for grappling with the "problem" of migration. The most important pattern in theoretical change, however, is that migration theory has steadily taken on new issues in migration. That is, to return to the hypothetically multidimensional grid of migration evoked earlier in this appendix, one may say that theorists have steadily taken on new types of interactions within that grid. As a result, the direction of theoretical advance is not so much that of new theory replacing the old, but of continuing the advance of theoretical work through the grid and, in particular, developing useful ways to link up existing theories. Viewing migration studies from this perspective, one may argue that the assembly of analytical work completed during the last century provides a basis for developing a more sophisticated and more comprehensive set of analytical statements on the process of migration. Expanded collaboration in the study of migration may be very rewarding.

Conclusion

To return to the questions at the beginning of this appendix, we can now offer some summary responses. *What starts migration?* Migration begins within communities of departure, but it also begins with the demand for migrants from communities of settlement; the latter becomes more pronounced as communication improves. At any stage, migrants include both the voluntary and the involuntary. *What sustains migration?* The continuing production of departures, the continuing demand for immigrants, and the effectiveness of networks and institutions facilitating movement. *What stops migration?* A declining development of migrants in communities of departure, a declining demand for immigrants in communities of settlement, and an increased cost of displacement. *What are the benefits of migration?* For communities of departure, migration can bring new resources. For communities of settlement, migration can bring additional labor and the fruits of that labor. For the migratory system as a whole, migration can bring learning and valuable exchange. *What are the costs of migration?* The communities of departure lose the persons and the energies of those who depart. For the communities of settlement, the arrival of migrants brings competition and conflict. For the migrants, mortality and other costs of displacement can be severe. The theories we have reviewed focus on various of these questions and responses.

The study of migration has advanced dramatically in recent decades in its breadth and depth. While tales of migration have been central to human society for all time, and while data have long been preserved on the directions and the numbers of migrants, scholars are now focusing much more systematically and successfully on migration and the interactions it brings. Migration has come to be understood as a basic and universal human phenomenon. Interdisciplinary discussions have led to identifying the many dimensions of this complex phenomenon. As a result, the parallels and links in migratory phenomena are being uncovered steadily. Major advances in analysis of migration have brought great advances to the study of migration and to identifying migratory phenomena. Migratory theory is complex and needs to be multi-layered, yet important advances have been made in determining regular patterns of migratory behavior. In some cases, support for study of migration has come with the intent of resolving some of the social conflicts that seem inevitably to accompany migration. Indeed, the research has been productive of new data and improved theory. Yet the advances in theory, while they may do much to explain the conflict and identify parallel conflicts in past and present, are not likely to prevent conflicts from arising.

The social complexity and variability of migration remains an unremitting challenge to its theorization. Sociologists Douglas Massey and Alejandro

Portes, working at different scales within the sociological literature, developed a debate on the scope of migration theory that is of wide relevance. Massey (1993), working on the large flows of migrants moving between Mexico and the United States with surveys and official data, sought to develop an overall theory that would encompass the principal patterns of migration as a social phenomenon. Portes, working with ethnically defined urban communities and their new migrant arrivals, using ethnographic methods, recognized the complexity and institutional specificity of migration and argued against any effort to create a general migration theory (Portes and Böröcz 1989). This dilemma can perhaps be raised to a higher level but it is unlikely that it can be resolved. That is, for a comprehensive understanding of migration as a social phenomenon, we need the most advanced and rigorous theory that can be developed. At the same time, to grapple effectively with the specifics of migration in individual communities, we need to subordinate theory to empirical analysis.

For world historians, this analytical overview of migration is a step forward in conceptualizing and theorizing one general human characteristic—migration. The study of migration thus provides – along with world-system theory—an early example of the organization of large quantities of world-historical data through an appeal to theory. The idea is to use theses on the dynamics of human migration that have been developed in one time or place and restate them so that they can be applied to other times and places, in the hope that the results will clarify the long-term and interregional similarities, differences, and developments in human migration. World-system theory, as developed through several decades of study, focuses on core regions at the macro level, tracing their expansion, contraction, and interaction (Wallerstein 2000). Global migration theory will be different and perhaps complementary in its character, in that it must reach out to explain tentacles of migratory relations across every region and at multiple scales. As these areas of worldwide study become more formalized, one can imagine that theories of other human patterns may eventually be developed at the world-historical level—for instance, for governance and family.

Bibliography

Basch, Linda, Nina Glick Schiller, and Cristina Szanton Blanc. 1994. *Nations Unbound: Transnational Projects, Postcolonial Predicaments, and Deterritorialized Nation States.* Basel.

Bodnar, John. 1987. *The Transplanted: A History of Immigrants in Urban America.* Bloomington, Indo.

Bourdieu, Pierre and Loïc J.D. Wacquant. 1992. *An Invitation to Reflexive Sociology.* Chicago.

Boyd, Monica. 1989. "Family and Personal Networks in International Migration: Recent Developments and New Agendas." *International Migration Review* 23: 638–670.

Breckenridge, Sophonisba. 1921. *New Homes for Old.* New York.

Brettell, Caroline B. and James F. Hollifield, eds. 2000. *Migration Theory: Talking Across Disciplines.* New York.

Brown, Lawrence Guy. 1933. *Immigration: Cultural Conflicts and Social Adjustments.* New York.

Coleman, James S. 1998. "Social Capital in the Creation of Human Capital." *The American Journal of Sociology* 94 (Supplement: Organizations and Institutions: Sociological and Economic Approaches to the Analysis of Social Structure): S98–99.

Curtin, Philip D. 1969. *The Atlantic Slave Trade: A Census.* Madison, Wis.

Davie, Maurice R. 1936. *World Immigration: With Special Reference to the United States.* New York.

Dennery, Étienne, trans. John Peile. 1931. *Asia's Teeming Millions: And Its Problems for the West.* Port Washington, N.Y.

Dingle, Hugh. 1996. *Migration: The Biology of Life on the Move.* New York.

Eltis, David, *et al.* 2009. "Voyages: The Transatlantic Slave Trade," online database, http://www.slavevoyages.org/.

Faist, Thomas. 1997. "The Crucial Meso-Level." In Tomas Hammar, Grete Brochmann, Kristof Tamas, and Thomas Faist, eds. *International Migration, Immobility and Development: Multidisciplinary Perspectives.* New York.

———. 2000. *The Volume and Dynamics of International Migration and Transnational Social Spaces.* Oxford.

Fawcett, James T. 1989. "Networks, Linkages and Migration Systems." *International Migration Review* 23: 671–680.

Foner, N. 2000. *From Ellis Island to JFK. New York's Two Great Waves of Immigration*. New Haven.

Gabaccia, Donna. 2012. *Foreign Relations: American Immigration in Global Perspective*. Princeton.

Handlin, Oscar. 1951. *The Uprooted: The Epic Story of the Great Migrations that Made the American People*. Boston.

Hansen, Marcus L. 1927. "The History of American Immigration as a Field for Research." *The American Historical Review* 32:3 (April): 500–518.

Hatton, Timothy G. and Jeffrey G. Williamson. 2005. *Global Migration and the World Economy: Two Centuries of Policy and Performance*. Cambridge, Mass.

Hochstadt, S. 1999. *Mobility and Modernity: Migration in Germany, 1820–1989*. Ann Arbor, MI

Hoerder, Dirk. 2002. *Cultures in Contact: World Migrations in the Second Millennium*. Durham, N.C.

Jenks, Jeremiah W. and W. Jett Lauck. 1911. *The Immigration Problem: A Study of American Immigration Conditions and Needs*. New York.

Kearney, Michael. 1986. "From the Invisible Hand to Visible Feet: Anthropological Studies of Migration and Development." *Annual Review of Anthropology* 15: 331–361.

Lesger, Clé, Leo Lucassen, and Marlou Schrover. 2002. "Is there life outside the migrant network? German immigrants in XIXth century Netherlands and the need for a more balanced migration typology." *Annales de Démographie Historique* 2: 29–50.

Lewis, W. Arthur. 1954. "Economic Development with Unlimited Supplies of Labour." *Manchester School of Economic and Social Studies* 22: 139–191.

Light, Ivan and Edna Bonacich. 1988. *Immigrant Entrepreneurs: Koreans in Los Angeles, 1965–1982*. Berkeley.

—— and Parminder Bhachu. 1993. *Immigration and Entrepreneurship: Culture, Capital, and Ethnic Networks*. New Brunswick.

Lucassen, Jan, and Leo Lucassen, Eds. 1997. *Migration, Migration History, History: Old Paradigms and New Perspectives*. Bern.

——. 2011. "From Mobility Transition to Comparative Global Migration History." *The Journal of Global History* 6 (2) 299–307.

—— and Patrick Manning, Eds. 2010. *Migration History in World History: Multidisciplinary Approaches*. Leiden.

Lucassen, Leo. 2005. *The Immigrant Threat: The Integration of Old and New Migrants in Western Europe since 1850*. Urbana, IL.

Mabogunje, Akin L. 1970. "Systems Approach to a Theory of Rural-Urban Migration." *Geographical Analysis* 2, pp. 1–18.

Manning, Patrick. 1990a. "Slave Trade: The Formal Demography of a Global System." In Joseph E. Inikori and Stanley L. Engerman, eds. *Slavery in the Atlantic*. Durham, N.C.

——. 1990b. *Slavery and African Life: Occidental, Oriental, and African Slave Trades*. Cambridge.

——. 2006a. "Cross-Community Migration: A Distinctive Human Pattern." *Social Evolution and History* 5: 2: 24–54.

——. 2006b. "*Homo sapiens* Populates the Earth: A Provisional Synthesis, Privileging Linguistic Data." *Journal of World History* 17: 2: 115–158.

Massey, Douglas S. 1999. "Why Does Immigration Occur? A Theoretical Synthesis." In Charles Hirschman, Philip Kasinitz, and Josh DeWind, eds. *The Handbook of International Migration: The American Experience*. New York.

——, Joaquín Arango, Graeme Hugo, Ali Kouaouci, Adela Pellegrino, and J. Edward Taylor. 1993. "Theories of International Migration: A Review and Appraisal.," *Population and Development Review* 19: 431–466.

McKeown, Adam. 2001. *Chinese Migrant Networks and Cultural Change: Peru, Chicago, and Hawaii, 1900–1936*. Chicago.

Moch, Leslie Page. 1992. *Moving Europeans: Migration in Western Europe Since 1650*. Second edition. Bloomington, Ind.

—— 2012. *The pariahs of yesterday. Breton migrants in Paris*. Durham and London.

Park, Robert E. and Herbert A. Miller. 1925. *Old World Traits Transplanted*. Chicago.

Pessar, Patricia R. 1999. "The Role of Gender, Households and Social Networks in the Migration Process: An Appraisal and Review." In Charles Hirschman, Philip Kasinitz, and Josh DeWind, eds. *The Handbook of International Migration: The American Experience*. New York.

Piore, Michael. 1979. *Birds of Passage: Migrant Labor and Industrial Societies*. Cambridge

Portes, Alejandro and Robert L. Bach. 1985. *Latin Journey: Cuban and Mexican Immigrants in the United States*. Berkeley.

—— and József Böröcz. 1989. "Contemporary Immigration: Theoretical Perspectives on Its Determinants and Modes of Incorporation." *International Migration Review* 23: 606–630

—— and Min Zhou. 1992. "Gaining the Upper Hand: Economic Mobility Among Immigrant and Domestic Minorities." *Ethnic and Racial Studies* 15: 491–22.

—— and Julia Sensenbrenner. 1993. "Embeddedness and Immigration: Notes on the Social Determinants of Economic Action." *The American Journal of Sociology* 98: 1320–1350.

—— and Rubén G. Rumbaut. 1996. *Immigrant America: A Portrait*. Second edition. Berkeley.

Ravenstein E. G. [Ernst Georg or Ernest George] 1885. "The Laws of Migration." *Journal of the Statistical Society of London*. 48: 2: 167–235.

——. 1889. "The Laws of Migration." *Journal of the Royal Statistical Society*. 52: 2: 241–305.

Sassen, Saskia. 1988. *The Mobility of Labor and Capital: A Study in International Investment and Labor Flows*. New York.

Stark, Oded. 1992. *The Migration of Labor*. Cambridge.

—— and David E. Bloom. 1985. "The New Economics of Labor Migration." *American Economic Review* 75: 173–178.

Taft, Donald R. 1936. *Human Migration: A Study of International Movements*. New York.

Thomas, Brinley. 1954. *Migration and Economic Growth: A Study of Great Britain and the Atlantic Economy*. Cambridge.

Thomas, William I. and Florian Znaniecki. 1918. *The Polish Peasant in Europe and America: Monograph of an Immigrant Group*. Chicago.

Thompson, Warren S. 1930. *Danger Spots in World Population*. New York.

Tilly, Charles. 1978. "Migration in Modern History." In William H. McNeill and Ruth S. Adams, eds. *Human Migrations: Patterns and Policies*. Bloomington, Ind.

Todaro, Michael P. 1969. "A Model of Labor Migration and Urban Unemployment in Less-developed Countries." *American Economic Review* 59: 138–148.

——. 1980. "Internal Migration in Developing Countries: A Survey." In Richard A. Easterlin, ed. *Population and Economic Change in Developing Countries.* Chicago

—— and Lydia Maruszko. 1987. "Illegal Immigration and U.S. Immigration Reform: A Conceptual Framework." *Population and Development Review* 13: 101–114.

Wallerstein, Immanuel. 2000. *The Essential Wallerstein.* New York.

Willcox, Walter F., ed. 1931. *International Migrations: Volume II, Interpretations.* New York.

—— and Imre Ferenczi, eds. 1929. *International Migrations: Volume I, Statistics.* New York.

Wyman, Mark. 1993. *Round Trip to America: The Immigrants Return to America, 1880–1930.* Ithaca, N.Y.

Zelinsky, Wilbur. 1971. "The Hypothesis of the Mobility Transition." Geographical Review 61: 219–249.

Further reading

Brettell, Caroline. 2000. "Theorizing Migration in Anthropology: The Social Construction of Networks, Identities, Communities and Globalscapes." In Caroline Brettell and James Hollifield, eds. *Migration Theory: Talking Across Disciplines.* New York.

Fawcett, James T. and Fred Arnold. 1987. "Explaining Diversity: Asian and Pacific Immigration Systems." In James T. Fawcett and Benjamin V. Cariño, eds. *Pacific Bridges: The New Immigration from Asia and the Pacific.* New York.

Gabaccia, Donna R. 2000. *Italy's Many Diasporas.* Seattle.

Harzig, Christiane and Dirk Hoerder, with Donna Gabbaccia. 2009. *What is Migration History?* Cambridge.

Kritz, Mary M., Lin Lean Lim and, Hania Zlotnik, eds. *International Migration Systems: A Global Approach.* Oxford.

Massey, Douglas S., Joaquín Arango, Graeme Hugo, Ali Kouaouci, Adela Pellegrino, and J. Edward Taylor. 1998. *Worlds in Motion: Understanding International Migration at the End of the Millennium.* Oxford.

McNeill, William H. 1984. "Human Migration in Historical Perspective." *Population and Development Review* 10: 1–18.

Petersen, William. 1958. "A General Typology of Migration." *American Sociological Review* 23: 256–266.

—— 1978. "International Migration," *Annual Review of Sociology*, 4: 533–575.

Ravenstein, E. G. [Ernst Georg or Ernest George]. 1876. "The Birthplace of the People and the Laws of Migration." *The Geographical Magazine* 3: 173–177, 201–206, 229–233.

Simon, Rita James and Caroline B. Brettell, eds. 1986. *International Migration: The Female Experience.* Totowa, N.J.

Taylor, J. Edward. 1986. "Differential Migration, Networks, Information and Risk." In Oded Stark, ed. *Research in Human Capital and Development: Volume 4, Migration, Human Capital and Development.* Greenwich, Conn.

Todaro, Michael P. 1980. "Internal Migration in Developing Countries: A Survey." In Richard A. Easterlin, ed. *Population and Economic Change in Developing Countries.* Chicago.

Zolberg, Aristide. 1989. "The Next Waves: Migration Theory for a Changing World." *International Migration Review* 23: 403–430.

Index

issues undergo study at each scale. For instance, the individual scale addresses the logic of each individual's choice and movement. The household scale refers to decisions by families that may affect individuals differently. The community scale may refer to communities of departure zones, arrival zones, of migrants, and others. At the regional scale one may address such major social movements as war and its flows of refugees; in recent times, the phenomenon of urbanization has become the single largest form of migration. At the macro level one may consider whole systems of migration, accounting for interactions from beginning to end. Diaspora communities, for instance, are analyzed at either regional or macro levels. Accounting for the social costs and benefits of migration takes one form at the level of individual migrants but quite a different form at the level of societies overall.

The range of issues to be considered in migration theory is thus very large indeed, and it is simply not possible to focus on all of them at once. To put it one way, each theory must impose a simplification on the overall process of migration, in order to clarify at least some aspect of migration. To put it another way, we can imagine that all the elements of migration can be formed into a multidimensional grid of migration. Such a grid, extending in many directions, would reflect the part that each element plays in the interacting processes of migration. The various dimensions of time, space, institutions, and social or cultural dynamics could conceivably be studied, three or four at a time, to give pictures of migration from various angles. Such theories might focus on immigration (Irish arriving in Boston), on emigration (sojourners leaving south China), on the voyage (the Middle Passage), on the labor market (Italian workers choosing between Buenos Aires and New York), or on institutions (border restrictions and creation of the category of "illegal migrant"). Each of these specific theories, if well designed, could support a useful analysis of certain aspects of migration. Thus, theories too can be set at varying social scales ranging from the individual to the global and from departure to the second-generation settler. In fact, we can note that migration analysis has centered on the study of immigrant communities. There is more to be learned about immigrant communities, but more still remains to be learned about other aspects of migration.

For times thousands of years ago, when data about migrations are truly scarce, we know mostly about the arrivals of migrants in lands of settlement—and sometimes only about arrivals. Such was the case with the Huns and the Bantu, who have been traced back respectively to the Hsiong-Nu of Mongolia and the forests of Cameroon. With further study, it has often been possible to discern the points of origin and the trajectories of such early migrants. Other details of migration processes require more complex analysis. Techniques in linguistics, archaeology, anthropology, genetics, and chemistry can all help in reconstructing migration histories (Lucassen, Lucassen, and Manning 2009). One may hope that the specific migration theories for recent times, outlined in the next section, can be linked to these techniques.

all the

walls

of   a

novel

belfast

sarah j. carlson

TURNER PUBLISHING COMPANY

Turner Publishing Company
Nashville, Tennessee
www.turnerpublishing.com

All the Walls of Belfast
Copyright © 2018 Sarah Carlson

This is a work of fiction. All the characters and events portrayed in this book are either products of the author's imagination or are used fictitiously.

Cover design: Olga Grlic
Book design: Meg Reid

Library of Congress Cataloging-in-Publication Data

Names: Carlson, Sarah J., author.
Title: All the walls of Belfast / Sarah J. Carlson.
Description: [Nashville] : Turner Publishing Company, [2019]
Summary: Wisconsin seventeen-year-old Fiona Kelly visits the father she never knew—and her half-brothers—in Belfast, Ireland, where she also connects with Danny, but their families' pasts may shatter what they have.
Identifiers: LCCN 2018040703| ISBN 9781684422524 (pbk.)
ISBN 9781684422531 (hardcover)
Subjects: | CYAC: Fathers and daughters—Fiction.
Family life—Ireland—Fiction. | Belfast (Northern Ireland)—Fiction.
Northern Ireland—Fiction. | Ireland—History—20th century—Fiction.
Classification: LCC PZ7.7.C4115 All 2019 | DDC [Fic]—dc23
LC record available at https://lccn.loc.gov/2018040703

9781684422524 Paperback
9781684422531 Hardcover
9781684422548 eBook

Printed in the United States of America
17 18 19 20 10 9 8 7 6 5 4 3 2 1

For Norah and Ewan

chapter one
Fiona

The plane broke free from a sea of boiling blue-gray clouds as we made our final descent into Dublin. Brilliant green pastures boxed in by hedges zipped under us. Just like I'd always imagined. The lady in front of me snapped a million pictures out her window. I wanted to too, but I didn't want to look like a total tourist. My favorite song by Fading Stars played on through my earbuds.

"Flight attendants, cross-check and prepare for landing," the captain's voice cut over Martin Benjamin's smooth voice.

My heart stuttered.

July 3, 2012. The day I'd meet my dad—my father, Peter, a man I'd never known—in the flesh. Yes, Mom and I had lived with him until I was two and a half, but I didn't remember a single thing about those years. And since then, there'd been nothing. Not a word from him in fifteen years.

And now he was down there. Waiting for me. Not the unshaven brute in a stained wifebeater I'd always imagined. A week ago, just minutes after I'd finished my last final of junior year, the truth had all come out. Mom had lied to me for a decade and a half; my "deadbeat dad" had always wanted to be in my life. Every time Mom had taken me to Olbrich Gardens, when I'd dropped my penny into the koi pond, I'd wished for a dad who would show me Jupiter through the telescope he bought me for my birthday. I'd never had that, and it was all thanks to Mom. I still couldn't believe she'd kept me from him. In a way, I understood her reasons, but...

The plane shuddered as we touched down. I was officially back on the island Mom had taken me and fled from. Tingles swelled from my stomach through my arms and legs.

"Welcome to Dublin Airport," a flight attendant with an Irish accent said over the intercom. She repeated it in Irish as the plane taxied past a row of other shamrock-marked Aer Lingus planes. Tall green letters spelled out *"Baile Átha Cliath, Dublin"* on the terminal we approached. Belfast apparently had an airport, two actually, but there were no direct flights from O'Hare, and Mom didn't want me navigating two layovers alone my second time ever flying. So Dad was picking me up in Dublin. The cabin filled with the clicks of unfastening seat belts and low voices. I pulled my messenger bag from under the seat in front of me and tucked my phone into it.

Following the slow flow of passengers off the plane, I wondered if the others would be waiting for me too. "The others" were Patrick and Seamus, my half brothers. I'd known they existed, but just as fabled, faceless beings. Patrick was seven years older than me, and Seamus three. Their mother, Dad's first wife, had died giving birth to Seamus. Mom was still their stepmom, legally speaking, since she and my father had never divorced. I even had a six-year-old nephew, Finn; he was Patrick's son. I couldn't believe all I'd missed out on. I was an *aunt*.